# DRAMA
# IN THERAPY

## Volume I: CHILDREN

*"We love the things we love for what they are."*

— Robert Frost

*Edited by*
GERTRUD SCHATTNER
RICHARD COURTNEY

*Foreword by* Theodore Isaac Rubin, M.D.

# DRAMA IN THERAPY

## Volume I: CHILDREN

DRAMA BOOK SPECIALISTS (PUBLISHERS)
*New York*

**Library of Congress Cataloging in Publication Data**

Main entry under title:

Drama in therapy.

    Includes bibliographical references and indexes.
    CONTENTS: v. 1. Children.—v. 2. Adults.
    1. Drama—Therapeutic use.  2. Child psychotherapy.
3. Psychotherapy.  I. Courtney, Richard.
II. Schattner, Gertrud.

RC489.D72D72        616.89'1523        80-15680

ISBN 0-89676-013-8 (v. 1)
ISBN 0-89676-014-6 (v. 2)

*Grateful acknowledgment is made to the following for permission to reprint previously published material:*

*American Journal of Psychotherapy* for "Play, Fantasy, and Symbols: Drama with Emotionally Disturbed Children," Eleanor C. Irwin, and for "Art & Drama: Partners in Therapy," Eleanor C. Irwin, Judith A. Rubin, Marvin I. Shapiro; *New Outlook for the Blind* for "Drama: A Means of Self-Expression for the Visually Impaired Child," Susan Aach; Speech Communication Association for "Developmental Drama for Brain-Damaged Children," Sue Martin; Jason Aronson, New York and *Acta Paedopsychiatrica* for "Dramatized Storytelling in Child Psychotherapy," Richard A. Gardner; *Journal of Rehabilitation* for "Drama: An Outlet for Mental & Physical Handicaps," Marvin L. Blumberg;

*and to the following:*

Viola Spolin for "Theater Games," copyright © 1980 by Viola Spolin; and Baywood Publishing Company for "The Actress as a Mental Health Teacher" by Hugh James Lurie, copyright © Baywood Publishing Company, Inc., 1973.

10 9 8 7 6 5 4 3 2 1   0   1 2 2 3 3 4 4 5 5 6 6 7 7 8 8 9 9

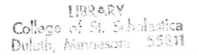

# CONTENTS

vi

THEODORE ISAAC RUBIN, M.D., a practicing psychiatrist in
New York City, is president and faculty member of the American
Institute for Psychoanalysis, a fellow of the American Academy of
Psychoanalysis, and a member of the American Psychiatric
Association and the Association for the Advancement of
Psychoanalysis. Recipient of the Adolf Meyer Award (Association
for the Improvement of Mental Health) and the Social Conscience
Award (Karen Horney Clinic), he lives in New York City and is the
author of twenty books including *Lisa and David, The Thin Book By A
Formerly Fat Psychiatrist, Shrink,* and *Compassion and Self-Hate.*

# FOREWORD

ALL THERAPIES have the common goal of returning the self to the self. This means the reestablishment of knowing what we feel, what we want, and having the ability to make free choices and to act accordingly with appropriate and good judgment.

"Acting out," in psychiatric parlance, invariably connotes destructive activity. To "act out" means compulsive, choice-less, impulsive, and often disorganized moves which are counter-productive and maladaptive. Neurosis, psychosis, and sociopathy are each marked by destructive and life-impeding "acting out" phenomena. The afflicted individual is "caught" in an "acting out" matrix or web, fed by unconscious conflicts and forces over which no control is effectively exerted. This matrix, if sufficiently malignant, accounts for the victim's entire life production and exploits all of his or her time and energy. In people who are healthier, who retain some measure of health and choice, "acting out" may be confined to sporadic destructive acts, maneuvers, explosions, and impulse activity.

Drama therapy represents a different kind of "acting out." Indeed, this therapeutic modality may well offer a uniquely effective instrument in both investigating sources of "de-structive acting out" and in remediation of various emotional disorders. I am immediately reminded of conditions in which "acting out" consists of great attacks and damage on constructive action of any kind. From my point of view, severe hopelessness, deadening of feelings, depression, resignation, fear of deeper feelings—especially of anger, all leading to inhibition and even to paralysis are forms of "acting out." Being unable to act in one's own behalf as a result of unconscious forces is then a form of "acting out" experienced through paralysis or no action at all.

We know of course that theatre has a long history as a therapeutic agent for people, indeed much longer than psychoanalysis and other modalities. We are also aware of the process of identification, empathy, catharsis, ventilation, and abreaction—in which we express our feelings as well as words. We are aware of the therapy which ensues and the relief enjoyed after a cathartic reaction takes place and in abreaction activity.

But the art and science of drama therapy offer the above therapeutic modalities and more. This is what this fine, comprehensive work is all about. Its papers are written by artists and scientists, and it has been integrated by editors who are artists, scientists, and therapists. Drama therapy, as conceptualized in this work, provides procedures, examples, and voluminous substance of "integrated or constructive acting out." Through this most serious and unique work we learn how to use the human proclivity for acting in the service of serious psychotherapy. "Integrated acting out" is highly organized and represents planned, cohesive tapping of inner resources designed to promote the cause of free choice and *constructive action*. People do not have to be scientists, therapists, or professional artists to enjoy the therapeutic benefits of involvement in drama. The play's participants enjoy the unique benefits of camaraderie in the cooperative effort necessary to the fruition of the production however modest or ambitious. Playing out a role as an actor can serve as a bridge to mobilizing inner resources in actual life. To involve one's self in creative process taps and activates inner resources.

"Constructive acting out" is then the subject of this important work. Its diverse experts have provided us with a significant contribution to understanding and relieving human misery. Through "constructive acting out" we may understand and dissipate "destructive acting out." Drama therapy gives the patient an opportunity to feel so much more of himself than other treatment modalities. Through acting out he can feel and activate his feelings. He can speak and hear his voice. He can move and feel his body as he moves. He can feel himself in relation to other actors. In short, he can experience the integrating use of his total self as an exercise in constructive acting and living.

These two volumes describe this fine, therapeutic instrument as applied to both children and adults. I am pleased that each group is taken separately because problems and solutions for each, while they have much in common, are also highly specialized. May I also point out that drama therapy as described in these volumes has the capacity to entertain although it is also a methodology for investigation and treatment. This work adds dimension to both fields, psychotherapy and drama, and in so doing rewards readers of all persuasions.

Theodore Isaac Rubin, M.D.
New York City

# PREFACE

THIS BOOK IS a collection of papers about drama therapy. It is in two volumes: the first about children, and the second about adults.

It is intended to meet a number of needs. First, there is very little published material on the subject and this book aims to fill the gap. However, even two volumes cannot completely satisfy this need and so, second, it is intended to stimulate further publications that might delve deeper into the different topics introduced here. As a result, third, the book is intended to cover as wide a spectrum as its length permits. Fourth, it aims at an international audience. The need for drama therapy knows no frontiers. Although the majority of chapters are written by Americans, there are equally distinguished contributions from Canada, Britain and elsewhere. Fifth, we hope that the book will interest a wide readership and that the subject matter will gain the significance in society that it deserves. It contains learned papers for the qualified practitioner and there are more popular articles for the layman and the student. Sixth, and finally, this book aims to provide materials for those areas of drama therapy where needs are greatest. To that end, we have included contributions of the highest quality which speak to the most immediate of these.

Both volumes have the same structure. Part 1 looks at Assessment, Part 2 at Special Problems, and Part 3 at Related Techniques. Part 4, however, differs: in Volume 1 it is concerned with Education, but in Volume 2 this part contains material on Theatre. No complete bibliography is given because specific references to each topic are included at the end of each chapter. However, we would encourage the interested reader to refer to the index where cross-references of topics will assist him in his further studies.

G.S., *New York City*
R.C., *Toronto*
1981

# ACKNOWLEDGMENTS

GERTRUD SCHATTNER wishes to thank Marcy Syms Merns for her untiring efforts on behalf of this publication, Karin Abarbanel, Ronald Christ, Barbara Eler, and Ramon Gordon for their help and valuable advice. Richard Courtney wishes to thank Ina Dumphie for secretarial assistance. Both authors are thankful to Rosemary Courtney and Edward Schattner, M.D., without whose editorial assistance and personal help the book could not have been written. Their special appreciation goes also to Rosemary Courtney for the preparation of the Index.

The publisher acknowledges permission to reprint articles as follows. In Volume 1: "Play, Fantasy, and Symbols: Drama with Emotionally Disturbed Children," by Eleanor C. Irwin, *American Journal of Psychotherapy,* 31, 3: 426–36; "Art & Drama: Partners in Therapy," by Eleanor C. Irwin, Judith A. Rubin, and Marvin I. Shapiro, *American Journal of Psychotherapy,* 29, 1: 107–16; "Drama: A Means of Expression for the Visually Impaired Child," by Susan Aach, *New Outlook for the Blind,* September 1976: 282–285; "Developmental Drama for Brain-Damaged Children," by Sue Martin, *Communication Education,* Speech Communication Association, 5205 Leesburg Pike, Falls Church, Virginia 22041, September 1977, Volume 26, No. 3: 208–213; "Dramatized Storytelling in Child Psychotherapy," by Richard A. Gardner, from sections of his book, *Psychotherapeutic Approaches to the Resistant*

*Child,* (Jason Aronson, New York), and sections from "Dramatized Storytelling in Child Psychotherapy," *Acta Paedopsychiatrica,* 41, 1974: fasc. 3, 112–15. In Volume 2: "Creative Dramatics: An Outlet for Mental Handicaps" (reprinted as "Drama: An Outlet for Mental & Physical Handicaps"), by Marvin L. Blumberg, *Journal of Rehabilitation,* 42, 6; "The Actress as a Mental Health Teacher," by Hugh James Lurie, *Psychiatry in Medicine* (Baywood Pub. Co., Inc.), 4, 2, Spring 1973: 183–90.

GERTRUD SCHATTNER is a graduate of the Vienna State Academy for Performing Arts and the Max Reinhardt Seminar for Dramatics. She was a lead actress under Reinhardt and Otto Preminger with Albert Basserman, Elizabeth Bergner, Hedy Lamarr, Peter Lorre, and Louise Reiner. She has also worked extensively as a translator of Pearl Buck, Richard Llewellyn, George Bernard Shaw, Luigi Pirandello, Thomas Wolfe, and others. In the United States she studied drama at Hunter College, Columbia University, and the Henry Street Playhouse, and trained in psychotherapy at the Alfred Adler Institute and the Moreno Institute. She was a staff member at the Adler Clinic and Post Graduate Center for Mental Health; chairman of play production for the Suffolk County Mental Health Association; recreation director and drama therapist for adolescent girls under the auspices of the Catholic Charities, Brooklyn, and at the Riverside Nursing Home and East River Nursing Home; director of her own Theatre for Young People; and instructor at Maria Ley-Piscator Creative Theatre and at the Lincoln Square Neighborhood Center. For thirteen years Gertrud Schattner has been senior drama therapist at Bellevue Psychiatric Hospital where she coordinates the program for volunteers for the entire hospital, supervising them as well as undergraduate and graduate students in drama therapy. She is also a faculty member of the Arts-in-Therapy Program, Turtle Bay Music School, New York City. Founder and first president of the National Association for Drama Therapy, she is a frequent guest lecturer on drama therapy.

# INTRODUCTION

I BEGAN TEACHING one of the first courses in drama therapy in the United States ten years ago in the Arts-in-Therapy Program of the Turtle Bay Music School in New York City. Each year, during the opening class, one of the first questions students would invariably ask was "What books should we read?"

Until now, my answer has always been the same: "There are no titles I can suggest, because there are no textbooks or guides to the field of drama therapy."

It was from this need and from my own wish to share my life's work and experience that the idea for an anthology of *Drama in Therapy* was born. Would it not be helpful in creating a recognized profession to find other people who might be doing similar work? The response, as I began searching for contributors, was most gratifying, and I received many articles from therapists working in the United States, Canada, Europe, Israel, all around the world. I was fortunate that I was joined in my work by Richard Courtney. To sift through the mounting wealth of material became a demanding task. As we prepared and organized the selections, we came to the conclusion that the pioneering work of the drama therapists was of such importance that the publication of two volumes, rather than the single volume originally intended, was certainly warranted. With these twin volumes now, after five years of preparation and research, we hope to advance the recognition of drama as an adjunct to psychotherapy as well as a treatment modality in its own right.

The more than forty contributors to *Drama in Therapy* have been drawn to the use of drama as therapy from various fields: education, psychiatry, theatre, speech, movement, and visual arts. Do these specialists have anything in common? Why do they do what they do? There is no single answer applicable to all. For some it is the love of drama itself. Others have observed the power of fantasy and creative expression to reach the mentally ill, the imprisoned adult, the disturbed child.

The reasons why I became a drama therapist and have remained one for twenty-eight years are simple, direct, and have evolved from my life experiences.

My early youth was spent as an actress on the European stage—a career that was interrupted by Hitler's invasion of Austria. During the war that followed, I lived in Switzerland, where my husband was an attending physician in a tuberculosis sanitorium for survivors of Nazi concentration camps. Most of these survivors were young men in their twenties. Physically ill, they were also disturbed and broken in spirit after the horrors of imprisonment. They were quiet and depressed, polite but lifeless as they silently paced the hospital corridors. Many of them died, not because of illness, but because they had lost all interest in living.

I was asked to help them by organizing their leisure time between the medical treatment and the long rests ordered by their doctors. But I wanted more for them than organized leisure time. I wanted to extricate them from their apathy, to make them realize that they were free to communicate, free to build a new life for themselves. Yet what was I to do? I was completely on my own. I had no textbooks. My only tools were my intuition and my experience on the stage. I decided that we would meet in small groups. We would read short stories and poems, and I, drawing on my theatrical experience, would introduce them to role playing.

Following some initial reluctance, certain patients became interested in particular poems that expressed feelings of bitterness and despair. The authors of the poems seemed like friends to the patients. This relationship became even more apparent when we decided to prepare a performance of a play by the great Jewish writer, Sholom Aleichem, about life in a small community in Poland—perhaps very like the villages where most of these men had spent their early years.

It would take still another book to describe how these dispirited young men began to wake up, to enjoy themselves, and to work together. Being involved in the play's production meant becoming part of life again, being needed as members of a group with a joint purpose, working towards a common goal, and being valued for their own accomplishments. During rehearsal they regained their memories, they lost their shyness, they discussed their roles, and they gradually became creative contributors to the art of acting and staging a play. Many of the men had not smiled in years, but drama gave them the gift of laughter again. Drama also gave them the chance to accept responsibility, to rehearse, to redo, to recreate, and, of course, to enjoy the reward of a successful performance.

A few weeks after that performance, one of my actor-patients came to see me. We talked. He told me a little about his childhood and about his recent experience in the concentration camp. He also spoke about what had happened to him through our drama groups and our desire to care for each other, guided by someone who cared. Not only did he wish to cope with the memories of horrors, he also believed that he had gained the strength and confidence to plan a future. Gradually, he had forgotten to hate. Not one of those young men had spoken so intensely or so personally before.

At the time, I did not know that I had taken a very small step into the unexplored territory of drama as therapy. Neither did I realize that my first attempt to use drama as an instrument in the healing process had started me down the road of a long learning process, a road which I am traveling still. Those silent men in Switzerland were my first teachers, and all through the years since, each encounter with a patient has added to my understanding of the wide range of human suffering as well as given me an opportunity to renew myself.

Later, in the United States, I spent ten rewarding years as

drama instructor in a home sponsored by the Catholic Charities. I worked with hundreds of girls. Most of them came from broken homes, and they were troubled by many different psychological and mental problems.

One girl I especially remember is Marie. She spoke only Spanish, was very slow learning English, and her remedial teacher had little hope for her progress. But Marie had a lovely singing voice, and she wanted to play the lead in our production of a well-known musical. "To play this part," I told her, "you must be able to understand and correctly pronounce the words you sing." Within two months, Marie was the best reader in her class. She was taken out of the remedial program, and she became the star of the show. I had helped Marie to learn English, I told myself. What a therapeutic success!

Then there was the Lincoln Square Neighborhood Center in New York, where I worked for eight years with a mixed group of children—the rich, the poor, the healthy, the handicapped. Little Donna walked with crutches because she had had polio. When asked whether she would agree to a rather risky operation that might help her, she said yes and, when the doctor asked her why, she said, "I want to be in our show, *The Wizard of Oz*." Donna underwent surgery, never used crutches again, and was the happiest munchkin ever to dance down the yellow brick road.

It was during the seven years that my husband was resident psychiatrist at Central Islip State Hospital that my interest in the field of mental health began. I had become chairman of play production for the Suffolk County Mental Health Association, and I numbered among my cast members psychiatrists, social workers, nurses, and theatre enthusiasts from nearby communities. Our greatest success was the production of *My Name Is Legion*, the well-known play based on the life of Clifford Beers, founder of the mental health movement.

One evening, I was asked to help direct a talent show presented by the hospital's patients. It was the first time that I had become involved with the severely mentally ill. I recognized the almost magical outlet that drama gave those patients and realized once again the curative powers of the creative arts in the treatment of the emotionally disturbed. I watched what happened to them when they were allowed to express themselves on stage. I saw the pleasure and gratification they experienced when they knew they were important—when, however briefly, they could be in the limelight, at the center of attention. I learned what happiness some of the patients felt when they believed that they had something to contribute and that they were part of a team. I saw that through drama they felt the freedom and the right to express feelings that had been dormant but could now come to light.

From the moment I first worked with psychotic patients, I knew that I wanted to remain in the field of drama as therapy, to explore it further, and to specialize in as many aspects of it as possible. Although I have worked with clients from the very young to the very old, in many different settings, my most rewarding experience has been the last thirteen years with the patients at Bellevue Psychiatric Hospital.

My road to drama as therapy is just one among many. The chapters in these two volumes present several other approaches to the field, from several different points of departure, by specialists in many different fields—education, sociology, psychiatry, the arts. Assembling these approaches for the anthology, however, I began to realize that merely publishing them in book form would not be sufficient to establish drama therapy as a recognized profession. Something more was needed, and a goal began to develop in my mind: the founding of a national association for drama therapy with the aims of setting the highest standards, promoting public awareness of the field, helping new drama therapists to get the best possible training, making colleges and universities aware of our objectives, and, most important, seeing drama therapy fully accredited as a field of special study.

In June 1979 this goal was partially achieved when the National Association for Drama Therapy was founded with me as its president. Subsequently the American Psychiatric

Association has recognized drama therapy by inviting our association as well as other creative art therapy organizations to be represented at a joint conference with the American Psychiatric Association. With this invitation, drama therapy has moved another significant step closer to acknowledgment as an important discipline uniting therapists whose backgrounds may vary widely but who share a single aim of achieving growth and health using drama as their tool.

Gertrud Schattner
New York City
1981

# DRAMA
# IN THERAPY

## Volume I: CHILDREN

# Part 1
# ASSESSMENT

Drama therapy can be used to help those with specific dysfunctions. It can also be used as a generalized "helping" so that people can increase their potential as human beings. It can be used with children or adults.

As a methodology, it is increasingly used. Dramatic play and creative drama, improvisation and role play, dramatic movement and theatre games—all are becoming commonplace in many forms of treatment.

This applies to virtually all "schools" of therapy. It matters little what is the theoretical background of the therapist: he can be a Freudian, Jungian, or Gestalt therapist; he can begin from transactional analysis or general semantics; or he can commence from anthropological or sociological theory. Whatever the approach, drama is being used more and more in therapeutic situations.

The reason is clear: *drama is the prime form of human expression.* It includes all other media: sounds and words, movement and dance, visual and plastic arts, as well as ancillary forms like costume, puppetry, and the like. In drama, the human being is acting "whole"—with his total self. It is the most *direct* form of expression whereas other media express only parts of the "whole" — what one sees (art), what one hears (sounds and music), and so on.

Drama is the complete expression of the total mental activity. It is the external representation of all that takes place internally. It is not partial: it is inclusive of the cognitive, the affective, the aesthetic, the psychomotor, the moral — indeed, all aspects of our inner life.

But is there a direct cause? How does the therapist tell from the dramatic action what is occurring in the patient's mind? This is a vexed issue.

Most therapists assume that the patient's attitudes and behavior are in some way caused by his inner life. For example, it is thought that the child who plays aggressively is displaying some form of internal aggression. Exactly what this internal quality is, and how it too was caused, is what distinguishes the different "schools" of therapy. But, as Anatol Rapaport points out:

> Frequently, the neurotic feels better after following any course of therapy that seems promising to him. Feeling better, he may also function better in relation to his work and to other people. Because of the strong subjective component of therapy of this sort, it is next to impossible to compare the effectiveness of different therapies.[1]

It is not the purpose of this book to evaluate the different "schools" of therapy. Indeed, as drama can be used with virtually every "school," it merely behooves the drama therapist to acknowledge that there are different interpretations possible and work with them.

But the drama therapist must *assess* two things: first, the needs of the patient, and second, what method to use at a particular moment.

Most drama therapists would say that they must, first, "get to know the child." But what does that mean? "Getting to know" means finding out things about the child and then making judgments about what to do. How do we do that? Needless to say, *there are no rules*. There are no absolutes in drama therapy. No one can say, "At this moment, with this age and kind of child, you must do *this*." People are not machines. They are complex organisms who do not respond to in-puts that result automatically in out-puts. Yet some generalizations can be made. Although in specific circumstances one drama therapist might do one thing and a different drama therapist another, some might well do the same thing — or, if not exactly the same, their judgments can be very similar.

Thus, although there are no rules, there are *criteria*. A criterion is a guide for judgment. Drama therapists have some criteria in common, but they also have their own criteria according to their point of view. Their personal criteria may be due to their backgrounds from a particular "school" of psychology, or due to the type of media they may emphasize. Yet they all have criteria which they share: the need for involvement, concentration and sincerity in dramatic action; the close parallel of actual existence and dramatic life; the "whole" representations given by dramatic symbols of mental activity; and the close relationship of the dramatic media with other creative forms — art and design, dance, speech, music, and the like.

What criteria should actually be used will largely depend upon the individual's own choices — his own value judgments and assessments. In Part 1, assessment with children is considered. In Chapter 1, Richard Courtney provides an overview of the problems, and raises basic questions. In Chapter 2, Barbara Sandberg and her colleagues provide one specific example of assessment from a particular point of view — the developmental. In Volume 2, a different viewpoint is given by David Johnson (Chapter 2) who is concerned with assessment for adults. Given this background, we would encourage the therapist to develop his own criteria which will emerge from his own practice with specific patients.

1. Anatol Rapaport, *Semantics* (New York: Thomas Y. Crowell, 1975), p. 391.

RICHARD COURTNEY studied under G. Wilson Knight and Bonamy Dobrée at Leeds University, England, where he was also director of their theatre group. He has been a professional actor, director, and designer (including work with the British Broadcasting Corporation), and an instructor in drama education and therapy since 1948 in England and since 1967 in Canada. His lectures and broadcasts have taken him to various parts of Europe, the United States, Australia, and Asia. Formerly professor of drama at Victoria and Calgary, he is now responsible for graduate work in arts and education at the Ontario Institute for Studies in Education, and is cross-appointed to the Graduate Centre of Drama, University of Toronto. He was president of the Canadian Conference of the Arts from 1973 to 1976, president of the Canadian Child and Youth Drama Association from 1971 to 1973, and a board member of the American Councils of the Arts (USA). Currently chairman of the Task Force on Arts and Education in Canada, Richard Courtney has published over a hundred articles, reports, and books—including *Play, Drama & Thought, Teaching Drama, The Drama Studio,* and (forthcoming) *Peoples in Performance: Perspectives in Drama & Culture,* and *The Dramatic Curriculum.* He is a member of the British Association of Dramatherapists, and a founding member of the National Association for Drama Therapy (U.S.A.).

*Chapter 1*

# DRAMA ASSESSMENT

Richard Courtney

*"'All hid, all hid;'—an old infant play.*
*Like a demigod here sit I in the sky,*
*And wretched fools' secrets heedfully o'er-eye."*
                                                    —Shakespeare

## 1 INTRODUCTION

Shakespeare well understood "the play within the play"—one
group of players watching some of their members performing
another play to them. In the playhouse, the perceivers become
critics. In life, they become drama therapists and drama
teachers.

Whether we are drama therapist, teacher, leader or director,
we all face the problem of "What do I do now?" But before we
can answer that question we have to deal with a prior one: "How
do I assess what is happening?" Before I can know what to do
next, I have to see how well the performers are doing at this moment. Therefore, the question of assessment concerns: (1) what
the actor is capable of achieving; (2) whether he is achieving it;
(3) what his achievement tells us about him; and (4) what his
achievement informs us about what should happen next.

## 2 PRIOR CONCERNS

Before we can make such assessments, however, there are some
prior concerns. Any assessment has a series of assumptions within
it, and they are criteria, goals and contexts.

## Criteria

We all have our own way of looking at the world, and drama therapists are no exception. A Freudian psychoanalyst may interpret child play, behavior or dreams in one way and a Jungian may understand the same data differently. Who is "wrong?" Neither of them. Both are "right" from their point of view, from their frame of reference. Each of them has his criteria, and these provide judgments which assess the patient; they lead to further judgments about what can be done next.

While this applies to therapists, it applies equally well to teachers. One may require students to learn "the facts." Another may consider that the prime purpose of education is to learn skills. Still a third may think that neither of these is as important as "becoming a better person."

Thus each one of us has our own criteria, and these lead us to our own particular goals.

## Goals

Each of us has two kinds of goals: (1) generalized goals — the over-all long-term aims we have in pursuing drama therapy; and (2) specific goals — the particular aims we have in one session.

Generalized goals arise from our main criteria. They answer the question: "Why am I conducting drama therapy?" I have examined drama goals elsewhere[1] but, in summary, we can say that the most common goals today are as follows:

(a) *Intrinsic goals* — that is, drama has value in and of itself — particularly to assist personality development and ways of coping with existence;

(b) *Extrinsic goals* — that is, drama has value for purposes other than its own — which enhance specific learnings (speaking, say, or creativity) because it provides inherent motivation[2] and transfers learning to other fields;[3]

(c) *Aesthetic goals* — that is, drama has aesthetic values — which assist people's abilities in dramatic form (i.e. in acting, movement, and so on).

Any particular drama leader will have his own balance between these three generalized goals, and his view will determine his specific goals.

Specific goals are the aims of the drama therapist in one session. For example, someone who studied psychodrama with

J.L.Moreno may have the generalized goals of freeing spontaneity and releasing *catharsis* through "acting out;" as a result, in one session he may have the specific goal of releasing the patient's feelings about his parents through multiple role playing. On the other hand, someone with Gestalt training may have the generalized goals of encouraging "wholeness" and developing potential; as a result, in one session he may have the specific goal of making the patient aware of the *now* through, say, acting a past event in the present. Interestingly, the same technique can be used by drama therapists with very different goals: mirror exercises, for example, can be used in many different situations and with different goals.

## Contexts

The drama therapist's criteria and goals are placed in the context of a particular session. *Criteria and goals operate within the context of an encounter.* The question becomes: will my criteria and goals work? The practicality of "what happens" can alter and change things from moment to moment.

Contexts of drama therapy are always different from each other. A context occurs when a leader meets another person (drama therapist/patient, teacher/student, director/performer). There is then an interaction characterized by three factors:

(1) *their "World View"* — that is, *who* each is, how he views existence and what criteria he has;

(2) *their "Meaning"* — that is, *how each gives meaning* to the actions of the other person ("When he says *this*, or does *that*, what does it mean *for me?*");

(3) *their "Intention"* — that is, what each considers *vital* in the encounter ("Of all the things he says or does, which are the most important *for me?*").

These three elements provide the multiple levels of interaction within the context, and they determine which criteria and goals are or are not effective.

Thus criteria, goals, and contexts are the matrix within which the patient and the drama therapist work. They establish the prior conditions for assessment.

## 3 STYLES OF ASSESSMENT

Criteria do not only affect goals. They also provide our "frame of reference" for our judgments. And as there are many criteria, so there are many ways of assessing patients and deciding what action will be of most help to them.

Drama therapy is an all-inclusive field, overlapping with many fields, such as psychiatry, psychology, sociology, social anthropology, and others. A drama therapist who works mainly from drama and psychology is liable to have different criteria (and thus different forms of assessment) from one who works largely from drama and sociology. While this makes drama therapy an exciting field, because new methods of assessment and different techniques are continually evolving, it can provide some confusions. Nowhere is this more clearly seen than in word usage. For example, "projection" in psychology indicates an act of attributing one's own feeling to others; in the theatre, on the other hand, it describes the size or force of the actor's affect in the environment. Thus when examining a particular style of assessment, we must take great care with both the criteria used and the language in which it is framed.

Some of the major styles of assessment are examined below.

## 4 DETERMINISM

Determinism says that there is cause and effect between mental meaning and dramatic action. That is, a specific thought causes a particular dramatic action (effect).

Determinists (like Freud and Marx) would say that cause and effect is like billiard ball No.1 striking billiard ball No.2 — the second ball cannot move unless it is struck by the first. Thus Freudians would say that if I dream of a house with promontories, overhangs, and the like, then this is a symbol of my thoughts about the female body. Assessments of drama therapy have a one-to-one relation. That is, if the child's drama displays $X$ then it is caused by the specific thought $Y$; it cannot be caused by thought $Z$. The connections between causes are then examined and an assessment made. This is an inflexible way to assess dramatic action.

The approach known as behavior modification is also based on cause and effect and is likewise inflexible. It states that in-put $A$ (stimulus) automatically produces out-put $B$ (response). Thus, if the dramatic behavior (response) is not what is desired, then a painful stimulus must be given to prevent its recurrence. The job of the drama therapist then becomes how to assess positive and negative reinforcers which will produce acceptable behavior.

Neither of these styles of assessment is common among drama therapists today.

## 5 CATEGORICAL & ANALYTIC

Until Einstein, the main method of securing knowledge was to analyze the material into its categorical parts. The main problem with this method is that the whole is usually more than the sum of its parts.

Ann Shaw[4] attempted a taxonomy of creative dramatics based on the work of Bloom and others. Taking categories of behavior (cognitive, affective) she brilliantly analyzed the writings on American creative dramatics. An assessment based on her work would see in the child's spontaneous drama its cognitive and affective elements; the drama therapist would then plan subsequent sessions to meet these categorical needs. Like a wise researcher, however, Ann Shaw indicated at the end of her study that the taxonomy seemed to miss "the essence" of the activity.

More interesting, perhaps, is the *Inventory of Dramatic Behavior*[5] of Gil Lazier and Joseph Karioth. The *IDB* is a taxonomic, content analytic device for coding behavior. Dramatic behavior is divided into categories and the number of each occurrence is counted. It is designed to delineate one-person improvisations under the following headings:

(1) *Time* — a measure, in seconds, of the total time spent for each improvisation;
(2) *Amount of Space Traversed* — a description of movement measured by counting the number of spatial units traversed by subjects in the course of each scene;
(3) *Number of Stops* — a cessation of gross movement constitutes a stop and is scored accordingly;
(4) *Dramatic Incidents* — a measure of the number of individual units of drama which comprise a scene;
(5) *Novel Dramatic Incidents* — a counting of those dramatic units conceived totally by the improviser;

(6) *Dramatic Acts*—the smallest discernible units of intended physical behavior in the scenes;

(7) *Repeated Acts*—a category in which dramatic acts immediately repeated are scored;

(8) *Characters Created*—the number of imaginary characters created are scored.

*IDB* permits the improvisations of hundreds of subjects, each performing three scenes, to be coded by categories and processed through computer programs in order to ascertain norms. Thus assessments can be made by comparing the dramatic behavior of a patient against the norms discovered.

## 6 EXTRINSIC

There are countless extrinsic methods of assessment, and we shall merely examine those most commonly used.

One method that can be used in conjunction with drama therapy is sociometry.[6] Individuals in group drama express their preferences for each other in terms of companionship or working partnership. They are always asked concrete questions, such as "Whom would you best like to create an improvisation with?" Preferences can then be correlated and assessments made of: pairs chosen by no one else but each other; cliques; chains of friendship; popular stars; and unchosen isolates. Such assessments, however, are only valid in that specific group; a child who is isolated in one group may be popular in another.

Another method of growing interest is proxemics.[7] This assesses the personal space used by humans, and considers the intimate, social, and personal distances in different cultures. Specific assessments can be made of body axis or orientation, kinesthetic factors, touch code, visual combinations, and so forth. Studies have shown, for example, that: there are differences in the use of space between those who are "normal," the aggressive[8] and the schizophrenic;[9] females have a greater awareness of body feelings, and a more positive acceptance of them, than males.[10] Assessments can be made, therefore, between "normal" and abnormal behavior in dramatic actions.

Perhaps because drama therapy is related to creative drama, some assessments have been made from the field of creativity.

While some valid relationships can be made, unfortunately many are limiting. For example, Torrance's "Just Suppose" Creativity Test[11] has, as assessments:

(1) *Verbal Fluency* — score reflects the test taker's ability to produce a large number of ideas with words.

(2) *Verbal Flexibility* — score represents a person's ability to produce a variety of kinds of ideas, to shift from one approach to another, to use a variety of strategies.

(3) *Verbal Originality* — score represents the subject's ability to produce ideas that are away from the obvious, the commonplace, banal, or established.

Clearly, such creativity tests assess only a small element of the dramatic: the verbal.

It can be seen from these few examples that assessment from other fields, while they may be valid in their own terms, usually provide only a partial understanding of what is happening in drama therapy.

# 7 DESCRIPTIVE

Because so many of the above assessments imply bias (that is, they assess in a limited way, examining only what they are looking for), attempts have been made at value-free assessments. These are usually descriptive rather than prescriptive.

## Phenomenological

The appeal of phenomenology is to "look at things as they are." Husserl[12] acknowledged that *any* assessment is value-laden but, in order to be as impartial as possible, *description must occur before assessment.* A phenomenological description describes phenomena as they appear *to me.* But I try to describe them with the least bias possible — without any preconceived categories to get in the way and create bias.

Elsewhere I have put forward the *Phenomenological Dramatic Description*[13] which attempts a sequential description from the empirical to the present (*noetic*) and to the past (*noematic*). Such an approach should be made *before* an assessment. It is a salutory experience for a drama therapist, teacher or leader, to "go through the exercise." It leads us to be aware of the patient and his dramatic actions in new and fresh ways.

## Check Lists

A simple empirical method is the check list: a list of dramatic characteristics which can be checked off as they occur. Assessments can then be made by collating information from the checks.

One such is the *Developmental Drama Check List*[14] given in the Appendix. This is a check list related to specific developmental stages in childhood, and relates to the developmental assessment style described in (9) below.

## 8 DRAMATIC

Assessments from the field of Drama/Theatre appear to be of two main types, related to the major theories of acting in the twentieth century: those of Stanislavsky and Brecht.

## Dramatic Involvement

For Stanislavsky, the actor had to be immersed in his role. Most Western theatre today is of this style.

Brian Sutton-Smith and Gil Lazier have developed an *Assessment of Dramatic Involvement* Scale[15] as follows:

(1) *Focus:* the continuum from focused to distracted as follows:
   (a) how engrossed the child is in the dramatic task;
   (b) how convincingly he seems to be engaged in the performance of his "as if" behaviors.

(2) *Completion:* the degree to which the child completes the basic task.

(3) *Use of Imaginary Objects:* the capacity for creating convincing and palpable objects through physical means and conveying their properties (size, texture, weight, temperature, function, shape) in a consistent manner.

(4) *Elaboration:* the creation of new ideas in addition to those necessary for the dramatic task.

(5) *Use of Space:* a continuum between sufficient space to allow for the action, and the tendency to use a confined space when larger space is available.

(6) *Facial Expression:* the child's ability to convey the emotions of a character within the limits of the dramatic task.

(7) *Body Movements:* as they are appropriate to the dramatic situation, the particular character, and its success in com-

municating contextual messages.

(8) *Vocal Expressions:* in terms of emotional relevance, variety and vocal projection.

(9) *Social Relationships:* the actor's awareness of and reaction to other participants in the dramatic situation; that is, involvement with others in a convincing manner, and revealing his awareness of others in the group.

The *ADI* Scale can make assessments in terms of psychology or of drama. In terms of psychology, children appear to vary in their ability to focus in drama: distractability, impulsivity and hyperkinesis, and tolerance of fantasy are some such conditions. Consistency in the use of imaginary objects seems to relate to non-distractability. Appropriateness of facial, verbal, and gestural expression may point to abilities in other styles, and the social relationships revealed in drama may well relate to competence in social interaction, empathy, and insight. In terms of drama, there appear to be specific stages of development in each of the nine areas which increase the child's involvement in the role.

## *Representation*

In contrast, Brecht's theory of "alienation" does not expect the actor to be immersed in the role.

Where drama is used in therapy or education, the Brechtian approach is best exemplified by Dorothy Heathcote.[16] Of her it has been said:

Dorothy Heathcote is not primarily after illusion, nor empathy culminating in *catharsis* nor a psychologically justified realism of presentation. Her mode of working leads to an emphasis on the rational and reflective aspects of drama so that what is observed is an event which can be assessed and objective conclusion reached.

The rules of drama:

(a) that there shall *be seen to happen* — via some form of personification — a living moment of concern to humans;

(b) that persons shall *interact* either in themselves or with their environment;

(c) that the place of interaction must somehow be defined
    and *create limitations* upon what can occur;
(d) that *distortion of viewpoint be permissible* in order
    that some strands of the event be stressed and others
    avoided. In other words, in a selected framework of
    place, emotion, style of life, a limited portion of
    human experience and endeavour can be revealed in
    action by persons who stand for those represented;
(e) that from the interaction and re-enactment there shall
    be some *easement* or *development* of such situations.
    Life shall progress—move forward—as in reality it
    does;
(f) that all present realize that it is a re-living or *represen-
    tation of living* and *not* the actuality of reality.[17]

For Dorothy Heathcote, what is required in a drama therapy session is life accommodation and imitation processes akin to the
role playing processes in life. Theatrical techniques and skills are
not necessary. Rather persons behave, demonstrate or indicate
what *they* would do if faced with the problem of the "other"
character. He or she *assumes an attitude rather than a
character*—lives through the problem rather than the personage.

On this view, assessments are made as to the degree to which
the child meets the six rules of drama. For example, does the
child in drama therapy develop the situation, move it forward, as
well as we do in life? Does he *represent* living, or is he *involved* in
the drama? These assessments are very different from those of
Sutton-Smith and Lazier.

## 9  DEVELOPMENTAL
It is normally assumed that people progress: that they develop
through life, that they grow from what they *are* to what they
*become*. During this century, developmental psychology has
become increasingly influential, particularly through the
cognitive work of Piaget.[18] Although some developmental studies
have been made of the affective and aesthetic, little has been
done to discover the developmental stages for drama. Peter
Slade's pioneer work[19] has yet to be followed up.

## Approaches

Some developmental assessments can be made from both the
*IDB* and *ADI* Scales. For example, in each of the categories of the
Scales, the drama therapist can ask: Does the patient get better in
this category with time? It is also possible to show how patients
with specific problems progress. Thus progressions of
schizophrenics have been examined in visual art by Frances
Celentano[20] while David Johnson assesses their dramatic development in Volume 2.[21]

Gavin Bolton[22] has proposed three developmental stages of
dramatic action related to symbols. He has indicated that drama
is not simply "doing" — that it is not even simple action. He
distinguishes three degrees of symbolization leading to drama:
(1) *Concrete* (signifier): the practical meaning of the action —
    that is, the meaning is *bound* to the action. For example:
    when the giving of an object in an improvisation simply
    means giving an object.
(2) *Abstract* (proto-symbolic): problem-solving and decision-
    making. For example: the surface meanings of the events in
    the improvisation, the problems that have to be solved within
    it and the decisions to be made.
(3) *Abstract* (symbolic and dramatic): the value-laden concepts.
    For example: the actions are connotative — the concrete ac-
    tion has many meanings that accrue to it.
Although assessments of such symbolic developments can be
made, they can be achieved without reference to developmental
age stages. A different version of this style of assessment is the
*Dramatic Process Observation Scale* of Barbara Sandberg, given
in Chapter 2.

## Developmental Drama

I have elsewhere put forward a theory of dramatic imagination[23] which indicates developmental drama age stages and
methods of assessment. In summary, this is as follows:

### THE MENTAL PROCESS

The work of the mind has a three-fold process:
(a) We *perceive* things. We see, hear, touch, smell, taste, and

move — each sense gives us information with which the mind works. By increasing our awareness, we increase the information we gather.

(b) We *transform* this information "in our heads." We make sense out of our perceptions. We reorganize the information so that it fits to our existing mental patterns and, thereby, we can deal with it. We do so by imagining.

(c) We *act* with what we think. As children, we must do this in physical action — this is why small children can hardly ever be still. But when we are older, we do not have to do so physically: we can do it "in our heads."

This three-fold process happens instantaneously. Indeed, it is so immediate that an act is at once a perception. The process is reversible. In other words, what we *do* becomes immediately what we see, hear, feel, taste, smell and move.

DRAMA & MIND

Drama is an integral part of this process. It is what provides mind with its dynamism, energy and motivation. It is the prime way to externalize imagination.

Drama is impersonating. It is *acting "as if."* It is Laurence Olivier in the role of Hamlet, the teenager acting like a hero of the popular media, or the small child pretending to be a bear. But it is also, at the same time, *thinking "as if."* You cannot do one without the other — no matter if you are Olivier, or a teenager, or a child. How we think determines how we act.

There is a developmental sequence to dramatic thinking and acting in the young child, as follows:

(a) *Identification.* The baby identifies with his mother. By being fed, handled, and loved, he comes to feel *for* her — to develop empathy. But he has yet to distinguish himself from her: he does not understand the difference between inner and outer — between his inner "felt world" and the environment.

(b) *Play with "mediate objects."* He begins to develop interests in "a cuddle": a bit of cloth or piece of stuff which he handles, sticks in his mouth, and loves. He learns to do two things with it: while he loves it (picks it up, sucks it, etc.), he discovers he can also repudiate it (throw it down, give it away, etc.). Provided his mother is sympathetic at this time, the baby uses these "mediate objects" (which are mid-way between the subjective and the objective) to distinguish the inner from the outer. He imagines — sees possibility.

(c) *The Primal Act.* At about ten months old (universally, and in all cultures) the baby impersonates. He first pretends to be his mother, then himself, and then by degrees all other people and things. This is a sudden change: it is the moment when parents recognize that their baby has become a child. The baby has learned: (1) to distinguish the inner from the outer; and (2) to master the outer by an inner impersonation.

(d) *Substitution.* The child learns that one act can substitute for (can "stand for") another. That is, for a gross act ("I *am* my mother") he learns to substitute a *part* of that act: "I am my mother *sounding*," or, "I am my mother *moving*." As Gombrich indicates, a substitute occurs when the child can use it — its function makes it important.

Another element in substitution is Peter Slade's distinction of personal and projected play. Personal play is acting with the whole self — impersonating with one's whole being. Projected play occurs when the inner impersonation is projected outwards onto an object (a stick, say, or a doll) and moving that "as if" it is the self.

Substitution continues throughout life. Through it, we develop our own personal mental structures. Piaget has shown that in mental structures nothing is ever new — what arises has been built upon what already exists. Thus identification and impersonation are built into all later forms of thought. In other words, they are the *feeling* base for all other forms of thought and action.

## PLAY & THE ARTS

The child naturally grows towards adulthood through the medium of play. It is his way to grow and to learn, and he develops a complex and complicated series of mental structures through substitution. Things that "stand for" other things become signs, symbols and, eventually, abstract thought.

He also develops through the arts. He plays with artistic media: with his voice and a drum (music), with his body (dance and drama), with a brush and with mud (visual and plastic arts). These have evolved from the primal act, but he learns that instead of direct impersonation he can uses substitutes:

(a) Generalized movement — which leads to dance, then to three dimensions, and then to two dimensions.

(b) Generalized sound — which leads to music, then to speech and language, and then to literature.

In this sense, drama is the generic base for all of the arts.

It also accounts for why children can express themselves easily in different artistic media, moving fluently among them all.

## DRAMA & PERSONALITY

Drama builds our personality. It is psychologically healthful because imaginative dramatic thinking and spontaneous dramatic action help us to fulfill our potential. Drama develops ego-strength.

With the baby, this happens developmentally:

(a) *The "I am" experience.* This is given through love, feeding and handling, by the identification process.

(b) *The "I do" experience.* This is provided by play with "mediate objects."

(c) *The "I create" experience.* This occurs with the primal act, enabling the child to feel mastery over the external world — as though he is creating events in the environment.

The particular way in which we achieve these three steps establishes our personality, and the core elements of our character.

Throughout life, these three steps re-occur. At any moment in our lives, we all need to re-activate them. In order to function well in the world, to have mastery, to be competent in any aspect of existence ("I create"), I must also feel that I can "do" — and that, in itself, depends on the strength of the "I am" feeling. Encouraging play and arts activities provides such reinforcement for the child. Adults who doubt their abilities need to return to these steps — to engage in drama therapy.

On a personal level, drama therapy always returns to the elements we have described above: to perceptual awareness, imagining and transforming, and acting; to how the inner "felt world" relates to the environment through dramatic action and its substitutes; to arts processes; and to the paradigm, "I am, I do, I create" as the foundation of ego-strength.

## DRAMA AS SOCIAL ACTION

Spontaneous drama is the way we relate to the world. Improvisation in life creates our dynamics with others. Impersonation is "putting ourselves in someone else's shoes": our imaginative thought projects outwards towards the other person, breeds an empathetic response and, thus, becomes the basis of human communication. By thinking "as if" we are the other person, we try to relate our dramatic actions to him and, thereby, communicate.

Yet we do not communicate simply by the words spoken. Communication is the total dramatic context: the speech and intonation (our sounds), the gestures and bodily expression (our movements), and the total personality (our Being). Moreover, my sounds, movements, and Being *meet with* yours. As Martin Buber would say: communication is a genuine "dialogue" — and a dramatic dialogue at that.

## DRAMATIC FEEDBACK

Yet drama also feeds back the view which the world has of us. It can approve or disapprove of our actions, and this can affect our ego-strength. As Keith Johnstone indicates,[24] drama is always about status: in any dramatic situation, moment to moment, two people are always "master and servant" like the old *commedia dell'arte*. Continual disapproval attacks our sense of self. Then, if our personality is not strong enough to cope, we need to return to earlier dramatic structures in order to recuperate — to re-build who we are, what we do, and how we create.

## ASSESSMENT

The implication of this theory of dramatic imagination for assessment is manifold. Questions of assessment have to be asked within the following frames of reference:

(a) *The Mental Process:* what are the levels of the individual's perception, awareness and concentration? what is his manner

of relating perception, transformation and action?
(b) *Drama & Mind*: how does he relate thinking "as if" to acting "as if"? what is his level of identification and empathy? does his relation to objects have a subjective or objective emphasis? to what level of substitution does the patient regress and what form of substitution can assist him to develop?
(c) *Play & the Arts*: which medium is the patient now most comfortable in? can other related media be used to assist him? what is the patient's relationship to process and products in specific media?
(d) *Drama & Personality*: at what level of the "I am, I do, I create" paradigm does the patient operate in drama/sound/music/language/movement/dance/dimensions, and what are his differences? in what ways does his "felt world" relate to people, events, circumstances and things?
(e) *Drama as Social Action*: how well does the patient communicate in each of the specific media? within each, does he treat other people as objects or as persons?
(f) *Dramatic Feedback*: in each medium what is the status the patient places himself in? does experience in a medium that gives him status improve his feelings about himself in other media?

These are merely a few of the questions of assessment that arise from developmental drama. They can be related to the *Developmental Drama Check List*, given in the Appendix, should such questions need to be asked in terms of age stages.

## 10  CONCLUSION

Assessment is not evaluation. It is concerned with judgments the drama therapist can make about the present state of the patient and methods of assisting him.

However, the many styles of assessment can lead to confusion. Which one to use depends upon you — upon your criteria, goals, and the contexts you find yourself in. Each drama therapist must choose for himself. Only then can his assessment be a true reflection on his own view. When Brian Way said, "Start from where you are," he did not merely refer to the improviser — he also meant the drama leader.

# 11 APPENDIX
# DEVELOPMENTAL DRAMA CHECK LIST

*Check*

## 0–3 Months
Skin & touch sensitivity
Empathy with mother
Mouth & hand play
Sound repetition & vocal play
Surprise at face

## 3–6 Months
Postural cues
Movement repetition
Interest in bodily things
Interest in faces
Interest in colors
Play with food
Play with toys
Excitement at familiar things
Laughs at surprise
Moves & "sings" with parent
Crescendo ("This Little Piggy Went to Market")

## 6–12 Months
Crawling/walking
Development of personal circle around body
Pretends to be mother ("the primal act")
Anticipates climax
Makes others audience
Clear purposes, goals
Demands attention
Repetitions
Sound games
Gestural language

*Check*

Explores objects — realizes their existence
Delight at outcome
"Peek-a-boo"
Jokes

## 1–2 Years

Insatiable curiosity
Mischievousness
"Me" and "mine"
Exchange with others
Words developing
Dances
Pretense actions
Makes toys pretend
Pretends objects are toys
Relates toys to one another (doll in another toy)
Makes exits & entrances
Carries treasures about
Crayons in fist
Being chased or chasing
Explorations: length/weight/number/size
Makes rules
Makes music in time, rhythm
Makes "homes" (boxes, cloth)

## 2–3 Years

Movement flexibility: speed, rhythm, up/down, front/back
Strategies (offers, bargains)
Running commentaries
Sentences develop
Complete sequences of action (time)
Personifies parent routines
Time: "in a minute"/"in a little while"
Group choral games
Crayons in fingers

*Check*

Joins toys in pretense
Changes roles
Narratives continued
Hide and seek/"house"/tag

## 3–4 Years
"Why?"
Puzzles ("it fits")
Takes turns, sharing
Group games
Good gross motor control
Early grammar
Exaggerated stories
"Follow the leader"
Space differences made
Participates in narratives
Matching games (buttons/boxes)
Makes pretense environments
Runs from "monsters"
Dressing up
Pretense emotions
Groups of characters played
Acts problems/fairy tales

## 4–5 Years
Fine motor control
Secrets, surprises
Grammar develops
Group pretense play
Early conscience
Friends and enemies
Seeks approval from peers
Highly imaginative roles
Different voices
Symbol distinguished from reality

*Check*

Gymnastics
Free movement to music
Relay races/creeping
Pretends to tell the time
Games of order ("Ring around a Rosy")
Play rituals (possession, sequences)
Consciousness of roles of others
Puppets
Anticipates future
Invents narrative
Begins to learn to avoid aggression
Relies on own judgment

## 5–7 Years

Learns time beat
Boy/girl/baby play (sex)
Group play
Groups move in large circles
Role flexibility
Social roles begun (teacher/pupil)
Caricature
Games of acceptance ("Farmer in the dell")
Playful conversations
Improvises movements, objects, characters, situations
Analogy/animism
Difficulty in distinguishing fantasy & reality
Makes costumes/clay models
Chasing & running games
Left/right awareness
Realistic themes
Episodic plots (picaresque)
Movement: "big/small/grow"

## 7–9 Years

Highly creative dance
Can write well

*Check*

Play with mechanical toys
Collections, crazes, hobbies
Sense of fairness
Card & board games/creates own games
Feeling for ideas of others
Plays exaggerated roles
Distinguishes fantasy & reality
Plots: exaggerated/realistic/surprises/myths/legends/occupations
Establishes improvised speech/rich flow/nonsense talk
  (gibberish)
Puppets & puppet theatres
Groups play in small circles/spirals
Games of dominance ("King of the castle")
Increased grace/speed
Large group improvisation/pairs/solos/leaders emerge
Ball games
Cumulative plots/long endings/abrupt finishes
Group play in horseshoe shape begun
Love of detail

## 9–13 Years

Movement: changes in direction/focus/near & far
Increased clarity in gesture & body shape
Handicrafts
Very cooperative/independent
Winning/losing games
Intellectual games (charades)
Informal concerts
Growth of hypothesis/classification/historical sense
Small group improvisation/good partner work
Fluent speech
Language more important
Creative writing
Small scripts used in some improvisation
Invention of own languages

*Check*

Use of private codes
Plots of climax and conflict
Themes: animals/adventure/occupations
Emotional characterizations
Social role playing increases/social playmaking
Increasing need to "show"
Explores real in possible
Space: horseshoe shape developed/end shapes explored

# FOOTNOTES

1. Richard Courtney, "Goals in Drama Teaching," *Drama Contact* 1, no. 1 (May 1977): 5–8.

2. Richard Courtney, "Human Dynamics: Drama and Motivation," (Toronto: Ontario Institute for Studies in Education, 1977).

3. Richard Courtney, "Drama and the Transfer of Learning," (Toronto: Ontario Institute for Studies in Education, 1977).

4. Ann Shaw, "A Taxonomical Study of the Nature and Behavioral Objectives for Creative Dramatics," *Educational Theatre Journal* (Winter 1971): 361–72.

5. Gil Lazier and E. Joseph Karioth, "The Inventory of Dramatic Behavior: A Content Analysis Technique for Creative Dramatics," (Tallahassee, Fla.: Theatre Science Laboratory, Florida State University, 1972).

6. Jacob L. Moreno, *Who Shall Survive?* (New York: Nerv. Dis. Pub. Co., 1934).

7. E. T. Hall, *The Hidden Dimension* (New York: Doubleday, 1966); idem, *The Silent Language* (New York: Doubleday, 1959).

8. A. F. Kinzel, "Body-Buffer Zone in Violent Prisoners," *American Journal of Psychiatry* 127 (July 1970): 99–104.

9. D. F. Duff, M. J. Horowitz, and L. O. Stratton, "Body-Buffer Zone," *Archives of General Psychiatry* 11 (1964): 651–56.

10. John C. Stockwell and Clarence W. Bahs, "Body-Buffer Zone and Proxemics in Blocking," *Empirical Research in Theatre* 3 (Summer 1973): 27–40.

11. E. Paul Torrance, *Torrance Test of Creative Thinking: Norms-Technical Manual* (New Jersey: Ginn & Co., 1966).

12. Edmund Husserl, "The Idea of Phenomenology," in *Edmund Husserl and the Crisis in Philosophy*, ed. Quentin Lauer (New York: n.p., 1965); idem, *Ideas* (London: Macmillan, 1931); idem, *Cartesian Meditations* (The Hague: Nijhoff, 1960).

13. Richard Courtney, "Drama & The Phenomenological Description," *Discussions in Developmental Drama* 3 (February 1973): 12–25.

14. I am thankful to Mrs. Roberta Emery, Goosey Gander Kindergarten, Victoria, B.C., Canada, for her assistance in the development of the early stages of this check list.

15. Brian Sutton-Smith and Gil Lazier, "Psychology and Drama," *Empirical Research in Theatre* 1, no. 1 (1971): 38-46.

16. Dorothy Heathcote, "Drama and·Education: Subject or System?" in *Drama and Theatre in Education,* eds. N. Dodd and W. Hickson (London: Heinemann, 1971). Betty Jane Wagner, *Dorothy Heathcote: Drama as a Learning Medium* (Washington, D.C.: N.E.A., 1976).

17. Oliver Fiala, "An Artistic Affinity: Notes on Dorothy Heathcote's and Bertolt Brecht's Modes of Work," *National Association for Drama in Education Journal* 2, no. 1 (June 1977): 29-32.

18. Jean Piaget, *Play, Dreams & Imitation in Childhood* (New York: Norton, 1964).

19. Peter Slade, *Child Drama* (London: University of London Press, 1954).

20. Frances Celentano, "Progression in Paintings by Schizophrenics," *American Journal of Art Therapy* 16, no. 2 (January 1977): 68-73.

21. See vol. 2, chap. 2.

22. Gavin Bolton, "The Process of Symbolization in Improvised Drama as an Art Form" (Paper privately circulated, 1977).

23. Richard Courtney, "A Dramatic Theory of Imagination," *New Literary History* 2, no. 3 (Spring 1971): 445-60; idem, "Imagination & The Dramatic Act: Some Comments on Sartre, Ryle & Furlong," *Journal of Aesthetics & Art Criticism* 30, no. 2 (Winter 1971); idem, "Imagination & Substitution: The Personal Origins of Art," *Connecticut Review* 9, no. 2 (May 1976): 67-73; idem, "Dramatic Action: A Genetic Ontology of the Dramatic Learning of the Very Young Child," *Journal of the Canadian Association for the Very Young Child* (Spring 1977): 16-21.

24. Keith Johnstone, "Status Transactions and Theatre," *Queens's Quarterly* 82, no. 1 (1975): 22-40; idem, *Impro* (London: Faber and Faber, 1979).

BARBARA SANDBERG, Ed.D., is an associate professor of theatre and creative arts therapies at William Paterson College, Wayne, New Jersey; and has been an adjunct instructor at Teachers' College, Columbia University. She is a member of the American Theatre Association's panel on research in theatre education.

*Chapter 2*

# A DESCRIPTIVE SCALE FOR DRAMA

Barbara Sandberg

*". . . to hold, as 'twere, the mirror up to nature; to show virtue her own feature, scorn her own image, and the very age and body of the time his form and pressure."*

—Shakespeare

## 1  INTRODUCTION

The mirror of drama reflects our development through all the stages of life. As we grow and become, positive reflections help us to view ourselves and others—we see our diversities and potentials. Some of us, sadly, only glance at the mirror and look at a wavy "fun house" image—our growth in self-awareness has been marred by mistaking ourselves in the negative reflections others have shown us.

It is the task of drama therapy to find ways for positive reflections as well: to draw from the discipline of an ancient art the awarenesses which help us to wholeness; to help us see environments and lives which are satisfying and worth living. Drama is a process that is virtually inseparable from ways of human growth; it is a way of learning to use experience effectively. As we dramatize personae in play, we are saying, "I am different from others," and also, "I am like others." In sensorimotor play, we test and reflect upon the varieties of sensory stimuli available to us. On the basis of these perceptions, we create our inner world, and this allows us to decide who we are, and how we feel about others.

29

Drama therapy acknowledges these ways of growth through planned methodology which unites the seemingly paradoxical states of *doing* and *distancing*. Drama therapy occurs when: (1) a person is involved, and aware of the involvement, so that he is focused on the action; and, at the same time, (2) he is distanced from what he is doing. In drama, life has not swept us along in our unawareness; we have captured a moment and held it dramatically, based on our own experience. We own this space in time because we have perceived it; we own the self-knowledge because we have created and experienced it. In analogizing our experience to another person, place, or thing, we broaden our own self-understanding.

As we structure our awareness through the immediate dramatic process, we engage in a global perception because, while we are acting it, it is difficult to separate the knowing, feeling and doing from the reflecting about drama. In the drama, all is unified. As we assume personae interacting in a given time or place, we integrate our perceptual experience and forget ourselves in the playing. It is only through reflection on the process that we begin to see a configuration of the way we are: we play with a purpose — self-understanding. This is a paradoxical situation, but:

> The German language has a word for it: *Spielraum,* which is not conveyed in a literal translation such as "playroom." The word connotes... *free movement* within *prescribed limits.* This at least establishes the boundaries of the phenomenon: where the freedom is gone *or* the limits, play ends. Such a polarity also seems to adhere to the linguistic origins of the word *play,* which connotes both carefree oscillation and the quality of being engaged, committed.[2]

Planning, doing and reflecting provide the structure for drama therapy (they are the "prescribed limits"); the process (or "free movement") is the playful interaction between therapist and group (or individual) as they engage in the "as if" of drama. It should also be added that planning, doing and reflecting are inextricably linked: as effectiveness in expression is achieved, reflection becomes a more and more important focus of the playing.

How one achieves this phenomenon through process is too large a scope for one chapter. One possible framework for doing so, however, is presented here in the form of the Dramatic Process Observation Scale. This may provide a focus for reviewing and assessing elements of structure and process—a "mirror" for developing dramatic interactions.

# 2  THE DRAMATIC PROCESS OBSERVATION SCALE

This Scale has been conceived as developmental: the categories of (A) stereotyping, (B) imitative, and (C) creative and communicative behavior indicate the usual beginnings and hoped-for aims of drama in an educational or therapeutic context. These levels of development are then translated into five areas of dramatic focus: (1) role playing, (2) plot action, (3) theme, (4) use of space, and (5) reflection. The Scale has proved useful in assessing either group or individual behavior. However, it should be noted that individual assessments usually remain consistently within one category while group assessments may show a mixture between categories.

The categories and areas of focus are subjective and generally descriptive, rather than empirical and experimental. The Scale is not intended to be a means for classifying behavior. Rather, it is hoped that the Scale will be used as a mirror for people to learn to see themselves as they grow in self-understanding through drama. It has been used for initial assessments for therapy, and with groups and individuals as a mirror for reflecting development of dramatic expression. (Generally speaking, however, this last application should never be made of the Scale until the group or the individual has reached the point beyond stereotyping—which means involvement in both the doing and the reflecting.) (See Fig. 1.)

# 3  STEREOTYPING AS DRAMATIC BEHAVIOR

Stereotyping means withdrawal from fear of exposure to censorious eyes: it is defensive towards awareness of self and others. It may possibly be caused by initial inhibition in "performing" with an un-

| THE  DESCRIPTIVE  CATEGORIES | STEREOTYPING RANGE (1 - 3) | 1 AWARENESS OF THEME: "Cops and robbers" effect: rigidity in conflict solution. Tendency to solve conflict by physical aggression. No awareness of relation of theme to other dramatic elements. |
|---|---|---|
| | | 2 ROLE TAKING & PLAYING: Rigid role behavior, inhibited and stilted awareness of body movements and language. No ability to "take on" a characterization. |
| | | 3 CREATION OF PLOT: No awareness of beginning, middle and resolution of conflict. Tendency to categorize action in terms of "good and bad." |
| | | 4 USE OF PHYSICAL SPACE: Static and uncontrolled movement in a given area. No awareness of "personal"space. |
| | | 5 EVALUATION & REFLECTION: No response. |
| | IMITATIVE RANGE (4 - 7) | 1 AWARENESS OF THEME: Engaged in action for sake of "what happens next." Possibly an awareness of narrative line but no recognition of relation of plot to theme. |
| | | 2 ROLE TAKING & PLAYING: An attempt to respond to stimulus and motivation appropriately. Noticeable approval-seeking. |
| | | 3 CREATION OF PLOT: Cooperating in inventing appropriate plot and solving conflict without aggression — noticeable engagement in the "as if." |
| | | 4 USE OF PHYSICAL SPACE: Unimaginative perception of relation of space to self and others: strict defining of "territories." No ability to perceive the whole. |
| | | 5 EVALUATION & REFLECTION: Negative or positive statements ("I liked it," "I didn't like it"); little or no elaboration of detail. |
| | CREATIVE & COMMUNICATIVE RANGE (8 - 10) | 1 AWARENESS OF THEME: The ability to objectify and understand experience in order to structure dramatic experience through use of all the elements. |
| | | 2 ROLE TAKING & PLAYING: Coordination and confidence in ability to respond with effective verbal and nonverbal action to communicate character. |
| | | 3 CREATION OF PLOT: Ability to construct plot which amplifies and communicates thematic concern. |
| | | 4 USE OF PHYSICAL SPACE: Ability to focus on space as element of dramatic communication; creative use of total environment. |
| | | 5 EVALUATION & REFLECTION: Positive reinforcement; constructive criticism aimed at promoting better communication. |

*Figure 1, opposite:*
## DRAMATIC PROCESS OBSERVATION SCALE*
by Barbara Sandberg and Anne Battle

*For assessing group and/or individual
development in dramatic process.*

For rating observations:
1 to  3 describes Stereotyping
        attitudes and behaviors
4 to  7 describes Imitative
        attitudes and behaviors
8 to 10 describes Creative & Communicative
        attitudes and behaviors

*Copyright: Woodbridge Township School District,
Woodbridge, New Jersey, 1973, (PROJECT MOPPET).

---

familiar group, or by severe personality disorder in which the
individual has withdrawn from contact with others. Whatever the
cause, the symptoms have a certain familiarity: lack of ability to focus
or concentrate on dramatic action or character, inhibited movement
in the available space, and solving conflicts by physical aggression.
The degree and duration of the stereotyping will be dependent on the
readiness of the group or individual, in terms of mental health.

There will be limited or no ability to establish the dramatic "as
if." Suggestions for dramatic activities (verbal or nonverbal) will
be greeted with inhibitions to the point of inability to play. When
the therapist manages to motivate a plot action, the "cops and
robbers" effect often ensues with the "good guys" shooting the
"bad guys." (I have seen this occur, in varying degrees, with emotionally disturbed children, college undergraduate and graduate
classes. It appears to be a general initial response to dramatic process.) The group or individuals are at a loss in terms of handling
the "freedom" of the process and are unable to perceive the
"prescribed limits" of dramatic structure. At this stage, dramatic
behavior seems either extremely shy and withdrawn, or aggressive
and "acting out."

Hughes Mearns said that the following should guide the
creative processes of awareness:

*Acceptance.* We receive each crude product of creative effort, asking only if it is individual and sincerely meant. That procedure removes fear and sets up hope of success; and it stimulates marvelously the urge to create anew.

*Approval.* We find something to like in each effort. This is not just flattery, and it is not indiscriminate. One must approve only the original element, not the imitation of things read and heard or observed in the work of others. And such approvals must vary in intensity and always must be given sparingly. Instruction, meaning correction, has no discouraging place at this stage.

*Criticism.* When mutual trust has been set up, criticism may nearly always be profitable if it is associated with strong general approval; but there are two better places for criticism, the "low moment" when one is discouraged because of lack of technique, and the "cold moment," long after the effort when all interest is being tuned into a new creative venture.[3]

These "principles of creative learning" should become habits of mind and feeling for one who guides drama therapy or education. They form the basic attitudes of reflection on structure and process, and the drama therapist has a responsibility to model them as developing awareness for the participants. In the Spielraum of drama therapy, the therapist does not sit in the corner taking notes. In an interactive process, the therapist serves as an agent for *play:*

Anecdote: J. and I were having difficulty getting started. Our interactions in process were colored with acceptance, but I was having difficulty with giving approvals. J., an emotionally disturbed eleven year old, was fixated on stereotyped interactions where his superhero "good guy" outwitted and killed my villainous "bad guy." Finally, I told him I was "bored" with our sessions and "wondered if we could find something else to do." J. was amazed that I voiced my reaction and that I took our playing seriously. My "boredom" served as a springboard to better expression and communication because *I* had communicated my feelings; subsequently, we began to find approvals.

The basic approach to working with those on the stereotyped

level should be geared towards finding security and trust in process. The drama structures should be planned for feelings of success and discovery. An analogy: in painting a picture, one often
fills in the background and works towards the embellishment and
refinement of detail. So, too, in dramatic process, the details of
the "as if" (how a character speaks, specific props or costumes)
should come after the broader elements of drama are understood.
Movement and pantomime are good nonverbal ways of beginning. Verbal communication through character, for example,
means that the participant(s) must deal with the complex symbolization of finding the right words at the right time—an
embellishment difficult even at the creative and communicative
level.

## Sample Methodology at the Stereotyped Developmental Category

Movement Activity—establishing a movement vocabulary: (1)
Concentrate on the establishment of basic patterns of movement
(such as stretch, swing, bounce, strike, collapse, followed by
relaxation period in which you talk about the connections of feelings to physical actions); (2) Discuss how these actions may give
rise to images, with emphasis on positive and nurturing symbolic
actions (possible images—a seed growing, a chick hatching, the
sun rising). In addition to stimulating movement involvement,
the participant may wish to draw or write about his feelings as in-
fluenced by images (such as drama diaries).

When the participant reaches a degree of involvement with the
therapist and the process, signs of imitative development will
begin to appear. There will be more interest in developing the "as
if" and, concomitantly, the beginnings of a reflective and
evaluative frame of reference (this will be evidenced more in the
playing than talking about the process).

Stereotyped behavior can occur at any stage of dramatic
development, and may be a signal that the activity is too difficult.
Then the drama therapist must accept what has occurred,
acknowledge difficulties, and modify the activity. Stereotyping
always means that people are cancelling their creative options

because of fear of failure. The drama therapist must sense the needs of the participant and stimulate the "as if" and the reflecting on growth through the dramatic process.

# 4 THE IMITATIVE AS DRAMATIC BEHAVIOR

Imitative play is analogous to the free and unstructured dramatic play of the back yard or recess time: it is the type of play normal to the developmental socialization of childhood. It is spontaneous and "fun" — or "not fun" depending on such factors as who gets "mad" during the playing. There is real involvement in the playing, and the work of drama therapy is to retain the "freedom" while reinforcing the "prescribed limits."

In imitative behavior, the group seems a better framework for interaction than a one-to-one (participant and therapist) relationship. The latter may well be optimal for the early stages of stereotyping when a group may induce inhibition. (This would be especially true when working with the severely disturbed.)

The group involved in dramatic process is guided towards being supportive of and cooperative with its members. But unlike standardized forms of group psychotherapy, the group is involved in finding artistic expression for its wholeness. For example: a theatre game based on dramatic play, which has proved effective with groups at this level.

## Sample Methodology at the Imitative Developmental Category

Improvisation: Space Explorers. Participants are divided into groups of no more than three to five people. Each group: (1) creates a planet, and nonverbally conveys the *who, what* and *where* to a visiting team of Space Explorers (who may converse); (2) functions as a team of Space Explorers for another group's planet. In the activity, groups are always amazed at their regression to "good guys" and "bad guys"; frequently, the nonverbal communications of the Planet People are mistaken as the Space Explorers greet the unknown. Subsequently, the participants are often more able to recognize the need for a clear establishment of theme as a way of organizing plot actions, characters and space.

The confrontations in the play also help to establish a reflective group attitude: responses such as "I liked it," or "I didn't like it" seem inadequate. As groups learn to play and reflect on the playing, they become more interested in embellishing the "as if" of the planets; thus, believability and involvement increase. The improvisation demonstrates the structure of dramatic communication, the importance of a group cooperating to design the communication, and the opportunity for individuals to be creative within a supportive group framework.

The imitative stage is characterized by approval-seeking and somewhat superficial cooperation with the group and therapist. Frequently, ventures into the "as if" will either lack spontaneity (because of too much planning) or be chaotic (too little planning). The concern for "what happens next" is typical of this stage,and dramatic action (plots, characters, environments) may be copied from the latest popular television program.

Games with open-ended potential (such as Space Explorers) are good stimuli to develop the reflective. Videotape and playback of group interactions are especially effective; when combined with the Scale, a group may react very constructively. "Drama diaries" can record individual reflections on experiences, as well as perceptions of group leadership or membership.

At the imitative level, there is an adjustment to the situational demands of drama. Although better able to take part in dramatic action — especially in groups — the person may still have no real confidence or ability to effectively express the self. Criticism in the Mearns sense (the "low moment" and the "cold moment") may be beneficial.

*Anecdote:* A crossover into more expressive playing may be stimulated by a prop or piece of costuming. One boy suddenly got involved and believable when he wore a cape for his characterization of a mythic hero. At this point, he became responsive to the "as if"; his use of space was more effective, and he was able to respond in character. Until this point, he had avoided interactions with the therapist on the basis that "drama was no good because it wasn't real."

## 5  THE CREATIVE & COMMUNICATIVE AS DRAMATIC BEHAVIOR

The rational and irrational play of drama therapy offers possibilities for finding new solutions for old creative problems — and old solutions for new problems. As participants begin to feel "ownership" in the process, and the therapist's role becomes more integrated into the playing, they will take more responsibility for what is done and how it is done.

A group innovating in dramatic process will make no separation between playing and reflecting.

At this stage, there may be an urge to perform for an outside audience. If the drama therapist feels there is genuine innovation and artistry in the group, then performance may possibly be seen as the natural result of the process. Performing offers positive gratifications when the person is beginning to see himself as dramatically innovative and effective; but it may also mean the awkwardness of forgotten lines, losing character and missing entrances. These theatrical "mistakes" may loom twice as large to the person accustomed to the supportive atmosphere of the drama therapy group. Reflecting on an unsuccessful performance might well regress the participant to an earlier developmental level. I am aware of the dangers of performance for emotionally disturbed children: reflections from an audience, even though supportive, can be completely misinterpreted and could become an impetus to withdraw into stereotyping. The growth towards self-awareness through dramatic doing and reflecting is slow, and the process needs much nurturing. The demands of performance and formalization are often out of keeping with the informal, relaxed and supportive tone of drama therapy sessions.

## 6  ASPECTS OF DRAMATIC FOCUS

Within each of the descriptive categories of the Dramatic Process Observation Scale are areas of dramatic focus as follows:

### 1. Awareness of Theme

The theme, or central idea, is the conscious, ordered message to be communicated. It is expressed through role taking and playing, creation of plot, and the use of physical space; reflection and evaluation of these elements clarifies and refines the dramatic communication of theme. Emotional disturbance may create life themes which are pathologically subjective and destructive to the growth of self-awareness. The objective awareness of theme, through growth in communicative expression in dramatic process, may be seen as a central concern for drama therapy. It may indicate an understanding of the causative factors in the communicative intent; it certainly means a greater understanding of the structure of the dramatic message.

## 2. Role Taking & Playing

The ability to see things from another's point of view is central to our understanding of the self and others. Thus there must be: the ability to perceive a role as separate and different from one's own person; to spontaneously take on the character and characteristics of another being; and to understand things from their point of view.

## 3. Creation of Plot

The narratives of our lives form the basis for dramatic situations; through the creation and recognition of conflict, plot is developed. There must be a willingness and ability to see and understand experience, and to order these into consciously structured dramatic action.

## 4. Use of Physical Space

The uninhibited, spontaneous interactions with space shape dramatic communication. This is the conscious ability to define, alter and/or move through space as part of the involvement in the "as if" of drama.

## 7 CONCLUSION

The transformations from stereotyped, to imitative, to creative and communicative dramatic behavior are difficult to predict in terms of time. The drama therapist needs patience, skill in human interactions, and both artistic and aesthetic knowledge of the discipline of drama in order to start the therapeutic processes which lead to transformations in the way people see themselves in the reflective mirror of drama.

Research in drama therapy is just beginning. Increasingly, the behavioral sciences are indicating the need for new applications of an ancient, healing art. As Piaget says:

> Whereas other animals cannot alter themselves except by chang-
> ing their species, man can transform himself by transforming the
> world and can structure himself by constructing structures; and
> these structures are his own, for they are not eternally predestined
> either from within or without. So, the history of intelligence is not
> simply an "inventory of elements;" it is a bundle of transforma-
> tions, not to be confused with the transformations of culture or
> those of symbolic activity, but answering and giving rise to both of
> these.[4]

It is hoped that the developmental mirror presented here will stimulate further reflections.

The following case studies are descriptive reports based upon the use of the Scale. Barbara Eberhardt, Kathy Gaskins, Susan Hefler, and Cynthia Lightbody write from their unique back-ground and experiences. We searched together for ways in which drama therapy could positively affect the lives of emotionally disturbed children. In seeking to translate theory into practice, we discovered, collaborated, and came to individual and collec-tive realizations of what it means to practice drama therapy.

## APPENDIX 1:
## CASE STUDY/BARBARA EBERHARDT[5]

B. was a thirteen-year-old disturbed male. Because time was limited (5 months) I tentatively planned a series of structured events and intermediary objects to introduce theatre elements, build trust, and begin to know B.'s private world. Initially anxious about "drama," he presumed he would have to memorize and perform as he had done unsuccessfully in a school play some years before. He had to be weaned from his preoccupation of wanting/ not wanting to be a "star," and his prejudice that theatre was only done on a large stage before an audience. The challenge was to get him "to do," to take minor risks, and thereby reinforce the positive experience of exploring the self creatively through one or more of the dramatic elements. I began with simple tasks for playfulness and rapport (fantasizing to music, non-verbal transformation and movement games, doodles in a drama log, relaxation exercises, circus and animal games). Two dominant themes emerged: power-money-girls, and guns-knives. These themes erupted verbally, as interruptions of the task at hand, and in sharp contrast to his actual behavior which was meek, humble, eager to please, noncompetitive. Unable to use these themes directly as raw material for acting out, his fixation on them severely limited his ability to be involved in any of the suggested events. Since a major part of our experience together concerned these preoccupations, I will sketch here some of the interactions which led to *B*.'s beginning acceptance of and play with these themes.

Through the use of coordination exercises, props (intermediary objects), musical instruments, and theatre games, I looked for a link to spark his imagination and involve him in creative concentration. It began to be apparent that *B*. felt safest when assuming a radically different characterization from what he felt about himself. This occurred in short pantomimes: young tree, old tree, various animals, ancient miser, old woman. Our first concentrated interaction, lasting almost a whole session, occurred in the second month when he took on the role of a kangaroo, his favorite animal. He developed an unembellished plot of two kangaroos fighting for their lives against white hunters. Though unable to sustain the posture and balance of his character, he did remain concentrated, and resolved the conflict with an appropriate means of defense (kangaroo tail). This was also the first time that he allowed me to share the action and did not resort to the use of a gun or knife to terminate the conflict. This began a fruitful one month period of largely nonverbal acting out of animal characters, developing situations, toying with plots, and resolving conflict with the self victorious and in character. This phase ended as abruptly as it had begun.

Subsequently there was a pattern to our process together: bursts of concentrated creativity alternating with periods of uninvolved "rest," with no transition or warning from one phase to the other.

This rest phase was broken unexpectedly late in the third

month when I brought a piece of gold cloth to the session. After draping and handling it in a variety of ways, he threw it around his shoulders with a flourish and announced it was a cape. That action triggered a flow of creative activity. He entered a period of assertive leadership in which he suggested roles and situations. Example: he determined to play a prince who had to slay a dragon in order to win the princess. Rather than reacting defensively to a conflict situation, as he had in previous animal improvisations, he defined the plot and sought out conflict in order to win the prize, the princess. He determined areas of the room for specific actions, found objects to use as weapon, throne, dragon cave, and assigned me multiple roles. He now integrated the dramatic elements we had worked on earlier: the plot had a beginning, middle, and resolution; characterization and spatial arrangements remained constant; there was a high degree of interaction (including verbal interplay), total involvement in the process, and an experience of dramatic flow through an appropriate and satisfactory resolution. He visited the "king" and announced his intent with pomp and dignity; sought out the dragon and slew it; returned victorious with proof of the battle to claim his prize, which (for the first time as a human persona) he felt he deserved.

The "slaying of the dragon" led to the construction of a cardboard sword — a concentrated, detailed effort of drawing, cutting, and decorating. I felt B. might be ready now for a project, a specifically planned and rehearsed event to be repeated and refined, allowing him a more reflective relationship to the dramatic process. In the month that followed, we worked on coordination and characterization exercises, levels and planes of space, and the introduction of elementary stage vocabulary. One day B. arrived with a picture which he had had in his "private drawer" for some time: Perseus holding the head of Medusa. It seemed to have a great deal of meaning for him even if he could not articulate it and, though he was hesitant, he decided to use the story for his project. What followed was laborious and demanded a great deal of effort on his part, but each completed stage provided a secure foundation for the next. It was now the middle of the fourth month. He began the project by studying the myth, then outlined the plot and props needed in his notebook. He researched, designed, and constructed a shield (decorated with a Christian cross). Subsequently, he selected the location and size of the path of Perseus' journey, the mountain where Medusa lived, and the victor's return route. He was most concerned with the problem of Perseus/himself finding and killing Medusa without looking at her directly and risking being turned to stone. At times, he projected himself so firmly onto Perseus that I would stop the action to discuss other elements of the "as if" situation. At an early stage I had introduced the possibility of videotaping the scene; he was enthusiastic, but his anxiety level rose as we approached completion. At such times I moved away from the project entirely, or introduced another dramatic element. By the day of taping, props, costumes, scenic arrangements, characterization and sequence of actions were in order, but no clear beginning or end to the event had developed. *B.*, however, was not dissatisfied; for him, all the action lay in obtaining the head of Medusa. The taping went well. The actions and characterizations proceeded as *B.* had planned, modifying his earlier negative experience with "performing." His actual experience between "curtain" and "curtain" seemed to give him more satisfaction and confidence than watching and evaluating the tape.

Though still egocentric and largely unaware of the relationship of the improvised scenes to his preoccupations, in the course of four months, *B.* had taken the lead in creation of plot and character, actively sought suggestions and alternatives, had begun to understand space as an element of dramatic communication, and could differentiate between appropriate and inappropriate character responses to situations. He was beginning to develop and use dramatic structures creatively to reflect aspects of his experience and release frustrated energy through the elements of theatre.

# APPENDIX 2:
# CASE STUDY/KATHY GASKINS[6]

*A.* was diagnosed as schizophrenic at age ten. She was autistic and

had been institutionalized several times from eighteen months to
her current daytime attendance at a residential treatment center
for the emotionally disturbed. At other times, she lived either with
her divorced mother or her natural grandmother.

In our first three drama therapy sessions: she avoided eye,
physical and personal contact with me; her thinking patterns
were disorganized, as evident in her performance; she appeared
confused about her identity; and she ventilated her anger and
hostility destructively. In our opening sessions, we spent the first
fifteen minutes getting to know one another, and the last part of
the hour in spontaneous and random movements to varied beats,
produced either by *A.* using rhythm sticks, or with a metronome.
We used a "mirror game" and practiced eye contact for five
seconds, and then for longer, until we had built an easy rapport
between us.

We went from movement to a beat to movement with music.
Although still random and spontaneous, our movement focus was
on stretching and using our bodies in as many ways as possible.
She began to adapt to the music's suggestive qualities and express
in her movement the emotions she felt.

We began to pursue metaphorical movement: living and growing was the analogy most chosen by *A.* I asked her to keep the
experience short, and to project it in such a way that it would
seem real to others and herself. If the metaphorical movement
did not seem real, she was to stop and we would begin again. I
said it was most important that she believe in what she was doing.

I added several other components. First, we combined movement to a metronome beat with an analogy. Then we used movement to music and included analogies. Particularly helpful was
Saint-Saens' *Carnival of the Animals.*

Then we used the tape recorder to tell our own stories. *A.* could
not create a story in logical sequence, so we started by depending
heavily on popular pieces (for example, Rudyard Kipling's *The
Elephant Child*). We studied the construction and began recording our spoken parts section by section (i.e. beginning, theme,
middle, climax and end of story), and followed by a pantomime
of what we had spoken. We then used the verbalization and pan-

tomime together in each and ended by dramatizing the total story in sequence, though there were minor variations each time it was reenacted. The crucial factors were to progressively and systematically reach a dramatic goal, making the experience real for others, and keeping the action real to the participants.

*A.* then created her own story on the tape recorder. She chose the characters, the setting, and initiated the beginning action. We broke the story down into parts, worked over them verbally and physically, and then combined the verbalization and pantomime. We did not pre-determine how the story would proceed or end. *A.* usually followed the themes of the traditional stories with which we had previously worked.

Our last efforts were a complete spontaneous drama from beginning to end. This permitted greater input from *A.*'s life experiences; for example, her confusion about her name and origin was repeatedly brought out in her characterizations. Frequently she cast me in roles that paralleled her real life experiences. She could then observe alternate behaviors to those stimuli because, not being her, I did not respond in the same way as she did. Thus she could view herself and observe different ways of dealing with stimuli that might be directed towards her. This encouraged a more concrete realization of herself.

*A.*'s anger frequently showed itself: several times she had been sufficiently frustrated to attack one of her teachers. We discussed alternative ways to deal with anger and frustration. While this behavior was never displayed in our sessions, I tried to guide her to a more realistic resolution of these feelings. The drama permitted a detachment from the real life situation into one whereby she could convert her feeling into another action. The benefit was that she could deal with these problems at her own speed, in her own way, and with no personal invasion of privacy by me.

After six months, *A.* showed an increase in self-confidence when contributing to dramatic action. She was able to ask for physical comfort and attention during our sessions. Her physical abuse of her teacher stopped. She showed a greater ability in organizing and planning dramatic action, and in carrying the action successfully to a goal.

# APPENDIX 3:
# CASE STUDY/SUSAN HEFLER[7]

My task was to involve a thirteen-year-old emotionally disturbed boy, E., in the dramatic process. At our initial meeting, it was immediately evident that his hostility and intense anger at being asked to do anything other than what he was involved in at the moment had to be subdued first, before a working relationship could be established. Suggestions for dramatic activities were met with an inability to play, and his overwhelming anger, directed at no particular object, had to be harnessed and refocused.

After several weeks, tolerance of activity change (from classroom to drama session) began to emerge sporadically: he would enter less aggressively, a bit more accepting of this interruption of his life. Exercises involving movement were resisted as he had little awareness of his body and its existence in space. All verbal interactions alternated between aggressive, provocative attacks and lengthy disconnected lectures on historical topics (such as Egyptian civilization).

The first success was E.'s participation in imaginary object transformations involving some fine motor coordination limited to hand movement. He was comfortable within the prescribed spatial limits of a defined seated area; he was also not allowed to talk—his greatest defense against interaction—and he became visibly excited at his new mastery over the creation of and identification with that which was imagined. This small achievement, the ability to form space into imaginary objects of delimited size, shape and weight, initiated a tentative trust in me and the dramatic process. This acceptance was not constant and could not be counted on as a firm base which might lead him to imitative behavior. The really spontaneous involvement in playing (Category B) surfaced sporadically towards the end of our year together, but never consistently enough to enable behavior to be classified as anything other than stereotyped.

The peak moments which broke through into the imitative stage centered around his future career goals of becoming a lawyer. He would assume the role of lawyer and function "as if" he was being interviewed for law school. He recognized the need to clearly organize the plot actions: what was the interview going to consist of? when was he expected to take written tests? He delighted in assigning me character parts complete with specified mood and feeling. He rearranged furniture and space to create environment and, finally, in the last sessions he promoted himself to President of the United States, assigning me role, motivation and, even, dialect appropriate to his theme. But his themes remained pathologically subjective in their expression, and he was unable to distinguish projected fantasy from the ordered milieu of drama.

In play, we constructed dramatic conflict and attained appropriate resolutions to a myriad of national concerns ranging from the energy crisis to unemployment. Reflection and evaluation on these improvisations were always limited. Terse, one sentence comments on how he felt "superior" were all that could be elicited. This restrictive ability corresponds to the imitative stage of the Dramatic Process Observation Scale.

Since his enthusiasm arose from his ability to manipulate me rather than from mutuality, he was never able to proceed to truly cooperative interaction. His communication remained egocentric, stifling growth towards effective, innovative expression. Though able to take on roles, he was unable to reflect and objectify the experience. Aware of power within role, he used this as an end in and of itself. Though able to organize plot sequence, he retained unilateral control over organization of activities.

## APPENDIX 4:
## CASE STUDY/CYNTHIA LIGHTBODY[8]

M. was a highly verbal child who spun yarns: monsters, outer space, death and destruction were his favorite topics. His body image and coordination were extremely poor. He found nonverbal behavior threatening and difficult to focus upon.

In our first sessions, I mixed verbal and non-verbal tasks. The latter included mirrors, trust walks, walking on hot coals and soft moss, and so on. We also sat quietly with our eyes closed and listened to the sounds in the room: I asked him to concentrate on each one, and then have the different sounds hold conversations with each other.

Our beginning project was a play *M.* made up about a Lightning Monster. The story roughly paralleled a popular monster film. *M.* was obsessed with the violence which he associated with the monster (the part he chose to act). This play took several weeks and, when it was over, I asked him to tell me how the *monster* felt. He said: "I'm in great pain because of my wound. I've grown weak because of the amount of blood I've lost. The men didn't have to wound me if they wanted me to get away. They could have taken blind shots with their bazookas at my skull. I wouldn't like the shells hitting my body and I would have left... I hated them for wounding me."

I concentrated on non-verbal expression, and began each session with rhythmic warm-up exercises. These began as very simple movements (walking to a beat at different tempi) and progressed to free movement to music and "energy levels through movement" (i.e. inhaling and exhaling deeply with sounds while stretching). We moved on to pantomime, building from the simple to the complex until he could express non-verbally many moods and feelings and, finally, entire stories. Simple movements included mirroring, or throwing an imaginary ball back and forth and having the ball change from one kind to another — although he initially found this confusing, he developed the exercise well.

To stimulate his visual imagery, I gave him a nondescript object (such as an eraser), asked him to imagine it differently (say, as a kitten or acorn), look at it, handle it, and describe it verbally and non-verbally. To increase his concentration, I expanded pantomimes from a single action to a series of related actions — such as searching for a ring. I asked him to search for a real ring, then an imaginary one. We then discussed the differences of feeling between a real and imagined object: the real was easier at first; later, with practice, the imaginary one became easier. We worked a great deal on sense images. These involved him in hearing, touching, smelling, and describing things around him. I used exercises, sometimes with real people and sometimes with imagined ones, as follows: *Focus* — (1) watching a plane come in; (2) looking at a funny movie; *Seeing* — (1) enter a large room in which you have left your sweater; (2) go into a dark closet to look for your sweater; *Hearing* — (1) an explosion; (2) a small sound and trying to decide what it is; *Smelling* — (1) cookies baking in the oven; (2) something unpleasant and trying to decide what it is; *Tasting* — (1) a piece of chocolate candy; (2) a sour apple; *Touching* — (1) a piece of velvet; (2) something wet and soggy. *M.* pantomimed all the above actions. Then I added props (real candy, apple, etc.) and he reacted to them. I asked him to pantomime again with no props, and to feel the difference between "pretend," "real," and "pantomiming and experience." At first, his movements were rigid and self-conscious, but after reacting to real objects he found it easier to pantomime the same reactions without props. He seemed to comprehend actually "feeling" the pantomime.

We began to build action into the pantomime: "feeding the dog" became "coming home from school to feed the new puppy — how big is he? how much does he eat? how do you take care of him?" To the sustained action we added feelings: *M.* came home happy, fed the dog, got angry with it; then became the dog and slinked away whimpering; and became *M.* once again and was sad because he had hit the dog.

We pantomimed a longer story. We found a cave, explored it, found treasure, saw a monster and hid until it passed by, and we carried the treasure home. We discussed feelings, and he expressed them in various stages: happiness, curiosity, excitement, fear, relief, strain of lifting the treasure, relaxation and joy. He did well with the literal interpretation and lost a lot of self-consciousness about body movement.

We practiced the expression of feelings by using emotion cards — he would pick a card, act out in pantomime the emotion written on it, and I would guess the emotion portrayed. Then I would pantomime, and he would guess. This became one of his favorites, and we often used it for warm-ups.

For characterization, he would perform the same action as done by different characters: thus, as though visiting a gymnasium, he was a fat man, an athlete, and then a child who had never visited a gym before. With the story, "The Little Scarecrow Boy," he pantomimed a different character each time it was read;

with practice, he moved easily from one role to another.

In abstract pantomime (free movement to music) his favorite was *The Blue Danube* by Strauss. He found random movement to music very difficult but he tried hard. Then he created a story to music: when I played the music in small segments he began to focus much better. He said he chose *The Blue Danube* because it was happy and graceful; it made him think of water and boats rolling on the waves. He made up a story about the adventures of a blue whale while swimming along the river.

By the end of therapy, *M.* had made remarkable progress non-verbally. He was on the imitative level, but still had a hard time with innovative movements to music. At one of our last sessions, he beautifully pantomimed a leaf slowly uncurling and going through its life cycle (to *Clair de Lune* by Debussy).

Throughout the course of treatment, I interspersed puppetry which *M.* enjoyed. I used it as a reinforcement at the end of each pantomime project. His early puppet play was full of horrible monsters and violence; later, his monsters became helpful and benevolent, and his puppet family more loving and less violent.

In our final session, *M.* role played. His sister planned to move away to the country, and he was upset and angry about this. He played himself, then his father, then his sister — stepping into his sister's shoes, his anger changed to sadness, then grudging acceptance and, finally, understanding of her feelings and reasons.

During the five months of drama therapy, there was a marked improvement in *M.*'s imagery, concentration, focus, body awareness, and creative problem-solving processes.

## FOOTNOTES

1. Based on research at the Ittleson Center for Child Research, New York.
2. Erik H. Erikson, "Play and Actuality," in *Play and Development,* ed. Maria W. Piers (New York: Norton, 1972), p. 133.
3. Hughes Mearns, *Creative Power: The Education of Youth in the Creative Arts* (New York: Dover, 1958), pp. 245–46.
4. Jean Piaget, *Structuralism* (New York: Basic Books, 1970), pp. 118–19.
5-8. Barbara Eberhardt, Kathy Gaskins, Susan Hefler, and Cynthia Lightbody were members of the "Drama as a Means of Developing Communicative Awareness" Project, Ittleson Center for Child Research.

# Part 2
# SPECIAL PROBLEMS

Drama therapy with children having special problems has solid philosophic foundations. For the last two centuries, philosophers have been encouraging the use of dramatic play. Rousseau said that: "Childhood has its own ways of seeing, of thinking, of feeling, which are suitable to it; nothing is less reasonable than to substitute our own," while Froebel said that: "Play is self-active representation of the inner"—in other words, dramatic play *represents* the inner life. Although Freud said that "dreams are the royal road to the unconscious," child psychotherapists discovered that children better exemplified their inner world through play. As a result, throughout most of this century child analysts like Anna Freud, Margaret Lowenfeld, Melanie Klein, and Erik Erikson have consistently used play in their clinical work. In most cases, however, play was simply used as one of many methods with very young children, and less with maturation.

At the same time, British teachers were beginning to use spontaneous drama in education. Called "creative drama" or "child drama," it was used for two purposes:(1) to develop the child's self-concept so that (2) learning could be meaningful to the individual. In particular, Peter Slade came to use the term "drama therapy" to describe dramatic activity that led to "confidence, hope, feeling of security, discovery of sympathy, and concentration." However, it was not until the late 1950's that spontaneous drama was a commonplace in British schools, or that drama therapy was used systematically for children with specific dysfunctions. More recently, similar work in other countries has developed until, today, it is a major methodology not merely with children but with adults having special needs.

In this part, Sue Jennings provides an overview of the origins of drama therapy with children in Britain, describes current practices, and then her work with the physically disabled (Chapter 3). Peter Slade, in Chapter 4, discusses his work under three headings: (a) conscious and intended therapy; (b) constructive education; and (c) prevention. He then gives explicit examples of each, and also demonstrates how all three can be integrated in practical situations.

The next several chapters deal with *functionally impaired* groups. Marian R. Lindkvist delineates autism and shows how movement and drama together can assist children who suffer from this condition (Chapter 5). Eleanor C. Irwin examines case material of emotionally disturbed children (Chapter 6), and Julie Arden tells the story of one emotionally disturbed boy within drama therapy at a special school (Chapter 7).

The final set of papers deals with *organically impaired* groups. Sue Martin discusses the use of developmental drama with brain-damaged children (Chapter 8). Susan Aach shows how spontaneous drama can be a means of self-expression for the blind (Chapter 9), while Jackson Davis shows how theatre can be used with deaf children (Chapter 10).

In each chapter, the drama therapist discusses matters from his own criteria. For example, while Susan Aach approaches the blind child from creative methods, Jackson Davis is mainly concerned with performances by the deaf. A second factor is the need of the children: whereas Eleanor C. Irwin, Sue Martin and Julie Arden center their work on spontaneous dramatic play, Marian

R. Lindkvist acknowledges that the autistic child must be led through movement to the drama.

SUE JENNINGS, a dramatherapist and social anthropologist, is the author of *Remedial Drama* and editor and contributor to *Creative Therapy*. Secretary of the British Association of Dramatherapists and editor of their journal, she is course leader in drama therapy at Hertfordshire College of Art and Design, and holds a research fellowship in dramatherapy at St. John's College, York.

*Chapter 3*

# DRAMA THERAPY : ORIGINS AND THE PHYSICALLY DISABLED

Sue Jennings

*"Drama therapy is a means of helping to understand and alleviate social and psychological problems, mental illness and handicap; and of facilitating symbolic expression through which man may get in touch with himself both as* individual and group *through creativity structures involving vocal and physical communication."*

— British Association of Dramatherapists

## 1  ORIGINS & PRACTICE

The drama experience as known and practiced in simpler societies can be called a preventive mental health program through drama. This is beginning to influence thought and practice in the arts and caring professions in the West. While drama itself has been in existence in its many divergent forms for thousands of years, it has taken two decades of hard pioneering work for drama therapy to be accepted as a valid form of treatment and experience.

### *Background*

Drama therapy includes concepts from ritual and primitive art forms, the growth and development of theatre, theories of the creative process[1] and its effects on society.[2] The philosophy of drama therapy has been enriched by contemporary thinking in social anthropology

55

on ritual and symbolism. Other important influences have included analytic group psychotherapy, the growth movement and the newer therapies. There has been no lack of intellectual justification for the drama process in games and play, child drama, drama in education,[3] and psychodrama. However, until the sixties, theoretical justification made little impact on the clinical field which was looking for scientific proof to back up theory and practice.

But several influences came together in the late fifties and early sixties to help change the prevailing atmosphere. Peter Slade's historic contribution to the concept of Child Drama[4] cannot be overestimated. As a result, drama began to be recognized as an important part of the school curriculum, rather than a specialized extra after school.

Changes were happening in psychiatry, too, with the impact made by Ronald Laing and the Philadelphia Association. Maxwell Jones was developing his ideas of therapeutic communities. The fight was on for the educational rights of the mentally handicapped. The "human growth" movement began — encounter, sensitivity, gestalt, bioenergetics, Esalen. The traditional British scene was slow to react but many of these techniques have now become part of the establishment in psychiatry, psychology, management training, social work and other caring professions.

In America, dance therapy was the first to be recognized while, in Britain, art therapy and music therapy began to make their impact in the late sixties. Into this milieu came two organizations specializing in the therapeutic use of drama. Out of the Religious Drama Society grew Sesame which takes visiting groups into hospitals and runs training courses. One of their staff has also written a book on drama and movement in therapy.[5] I was personally involved with the other organization — the Remedial Drama Centre — with Gordon Wiseman and, later, Roy Shuttleworth. The Centre dealt with depressed and deprived groups in the neighborhood, as well as referrals from the education authorities and social welfare agencies. With the making of a training film and the publication of *Remedial Drama,* [6] progress was being made. Later, the Remedial Drama Centre developed into the Dramatherapy Centre and now operates as Dramatherapy Consultants, training and advising in the field.

More recently, the limitations of psychoanalytic, psychological and theatrical models were being realized and, in the quest for new structures, social anthropology began to have its influence. Just as Peter Brook took his theatre company to Africa and worked with an anthropologist, I took a long sabbatical and developed my anthropological training in fieldwork research amongst a tribal people in Southeast Asia. I spent two years looking for new rituals, new family and social structures, and evidence of drama being used unconsciously in preventive mental health.

The sixties and seventies have been questioning and challenging. Certainly they have been creatively revolutionary in the arts and therapy.

## Goals

First, drama therapy is concerned with the creative development of the whole person, physically, mentally and emotionally, through the drama process. Often problems can be understood or resolved spontaneously without situations being designed to solve specific problems. Roles can be tried out, relationships tested, self awareness as a social and political being can be discovered, and social skills can be learnt. Feelings can be explored and understood in relation to individuals and groups; and the creative process brings about aesthetic satisfaction, confidence and hope. But a balance must be kept between the needs of the individual and those of the group so that personal creativity can develop alongside social awareness.

Second, drama therapy is concerned with problem solving and is defined by its concepts and practices. These are wider than those of psychodrama. Techniques of psychodrama are used to examine specific problems, and this has far more acceptance by clinicians who utilize them as part of a specific therapeutic program.

Ideally, we should combine the creative and problem solving approach in our concept of drama therapy. If we focus on medical problems we tend to reinforce a medical model, often equated with sickness, rather than using creativity to find structures that will reinforce the more healthy aspects of the individual. Through creativity, we are enabling the joy and satisfaction to be experienced as well as the more painful areas.

In practicing drama therapy, we are presupposing that all people are creative and have latent talent with which they can express, communicate, pattern and shape their lives through symbolic interaction. Some people are more creative in music, others through visual art, both of which are more definable media than drama. The drama medium is less easy to perceive and define because the material is ourselves — our bodies, words, actions and symbols — and it is inclusive of all other media. Harness this and we have a veritable force.

## Practice

Drama therapy skills include techniques of psychodrama, sociodrama, theatre, dance, mime, movement, games, simulation, and improvisation in both verbal and non-verbal expression.

Whatever the distress of our clients, we are applying drama therapy to explore, first, the creative potential of the group. This may be through movement, dance, mime or verbal improvisation, play reading leading to role play, awareness games, guided fantasy, or dance-dramas exploring symbolic themes.

Where we start depends on the needs and expectations of the group. For example, drama gives a framework to explore problems of relationship that belong to a person's past or present; or we can look at the future, test our ambitions, and get in touch with reality as it concerns our potential. Many creative improvisations develop into personal situations relevant to people's own experience. If a situation involving leadership and dominance develops while improvising an underwater theme with music and sound effects, it might be "worked through" within the context of the improvisation itself. However, in one case it was necessary for me to be more directive. We stepped outside the underwater theme and used role play and sculpting to explore the group's feelings concerning leadership. From these came a personal psychodrama from one individual who was able to externalize his problem through family role play, egoing and role reversal.

However, we should not view improvisation purely as a means to specific therapy. It is important as a creative expression in its own right.

Another dimension of our work is helping our patients and clients to learn social skills: tying shoelaces with the mentally handicapped; learning the many forms of greeting and parting on a psychiatric ward; practicing going into shops, having a variety of responses from the shopkeeper, or rehearsing appropriate behavior in the outside world, for those about to be rehabilitated. Through research in education and play, it has been found that learning takes place more efficiently through "doing" rather than just by receiving information. Drama therapy provides very efficient learnings for the acquisition of these skills.

Through drama therapy, we have a medium for exploring ourselves and our feelings: to get in touch with those areas that have been blocked by tension; to re-experience childhood situations; to allow ourselves to be loved and to love; to be dependent; and to experience irrational rage. The whole range of emotions is there for us to explore and develop, and especially to come to terms with guilt feelings. Encounter techniques and sensitivity training are important, as well as simulation and improvisation of various scenes where these emotions are expressed. Often, it is initially easier to admit to these feelings when acting as someone else.

It is important that these dimensions of learning are perceived developmentally. That is, the creativity of the therapist stimulates the creativity of the clients and vice versa. The situation can be enhanced by the learning of a new technique, which brings about both a discipline and freedom. Important also is the fact that by teaching drama technique, one is giving one's client alternative methods of communication and expression.

## Why do we need drama therapy?

Society has always needed drama as the creative and ritualistic expression of a culture: that makes statements about its values, reinforces group identity, and reflects its ideas about the division of labour; that comments on politics or seeks to change it; that uses myth, legend and traditional story; that links drama with religion and belief systems; and that provides aesthetic experience for its people. Most cultures at most times have had a form of dramatic expression deeply rooted in their life style.

In Western society, man has become split between his mind and his body.[7] This results from the industrial revolution, modern technology, and man's technical awareness outstripping his capacity to change and adapt. His physical expression through the body is becoming more and more redundant. His mental expression is becoming more technical and complex. This applies not only in our educational system but also in our whole system of values and socialization. Contemporary society poses many dichotomies — the individual as opposed to group survival — yet the centralization of political power lessens the choice and freedom of the individual. Contemporary man is confused: in a world of technological development and seemingly limitless resources, as an individual he seems powerless. Man needs meaningful experiences through which he can retain some autonomy. Even his entertainment is observer-oriented rather than participatory: vicarious experiences of drama, movement, music and art do not satisfy him at either the emotional or the intellectual levels. Contemporary man must feel bereft because he no longer has a socially acceptable medium through which he can diffuse tension, reinforce his role, dissipate anxiety, instigate change, or discover an equilibrium within his social group, as well as satisfying his creative needs.

However, I must add a warning. It is easy to fob people off with ritual and pageantry, appealing to gross sentiment and self indulgence. We must realize that in drama therapy we have a very powerful tool that can be destructive (as well as constructive) if not used with responsibility. Properly used, however, drama therapy is a basis for personal and social change, as well as ritual satisfaction and aesthetic experience.

## The Reluctant Society

Difficulties within society have caused suspicion towards the notion of drama therapy and its integration into the day to day life of hospital, school or community.

Firstly, we are living in the age of the specialist — including all forms of artists and sportsmen — whose activities we vicariously enjoy rather than doing them ourselves. Society is now cut up into experts and non-experts: the notion of doing drama is compared with the professional theatre and, thus, a response from a drama class will often be "I can't act." As a result, ordinary non-experts do not "do" drama (or art, or whatever).

Secondly, drama is so akin to play that it is perceived, like play, to be the domain of children: as something we grow out of when we get older. Drama is often perceived to be childish rather than childlike. Occupational therapists complain to me that adult patients on their wards will not participate in drama because they say it is "kid's stuff." One has got to undo the long-term prejudices that prevent everyone joining in a drama session and enjoying it. But there is much work to be done in this area of "allowing" adults to "do" drama.

Thirdly, with the advent of small living spaces, home entertainment must be less active and more passive. Television is the ideal passive entertainment. There is just not enough room for everyone to join in — and the specialist does it better anyway!

In addition, if the artist is not elevated to a "specialist" then he is often an outcast because he is eccentric and living beyond the rules of "normal" society. Is it surprising that there is difficulty in accepting the notion of drama within society? Not only are we using skills which belong "outside society" or are considered too "specialized," but we are also using them with clients who, because of illness, deprivation or handicap are deemed to be outside the "norm."

For drama therapy to be accepted, it must change society's value system on two counts: in the methods and techniques that we use, and the people with whom we use them. Both changes have to do with alienation: that of both the client and the artist from the normal life of society.

The signs of change are encouraging. Many of the caring professions, such as occupational therapy and social work, now incorporate drama therapy into their training programs as well as in-service programs for their staff. Hospitals and related institutions are integrating drama therapy into their therapeutic programs. Very often, the internal staff—occupational therapists, social workers, nurses—run these groups while psychologists or a trained drama therapist is brought in from outside. The visiting specialist may present problems when integrating activities into an overall program. Ideally, each hospital would have a full time drama therapist, or one member of staff who is extensively trained, devoting the majority of his time to it. Special Education, too, is beginning to integrate drama therapy in both schools for the disturbed and those for the mentally handicapped and educationally sub-normal. Day release and full time courses are now being established in British polytechnics, colleges of education and art schools. Some hospitals run their own in-service training for staff, while educational authorities are employing drama therapists as consultants to train field staff.

Much has been accomplished in the last fifteen years, but there is still a long way to go. The most recent significant event in Britain was the formation of the Association for Dramatherapists and *The Journal of Dramatherapy*.[8] However, the Association, by its very structure, is seeking on the one hand to set professional standards and adequate training while, on the other hand, it is not trying to be elitist and exclusive. This is a very delicate path to tread.

## 2   GENERAL APPLICATIONS

"Drama for all" is important—whether people are deemed to be dysfunctioning or otherwise. There are many groups of people who manage to "survive": the twilight group who never quite get referred to any welfare agency; those whose lives are in a rut but who want to change yet do not know how; and the many who know there is something more to life but cannot begin to define it. To all of these people, and to everyone else, I would extend the idea of drama therapy; and I would hope that, in time, the notion of community participation drama becomes more developed and widespread.

There are various goals with dysfunctioning groups as well as the one common goal of developing creative communication. When working with the mentally handicapped, one is more concerned with social skill learning and stimulation. With the maladjusted, too much stimulation can be harmful, and the drama therapist provides secure frameworks for feelings to be externalized and problems to be worked through. The crucial step is to decide the goals of the group before designing the program. When working with adults, one must beware of approaching drama in a childish way — this will naturally cause resistance, not just with clients but with staff too.

Often, especially with adult groups, we must start with a very safe framework and I find that improvisation can be too threatening at times. I always use the yardstick of starting "where the group is at" and, if that means the security of sitting down and using a playscript, then that is where to start. The important thing is to know when the group is ready to move on: perhaps improvising from the scripted roles; perhaps improvising their own play though, initially, within a fairly tight structure. There is plenty to be developed from their feelings and thoughts about the roles they have played in the script; and it is only a step from such improvisations to the examination of "life scripts."

Many adult groups shy away from movement and seek the security of sitting still. However, I have found that one patient group needed sound effects for a radio play they were improvising and, soon, they were spontaneously getting up and down with alacrity. Adult groups will respond to dance-drama if the approach is at their own level.

The important guidelines for starting practical work are: (1) get to know the group and "where they are at;" (2) define the goals of the group; (3) try to balance the program with verbal and non-verbal work, stimulation and relaxation, personal role play and creative drama (not necessarily all in the same session).

One should aim for an emotional graph in a single session. After a peak of stimulation, the group should be brought down gradually (through music, or a verbal feedback session) so that the finish is calm. Nothing is more disruptive than to finish on a "high" when they leave the drama therapy group.

Do not expect "happenings." Developmental drama is far more healthy, and "happenings" tend to be contrived. Do not be surprised if drama moves into art and music. Some groups can find art or music therapy more creative than drama . It is not a case of either/or—rather, it is an emphasis upon one rather than another. Even so, I make use of art and music within drama: for instance, making and using masks.

I use the full range of dance, drama and psychodrama techniques, together with visual aids, masks, music and other effects when appropriate. Lighting is important. Often a group will respond more effectively if there is muted lighting—one coloured spotlight and the rest of the room in shadow. When these refinements are not possible, we have to work in rooms that are too big/small and with too little light. Improvisation is the answer, and often a client group will have creative ideas: for example, some harsh strip lights were converted to a warm atmosphere by pinning around them a hammock of orange curtain material. Screens can be used to divide space.

My criteria for the activity of groups are: (1) Safety: the safe place, safe music, ritual, predictability, reinforcement, etc. (2) Exploration: the stimulating environment, emotive music, provocative theme, etc. Any session must have a balance of the two. Some groups need more safety than others, and a few can cope with less safety and more exploration. Only the drama therapist's experience is a guide to this balance.

One must be sensitive to the needs of individuals and the group as follows: when silence is necessary; when to interpret and when not; when to allow long feedback sessions and a winding down period, or otherwise. All groups vary.

In setting up a situation, structures or models must not be superimposed that are too rigid or directive. Often these serve to fulfil the therapist's needs rather than the group's.

A word of caution to drama teachers working in remedial situations: never play at being therapist. You may well find a group ending up with a new problem rather than working through those it already has. If you are working in a diagnostic and interpretative way, then extensive therapeutic training is essential.

# 3  THE PHYSICALLY DISABLED

Drama therapy with the physically disabled can be divided into three areas: (1) the Multiple Handicap—both mental and physical damage; (2) the Physical Handicap—loss of limb, cerebral palsy, polio, etc., with no mental impairment; and (3) Symptomatic Physical Handicap—physical impairment caused by emotional problems, and sometimes symptomatic of neurosis or psychosis.

## The Multiple Handicap

Working problems with this group are often exacerbated by the frustration and despair felt by parents, teachers and nurses. Parents experience guilt, nurses feel inferior in status to their colleagues working with more "normal" patients, and teachers find work repetitive and progress slow. It is also mistakenly suggested that high intellectual capacity is necessary for participation in drama and so it is excluded from the activities of the more severely disabled.

In this work, there are three important goals (in addition to those given in 1. above): (1) as a learning situation for social skills; (2) as a means of getting in touch with, and expression of, feelings; (3) as a means of developing staff/child, parent/child, and child/child relationships. However simple the skill learning, it can be rehearsed through the drama process to both reinforce the learning and make the experience enjoyable. The learning will be directed to specific skills, therefore the structure will be comparatively tight. Eating, talking, teeth cleaning are all activities that can be experienced through play, through the imagination, and then applied to the real life situation. Because of severe impairment, it is too easy to allow the severely handicapped to maintain a dependency; staff end up treating them as children. Through the drama process, one has the opportunity for the development, as far as possible, of autonomous persons.

It is easy to forget that when a child is very damaged and, perhaps, cannot verbalize, that he or she still has feelings to express. Severe handicaps can create emotional problems—often through the reaction of parents, early hospitalization, or the ef-

fects of institutionalization. However severe the handicap, such
children's emotional needs are as strong or stronger than those of
the normal child. But their pathways of communication are very
limited. Many will never acquire speech or non-verbal communication through movement, touch and sound, but drama can
enable sorrow, rage, love and despair to be expressed. Physical
handling is important as a means of communication, of love and
trust, and to learn body image and balance. Many severely handicapped children are deprived of these in their early days.
Physical movement is important to prevent premature inactivity,
and for coordination and control.

Improvement in morale is crucial to maximize the progress of
these groups. In my experience, drama therapy is an important
way of achieving this because of its enjoyable quality.

## Physical Handicap

It is only in recent years that drama therapy has taken its place
in programs for the physically handicapped. Some physiotherapists in the past have said that the movement can be too stimulating, too generalized, or even "incorrect." The training courses
that we have run, however, have allowed physiotherapists to
integrate drama therapy into their own discipline, and they have
seen that it is not a question of either/or but of balance. Often,
the patient does not have the motivation or confidence to move at
all. Should the focus be taken off the handicap through creative
activity then often the motivation to move can occur spontaneously. One incident is relevant here. I was doing stories in
sound with a group of wheelchair children and one girl who had
never stood before became so involved that she stood up. When a
member of staff called out "Look, Mary is standing up!" she sat
down again and did not stand again for several weeks.

Drama therapy is important with these groups because:
(1) it can assist individuals to develop their bodies and limbs to
    their fullest potential;
(2) it can provide an understanding of emotional problems which
    may have been heightened by the handicap but are not neces-
    sarily its cause (perhaps stemming from early rejection at

home in the case of someone born with a handicap, or coming to terms with the trauma after someone has been damaged in an accident);

(3) it can assist people to adjust their perception of themselves and those around them, and pave the way towards healthy relationships.

Dance and rhythmic movement, even in wheelchairs, is important for the development of body image, self-image, creativity and confidence. It mobilizes and activates.

If staff and patients can see the handicap as a stimulus for ingenuity rather than a disadvantage, then many exciting things can happen. We have had fun-fairs and circuses with wheelchair patients. We have used costumes and been transported through time, we have made up faces and made masks — all the normal drama activities have been achieved with these groups. Importantly, through using their bodies less "directly" than in a physical training session, there has been a great sense of achievement.

People with normal intelligence who are physically handicapped suffer great difficulties and frustrations because they are aware of their disability. Using drama in a creative way can boost self-confidence and help them come to terms with their handicap. Energetic activities — such as football — when simulated through drama become possible for severely immobile people. One boy I worked with had exceptionally high intelligence but was unable to communicate verbally; yet he was able to find some fulfillment through creative activity which also satisfied his intellectual needs.

Drama therapy is also invaluable for emotional problems that overlay the physical handicap. Role-play, improvisation and psychodrama help in changing people's attitudes towards themselves and their preconceptions of how they feel the world looks at them.

## Symptomatic Physical Handicap

Everyone is affected by their early physical handling, and also by the attitudes of society towards both physical expression and "the perfect body." How we are held (even whether we are held at all), fed, dressed and bathed as infants has a bearing on how we develop as physical beings. Social norms of how to dress, walk and sit down influence our physical orientation and the degree of rigidity in the way we move. Moreover, the influence of technology has diminished the role of physical activity in our society and, thereby, the use of our bodies.

Despite the pressures of modern living, many of us learn to live with our bodies, maybe not wholly satisfactorily, but we get by. We may be aware of tension in body parts for which there are numerous pharmaceutical preparations. We may be anxious about the amount of physical violence in our society. Sometimes, there comes a point where a physical symptom can manifest itself—such as the loss of use of a limb—for which there is not a direct physical cause. Sometimes a person suffering in such a way may be referred for psychotherapy but such treatment does not necessarily mean that the symptom will disappear. Once insight and understanding have been gained, there may still be physical habits learnt over a long period of time that will now have to be re-trained. This is where drama therapy can be useful.

It provides the opportunity to re-experience the body: to experience its sensations and limits; to discover the optimum amount of tension necessary for alertness and action, and the point where tension itself becomes destructive. I do not propose to analyze the body signals and body language we express; that has been ably done by many, and is a necessary area of study in drama therapy. But we are all aware of the aggressive chin, the protected torso, the frozen posture, and so on. Very often, these have had their origins in early infancy through handling and role casting, or through the expectancies put onto us. Through drama therapy it is possible to re-experience the childhood situation and develop trust and dependency. It is also possible to work in body areas of extreme tension with guided fantasy. Technically, it is possible to work on the situation through drama therapy; or to continue work when psychotherapy has finished, or even alongside it; or, sometimes, to work initially in drama therapy and then feed information back to the psychotherapy situation. Techniques of dance, mime, movement, dance-drama, and projective play are all valuable in this area. I also use relaxation, massage, encounter techniques and sensitivity.

## Stereotyped/Compulsive Movement

Compulsive stereotyped movement, such as head banging, flicking, rocking and moaning, is common to many neurotic and psychotic conditions, emotional disturbance and handicap. There can be complete rigidity, catatonia and immobility.

In a previous publication, I suggested that man has a minimum ritual need which is normally satisfied with group rituals. This enables a person to achieve identity as an individual and as part of a group. Situations that are predictable and safe, that have rules and (hopefully) physical expression, are ritualistic. But the opportunities for these rituals are becoming less and, for the impaired, almost non-existent. I would suggest that, without adequate outlets, these rituals become inturned, self-destructive, isolated and exclusive.

In my experience, if ritual can be shared then its destructive intensity can be diminished and more satisfying group ritual expression can be developed. However, when staff try to interrupt the compulsive movements, they are usually performed even more and more vigorously. But tuning into the rhythm and moving, or making sounds *with* the person, forms the basis for the first communication—a shared experience in non-verbal communication which can be developed in a variety of ways.

It is not enough to discover our bodies and accept them without shame. It is also necessary to be creative with them. Through drama therapy this can occur in symbolic movement, dance, drama and related experiences. Our bodies are the medium of our expression, both verbal and non-verbal. However handicapped, let us develop their fullest potential.

## 4 CONCLUSION

I have discussed the background of drama therapy, its development, and its specific application to that broad area known as the physically disabled. I have tried to argue the appropriateness and need for this approach, and I have given guidelines for the structuring of sessions. But it would be a mistake to be over-directive and point to only one way of doing drama therapy. Such is its nature (like any other creative art form) that it must be flexible and adaptable.

Ideas breed ideas — and I find that, once this work has begun, it generates its own ideas and enthusiasm. Many staff have come to me, worried that they would run out of ideas, only to realize that they had not begun to tap the resources of their group. Creativity is a developmental process that has peaks and lulls but which never actually stops.

In living, growth and change come through risk taking. It is the same with drama therapy. It does take courage to take the first step — for both staff and client alike — but it is a step that can be limitless in its reward and enjoyment.

## PRACTICAL ILLUSTRATIONS
(multiple handicaps)

Peter was a three-year-old spina bifida with hydrocephalus attending a preschool special nursery for children with mixed and multiple handicaps.

It was uncertain to what extent he was brain damaged or whether he was withdrawn for emotional reasons. Initially he did not respond at all to music and movement; he would just sit and very rarely look at anything. As a last stimulus I decided to explore tactile objects and experiment with different textures: scrubbing brushes; egg shells; leaves; sand paper. I put these objects into his hands or against his cheek, and talked to him while doing so. His first response came when a piece of fern stuck to his fingers with the egg white that had come off the egg shells. It captured his interest as he rubbed it off his fingers and he started looking at and exploring his fingers as if he had noticed them for the first time.

This seemed to trigger off interest in other things. He started with movements to music, progressed to simple movement games and he then began to make speech sounds. After about a month, he was able to smile when it was time for his drama session.

At the same nursery we were using movement to music to develop new skills and spatial awareness. We decided to reinforce vertical space with pitch in music and sang the following:

High (stretch up high)   G
Low (reach down low)   G
Middle (come back to center again)   C   (Middle C)
Repeat
Down we go and up again (bend down and stretch again)
                    G, F, E, D, C, D, E, F, G,
    to High    G
      Low      G
      Middle   C

We also developed time songs which involved being grandfather clocks with arms ticking very slowly and then striking; clocks on the wall with middle size ticks and movement; and wrist watches with fast ticks and little finger movement.

These games were made up by the staff and students to fit the particular needs of the group.

With children who have severe mental handicaps I usually start with movement — gentle rocking and swaying to music; learning to roll and be rolled; to push and to be pushed; developing an awareness of body in space and of body strength. As a stimulus I use either drum beats or music with a strong simple tempo so that the children have time to assimilate the rhythm as they move; so often music is too fast or too slow to sustain the handicapped in movement. I always balance these sessions with contrasts between fast and slow; large body movement and more intricate movement, and so on.

# PRACTICAL ILLUSTRATIONS
## (physically handicapped)

A creative drama program was requested in a residential school for the physically disabled. Most members of the young adolescent group were in wheelchairs. The staff attended as well.

Our task was to provide a meaningful experience for the group
and to illustrate various contrasts of work to the staff who were
highly curious to see how drama could help such severely disabled
youngsters.

We devised a variation of the journey game (a journey theme is
invaluable because it has a ready-made structure of beginning,
middle and end and can encompass a high degree of stimulus and
de-climax to finish; the content can be as realistic or fantastic as
needed depending on the goals of the group).

We also wanted decision making and autonomy to be built into
the session. The actual stops of the journey on the magic carpet
we had worked out in principle before, but allowing time for
reaction and free expression within the structure.

The stops were: The Land of Sea and Shells (sea music, shells
of all dimensions and sand); The Land of Mud Puddles (mud
puddle effects, slurping music); The Land of Witches (fire,
cauldron); The Land of Princesses (theatrical jewelry and silk
drapes). Other props included a carpet, a jewel box and a map
with treasure marked on it.

We all gathered on the carpet, and our first task was to invent
the right word to make the carpet become airborne. This gave us
plenty of time for vocal warm-up, getting louder and louder in
order to leave the ground. Once in the air we all contributed a
running commentary on the things we were passing. Then we
touched down with a bump in the first land. We moved to the sea
music, handled and touched all the shells, and let the sand run
through our fingers. The wind started to blow stronger (sound
effect), and we took off before getting trapped by a storm. Our
second landing was to The Land of Mud Puddles and the magic
carpet began to get sucked into the swamp with all of us; everyone
helped one another as the mud sucked them in, pulling them to
the bank, but the magic carpet was lost to sight. We came to the
river, washed the mud off, jogged up and down to keep warm and
then crossed the river. We found ourselves in The Land of
Witches, and we were immediately pursued. One of the group
decided to join the witches and he got them to agree that we
could learn how to make up spells. (We felt it might be useful to

retrieve the carpet!) We still had our map with us; there was a big cross on it in The Land of Witches, but we decided not to mention it. We practiced our spells, and then went to find the cross. We dug there and found a huge chest of jewels. One of the witches gave chase when she saw us. We got back to the river — had to cross in convoy — then to the mud swamp. One of the people had invented a spell to retrieve the carpet. The witches were just in sight when we became airborne in a hurry and eventually we landed at the last land: The Land of Princesses. It turned out that the Princess had lost all those jewels, and she shared them with everyone. We all dressed up and danced in our wheelchairs before riding home and having a good sleep on the way.

As will be apparent from the story, a lot of imagination is involved; decision making, thereby encouraging autonomy; plenty of varied body movements; sensations (touch and sound); success factors (dealing with obstacles); fear (overcoming it when facing the witches); tension and relaxation, characterization and roles. The group and staff were exhausted, but the experience had been a positive one for them.

I frequently use escape themes with the physically severely disabled, feeling that the escape symbolically will help to fight feelings of being trapped by one's handicap.

The idea of being able to symbolically escape or to transcend oneself was experienced by a group we were working with in a Cerebral Palsy Center in Europe. We played a simulated football match, and the only difference was that we had an imaginary ball. All groups were involved either as team members or as crowd. One black girl who had been found in a mud hut in one of the colonies said at the end: "For the first time we can be the same as everyone else."

One favorite exercise with these disabled groups served not only to stimulate the imagination, but also to develop relationships and group work; it is called Change the Object. An object, such as a ruler or a piece of rod, is passed around the circle and people used it for anything that came into their minds. If the group is reasonably mobile then the object can be put in the middle of the circle and people will use it when an idea occurs to them: as weapons, musical instruments, brushes of various sorts, and so on. Soon the group started to use it as something that involved someone else and the beginning of relationships developed: a fishing rod, and someone else played the fish; a cricket bat, so someone else started to bowl. This pair work became important for starting communications within the group. Often it would then grow into group work, such as one person being the conductor and the others being the orchestra.

The following session was designed for an adolescent group with various degrees of handicap; most of them were wheelchair cases and some were brain damaged due to road accidents.

The theme I chose was color: to develop perception and decision making; to stimulate movement and extend the range of body skills.

I used long pieces of different colored chiffon, about 4 inches wide and 3 feet long. Initially we played the color warm-up game: the leader calls out a color, and everyone has to touch it. Then he calls out two colors, and people have to touch both at the same time. Even the most severely disabled could guide a helper's hand towards a colored square on a blanket.

I then introduced the scarves, and everyone chose his favorite color and said why it was his favorite color. We then explored movement, shapes and patterns, circles, waves, squiggles, small and large body movements. These scarves facilitate opening up and expanding the body.

We used the scarves to link with another person and to make patterns with him; then with people across the room to make a whole group pattern. Those who were more mobile began to explore the pattern. We then split in small groups and began to invent mobiles. Someone suggested that one person go into the middle and we make a maypole; this we did, plaited the scarves and passed them around even though we couldn't dance in and out. The session ended by people finding out the color of each other's eyes and grouping accordingly; then we relaxed to music and concentrated on colors in our minds' eye.

This session fulfilled all the goals that had been set out at the beginning, and also was great fun.

# FOOTNOTES

1. Jean Duvignaud, *The Sociology of Art* (London: Paladin, 1972).
2. Anthony Storr, *The Dynamics of Creation* (London: Secker & Warburg, 1972).
3. Richard Courtney, *Play, Drama & Thought: The Intellectual Background to Dramatic Education,* 3d ed. (London: Cassell; New York: Drama Book Specialists, 1974).
4. Peter Slade, *Child Drama* (London: University of London Press,1954); idem, *Experience of Spontaneity* (London: Longmans, 1968).
5. Audrey Wethered, *Drama & Movement in Therapy* (London: Macdonald & Evans, 1973).
6. Sue Jennings, *Remedial Drama* (London: Pitman, 1973; New York: Theatre Arts Books, 1974).
7. Jennings, "The Importance of the Body in Non-verbal Methods of Therapy," in *Creative Therapy,* ed. Sue Jennings (London: Pitman, 1975).
8. The Association for Dramatherapists (*The Journal of Dramatherapy*): 136 Oxford Street, Rugby, Warwickshire, England.

PETER SLADE, Vice-president of the Educational Drama Association and the British Association of Dramatherapists, was drama advisor to the Birmingham Education Committee, Birmingham, England, and director of their pioneer Drama Centre. A practitioner of drama therapy since the early 1930's, he is the author of *Child Drama, Experience of Spontaneity, Natural Dance,* and many other books and articles. In 1977 he was awarded the Queen's Silver Jubilee Medal, and has recently been elected Fellow of the Royal Society of Arts.

*Chapter 4*

# DRAMATHERAPY

Peter Slade

## 1  INTRODUCTION

Drama falls into three main divisions for the purpose of this discussion: (a) conscious and intended therapy, (b) constructive education, and (c) prevention. By conscious and intended therapy is meant all forms of carefully applied drama, such as psychodrama, and what I have called dramatherapy. Constructive education means here a wide and wise educational system, which not only includes the three R's but also allows time and opportunity for aesthetic discovery and practice, for training of the emotions and development and balance of the personality. By prevention is meant the elimination of unnecessary suffering by more thoughtful and knowledgeable behavior on the part of parents to children, teachers to children, children to children, and adults to each other. Drama has a part to play in all of these as an aid to confidence, hope, feeling of security, discovery of sympathy, and to concentration.

With all age groups we should be aware of treating the apparently obvious problem to be acted out as of paramount importance. It is of importance, but is not the only thing. There is, no doubt, a considerable realm which will be discovered in the future, connected with the "living myth." I have occasionally touched upon some outline of an imaginary story which brought a bright response from a person and, in sorting it out, have come to believe that the explanation of a sudden interest or unexpected revitalization could have been due to the coming near to what was a truly living myth for them — deep down inside.

There may be important ground to be covered here between drama and Jungian psychotherapy; but common to all age groups, a constant danger in psychodrama is a pedantic application of symbols in dramatic form. I am more and more sure that symbols cannot always be easily and helpfully applied in this open way. They are used certainly in an unconscious manner in drama of a therapeutic nature, and characters and situations can be seen to be linked with symbols, but it has not yet been fully recognized that imaginative, spontaneous acting is the "personal play" side of the dream. Symbols are thrown up, but there are many parallels which may be, as it were, symbols of these symbols, and through which the truth behind the original symbols is as readily stumbled upon.

The apparently haphazard or casually related train of events may represent a stark reality, so it is not generally necessary to be over careful to include symbols in suggested scenes. Adults, and particularly children, will often include them as their state leads them to do so. There are natural forms of drama which offer such opportunities of discovery for both patient and doctor, and it is these in the main that give us the best results under the three headings mentioned earlier.

This brings me back again to the child. Luckily, nature has provided a form of therapy. It is child drama. It is an art form in its own right, every bit as important as child art. My first book, *Child Drama,*[1] was an attempt to explain aspects of child behavior and to outline a simple method of therapy for educational purposes, simple enough for the ordinary teacher and parent to grasp if they will, so that so many unnecessary problems for children may, at least in part, be avoided. It is interesting to note that Piaget would appear to be re-proving many of the stages of development and points made.

I would very much like to draw the attention of medical specialists and psychologists to this method, for I believe it is the basis of an approach to health through drama for the young. If the norm is well known and recognized, it is far easier to recognize and place in proper perspective that which is abnormal, and that which is normal but slightly exaggerated. For instance, by applying sound in a particular way as an inspiration to drama, the use of climax on, say, a drum beat will induce children to run forward with joy, often uttering a cry. I have called this "running play." It was found that when some loud sounds were used in a certain school for maladjusted children, not only was a child inspired by this method to run within the confines of a room, but it was so successful that he vaulted through the window and absconded. It is, therefore, valuable to know what is likely to happen, so that you can be careful how much to use and when!

You can only know by knowing the norm. You do not normally offer exciting climax noises to hyperactive children. In the same way, some people might think that some little person was abnormal because he did a tremendous amount of killing in his drama. All children kill in their drama; it is a form of overcoming, a sign of success. The killing is not abnormal in itself, but you might judge that a great amount of it in play might be a signal of a need for success.

There is one very important thing which the grown-up who knows the full detail of behavior in child drama can add to the various ways in which children use sound. It is de-climax. It is a way of helping to change the mood of a scene from violent to calm by use of an accompanying sound. It is a way of offering a deep moment of peace to minds which in other realms find great difficulty in discovering it. Peace is one of the most difficult things to find in these days, when the pace of life is so fast. I have used de-climax by beating a table loudly, and bringing the sound slowly down until I was able to be heard in a whisper across a big room in Manchester where 180 people gathered, and have managed to calm a brain-damaged child by using music in the same way. Conversely, other teachers in the same home, using this method, have achieved considerable success, in conjunction with other forms of treatment, by using dramatic climax in the right way to aid withdrawn children.

As far as education is concerned, de-climax is a way of preparing children for the next lesson. If there has been a great deal of exuberance in an active period of personal play, it is essential that the lesson be brought to a calm ending; otherwise children cannot be ready for projected activity, i.e. learning and study. It is one amongst many things which this method of child drama has added to the general notions of activity in education. The arts must be integrated with the rest of education, or they may be a nuisance, but when integrated, they bring a renewed strength unto themselves also, because the house is not divided against itself.

There are two main qualities in the drama that I am trying to describe: absorption and sincerity. There can be tremendous absorption in the task done and a tremendous sincerity about the way of doing it. Both these, in time, can become habits of the personality, affecting such things as ability to concentrate, remember and learn; and the sincerity brings out the fundamental in things like truthfulness and honest behavior. In dealing with delinquent boys, I have found that it is possible to help them by becoming absorbed in the drama to such an extent that potentially dangerous weapons can be taken right out of their hands during their acting. The scene is then played through, and nobody gets hurt.

It is never very valuable to talk in mere theory, without giving some case work, so here are some examples:

## 2 OVERSTRUCTURING

At one school for the educationally sub-normal, they had been experimenting with psychodrama and imposed Freudian symbols. The psychiatric social worker had reported that a somewhat disturbed child's home was "awful" and that there was a drunken father, of whom everyone was afraid. The doctors visiting the school, therefore, started to impose structured situations about fear and hate of the father. The child became worse and showed signs of violence.

They called me in and accepted a six week course, doctors and staff alike. I started ordinary child drama with most of the children by making simple suggestions about what to do, not showing how. There were special sessions with three small companions for the disturbed child mentioned. In all sessions of active "personal" play, fathers appeared as kind and loving, if sometimes loud and commanding. I compared this with the box test ("projected" play) where one suggests the rooms of a house by squares on paper. By asking various questions, you obtain general attitudes of affection or fear about who wants to sleep near whom, as the child puts marks in the squares. In art also, father appeared as a loving figure. Finally I was convinced, and said to the staff, "You are treating this child all wrong. Although he gets drunk, the father is the only person this child loves and you are keeping him away both in the dream world of play and in reality."

Treatment continued on my lines only and the child improved considerably, became happier, started to learn lessons and ceased bedwetting.

## Geoffrey

Geoffrey lived in a street in a big city. He had no parents, and his foster mother was a bus conductress and away most of the day, so no one saw whether Geoffrey went to school or not, or what he did. What he actually did was to race up and down the road, firing at imaginary enemies and throwing atomic bombs. (This is the wild drama of the streets.) After a time he began to imagine that most of the grown-ups who looked out at him through windows were the enemies, and he found it more fun to throw large stones at these enemy faces, because the bomb then exploded with the climax of the shattering glass.

Other children began to be involved with Geoffrey, and there was going to be serious trouble unless somebody did something about it. So we took the gang into our garage and let them use it, and part of the downstairs of the house. Slowly we managed to interest them in making tremendous noises of all sorts for different explosions, and then weaned them off to violent imaginary attacks in the garden, with only one rule—that nobody should ever actually touch another person and that all weapons should be imagined. Cowboys, pirates and gangsters were all played out to violent hot jazz. Behavior in the whole gang began to improve at once, because someone had shown them how to let off steam with all one's energy, but to keep within a realm which did not cause trouble to other people. This would be alternated with types of music which calmed them considerably, and the volume control would be brought down until we could hear silence between ourselves. This silence would be prolonged until some child became restless and the spell was obviously broken.

There were two particular children that I very much wanted to save in this group, and they undoubtedly benefited. I cannot pretend to know what happened to Geoffrey because we left the vicinity, so I don't know whether he finally went to prison or not.

## Claude

Claude arrived at my drama center. He brought two companions with him—one large, incoherent boy, another quite small one. The small one had the unenviable position of being a sort of gangster's moll to Claude, and occasionally both the older boys would knock him about slightly; but there was obviously a sort of affection also, and intimations of homosexuality. When they first came, all three were unable to concentrate for more than two seconds, or to say any consecutive sentences without going off into guffaws. Any suggestion that they do something or keep to one part of the room was an immediate inducement to go to another part of the room. So we evolved something we called "fielding;" it was rather like cricket. Roughly, the arrangement was that grown-ups would stand round the room, not too obviously, and close in slowly on Claude and his two friends so that if they wanted to shoot off to another place there was somebody in the way.

I remember the climax came one night when someone had asked Claude to do something in the middle of the room, so he started shooting off to the far end instead and I was between him and his objective. I remember the meeting of our eyes, and the feeling I had that I was truly alone with a sort of wild bull, but I felt that this was "it" and I think Claude felt so too. I stood where I was, obviously in his way. He slowed up and we stared at each other for some time. I am very glad to say that Claude gave way first and returned to the center of the room. At this moment a very important thing happened to him: he had failed to disobey. The only alternative to failing to disobey in these circumstances is to obey by mistake.

We found that a person who obeyed by mistake several times began to discover that obeying did not do one frightful harm after all, and, somewhat slowly, we began to get cooperation by these means.

Now let us turn to the use of absorption: one evening Claude was playing a violent scene with the younger boy. He caught the boy's hair, and looked as if he was going to slit his throat with a rather odd implement that he had in his hand. I came up and sat on a rostrum block near him in the middle of the scene and quietly but firmly grabbed Claude's wrist. Claude said: "Wotcher doin' that for?" I said: "I think Tommy looks better with his hair on, don't you?" Claude said: "Looks bloody silly to me anyway." I said something like: "Well, I think we'll play it with his hair on, if you don't mind." We then, all three, played the scene through. The boy remained with his hair clutched, but without it being wrenched out; Claude brandished the terrible weapon; I held his wrist tight but did not intervene in any other way. And just as he was apparently about to crown the younger boy, somebody deftly came up from behind and removed the actual weapon. Claude was so immersed in the scene that he brought down an imagined weapon of air on the younger boy's head. In this way the scene was played through, and Claude discovered — perhaps for the first time — that it was possible (just as Geoffrey had) to have full emotional outflow without, in fact, causing physical damage. (Although many psychologists remind us that, in a way, dream and reality are one, I wonder whether there aren't certain realms in which some decision about what is dream and what is reality is not healthy to everyday life, or at least to a perspective of it.)

Claude improved so much that he became cooperative and was able to be trusted to go off and make up his own drama. It is interesting to note that, although he was fourteen or fifteen years old, the pattern of his imaginative play was what would be expected from an eight or nine year old child. To be playing in the pattern of an eight or nine year old when you are, in fact, fifteen in actual age, shows that you must be in a very uncomfortable state. Either you stopped somewhere in yourself, or you are journeying back to find the way on. In either case, the realm of personal play can help here.

Claude did finally get sent to the "big house," but when he came out he returned to the Center as the only place "where grown-ups had treated him right," and "Ah brought some sweets for the kids." I didn't like to ask where he got the sweets from, but we thought at least it was a move in the right direction that he had thought of doing anything for anyone else. (The latest news is that Claude and his former companions are well-behaved van drivers.)

## 3   BACKWARD READERS

I try to give backward readers hope, then triumph. Jane, age nine, was becoming distressed by parents at home and pressure from teachers. She was sent to me. I said, "Can you read this book?" Jane: "No." Self: "Then let's find a book you can read." Jane: "Can't." Self: "What do you bet?" Jane: "Don't bet, its nor-ty," but a slight smile appeared. Self: "Now let's imagine there are shelves of books here. I'm going to take one and read it to myself. You take one and read out loud." (My hope process.) After some gentle encouragement Jane began to improvise as if reading, from a book that was not there. I then said, "Oh, that's lovely. May I try reading your book?" I put mine down and, with a smirk and a hot hand, Jane handed me her imagined book. I began to "read." But Jane broke in: "No, that's all wrong." Self: "Oh, aren't I stupid, I can't read your book!" Jane: "No you can't (triumph)." I picked up the first real book and said, "Now isn't it funny, you can't read this book of mine and I can't read yours. Actually, I think it's rather nice, it makes us equal doesn't it?"

A number of sessions later she began to teach me to "read" her book and my improvisations were accepted. Still later, the strained expression began to leave her face and I knew the time had come for her to try to read my (real) book. This sort of motivation has proved successful in many cases.[2]

# 4    FOR CONFIDENCE IN SELF

*(Used with backward and depressed children, adult neurotics, long stay schizophrenics, and in prisons.)*

I use slow music, possibly Debussy, and say, "Paint your name on the clouds; every single one of us is important, so paint it really big so everyone can see. Good. Now paint 'I am ME' and underline it — very big that must be. The clouds cover the whole hall, I think." Later, with children, I might decide that now is the time for the clouds to clear. They look happier this week, so I perhaps turn them all into airplanes to paint their name on the blue sky with exhaust or golden sundust. They would then do this wonderful running play, as described in *Child Drama*,[1] with arms outstretched, wheeling and circling and making S and 8 shapes to my accompaniment on a tambour. Then capping their noise, an important point, I would bring the sound slowly down in a de-climax until silence reigned and we could discover peace together. Perhaps the airplanes would clean their teeth and go to sleep.

# 5    FOR CALMING ANXIETY AND STRESS

*(Used with young children, but a lot with adults, harassed teachers, people in industry, students and older children worried by examinations.)*

Self: "Everything is in such a rush these days. We never seem to have time to think or notice small things around us, perhaps even beautiful things. So when the music comes, move round the hall, touching, feeling and stroking things you find there. The curtains may be warmer than the metal, the brick rougher than the floor. Discover it all in your own time." I fade-in slow music on a record player and allow plenty of time. Then: "Now try stroking and touching in time to the music." Later: "Now shut your eyes, turn away from the objects and recreate what you have been doing, as if the objects were still there. Try to remember what they were really like." This is useful for actors in developing a picture of ac-tion and, for the mentally handicapped, it can be linked to visual image and memory training. It interests me that, with the remembered objects, the movement seems to be more beautiful as a rule than when done in actuality.

Similar experiences can be offered in discovery of sound, by gently tapping, scratching, etc., objects in the immediate environment. One can then select sounds and build them together—tinkle, stamp-stamp, slow scratch, plonk. Longer "sentences" of this kind can be either turned into an elementary band, music for a circus, or associated with word, letter and ultimately sentence structure for the backward, brain-damaged or those adults who have suffered a stroke.

It can be followed by outlining chairs and drawing people, an inch away from their outline, for those not actually ready to touch. It may be noticed that some patients show signs of giving love, sympathy or affection when drawing a close outline with a partner to calming music, but become aggressive when they actually touch. For some people touch is a very delicate matter. Careful timing for the occasion may be important.

## 6   SPEECH AND BACKWARDNESS IN JUNIOR CHILDREN

If my suggestions of the difference between personal and projected play have been understood, it may well be seen that a natural progression would be from play with objects towards activity where symbols represent those objects. (It is easier, after all, to reckon in numbers in a bank account than to carry actual bags of gold about with you. Adults therefore give traditional significance to such things as letters and numbers and expect all children to understand the process. Unfortunately they do not.)

I seem to have helped a good many people down the years, of various age groups, by indulging in personal play and actually getting up and being the number or process themselves. It is important to feel the thing in three dimensions, so to speak.[3] Thus the employment of "ladders" on the floor, and going "up" and forward for plus feeling, and "down" and backwards for minus, seems to help.

In the middle 1930s, I was using shopping scenes and domino marching. Marching in pattern shapes to record music, say four and five coming together. Halt. Let's count ourselves. We do actually make nine. March away again and we have substracted, etc. One professor who saw it once said, "My goodness this is exciting, do you know what you are doing?" "Just one backward child trying to help other backward people," I replied. "No, no," he said. "You are doing something much more important, you are teaching them the fivishness of five!" Think of that.

In backwardness of speech and foreign languages, I use jabber talk — a made up language. I have used it with adult actors since my first professional companies in 1931 for emotional content of sound, but in therapy I want to stop that awful wall growing up inside a person when isolated in inability or shyness. If the wall becomes too high, you just cannot talk. So I encourage people in that state just to jabber loud. Then talk to a partner. Then try to mean something. Then to express emotion. Then add a few words of English or French, and behold, you can speak!

With shy Pakistanis in our schools, I sometimes pass near them when everyone is jabbering and say quietly, "Speak in your own language if you want to." They then jabber in theirs, and the rest go on jabbering as Martians, or French Martians, and no one knows the difference. Later one can jabber as an Indian, as a Spaniard, as an Italian or a German, so you approach the feel of sound. This is the very heart of language before or parallel with learning the words. It often seems to work. And, in the case of three dimensional mathematics, return to the actual symbol often brings further understanding after "being" the thing in personal play.[4]

Lonely talking can also stop the wall building up inside. This is the term I give to putting on a record, then talking to the music, trying to feel its intention, logic or emotional value. I used to improvise poetry this way when in despair at boarding school. Another delightful self-treatment is to declaim in the bathroom. Pompous statements and textual quotations always sound much better in there.

# 7 EDUCATIONALLY SUB-NORMAL AND SOME SEVERELY SUB-NORMAL

*(Fifteen children about 8 years of age.)*

I use a mat or sometimes a chalk circle as a base of security, "home." We are going out to touch a snowman, hand in hand.

We go out. "Ooh it's cold. Snowman is over there." We all walk
over the room and touch an imaginary snowman (i.e. I do, or
anyone else who can extricate a hand). Then we have to go
"home" again. Turning round means extricating and then re-
clutching hands. It may take quite a time. No hurry. Off we go
"home." At home we hug. Then we try again and again and
again.

The aim eventually is to see if anyone can go without holding
hands and turn round without holding hands afterwards. This is
a triumph. Later we may manage to build a snowman together or
make me into a snowman, or have a snowball fight to drum beats.
If we can do that and not fall over, it will be like seeing a miracle.
This sort of triumph always moves me tremendously. I suddenly
feel I love all the world. The children generally look transfigured
with joy, too, at so momentous an achievement.[5]

# 8   TRACKING, BALANCE AND VISUAL IMAGE

Some patients understand about movement, but their bodies will
not carry out their mental intentions, while others have quite
capable bodies but their minds cannot give the command. Visual
image, space relationships, tracking etc., all come into the picture here. Tansley did a lot of work on simple obstacle tests in Birmingham, England. I helped a bit here by including simple drama
situations. One child had learned how to walk along an upturned
bench, turn head-over-heels and spring up afterwards. I suggested he was walking a tight rope on the bench and that he
should spring up and try to run after the ice cream van before it
was too late. By giving purpose to the exercise in this way for the
child, he gained enthusiasm in how to use what he had learned,
even taking a step backward then forward again on the "tight
rope;" after the head-over-heels he ran, however falteringly,
across the room for the first time in his life and collapsed laughing
in sheer delight at his achievement.

Nervous children will often climb faster and higher, if involved
as a cop in a chase with a criminal, too, or the sheriff and
outlaws. The more they enter the creation the less room there is
for fear.

## 9   PHYSICAL HANDICAPS

With the blind I have used stamping and knocking to indicate geographical areas of a room. With the deaf I have developed stylized dance, sometimes based on sign language. They cannot lip read with me easily, as I have such a crooked mouth, so we often have to have an interpreter. With handicaps requiring wheelchairs, my suggestions elsewhere have been for jousts — "knights in armour" with paper spears. I also remember three stately "kings" entering slowly in chairs to Delius' music, sitting with great dignity as they visited the crib in a Nativity play.

At the old Peter Slade Studio in London, I used to have improvisations on newspaper stories. One woman would only take the part of a parrot because her voice was weakening. I managed to sign to someone to put the volume up and I put a microphone very close to her mouth. When the tape was played back, she sounded as strong as the others. This gave her such hope that she began to try again and for a while became the leading actress in the group till her physical condition prevented her from coming. Other examples in detail appear in *Experience of Spontaneity.*

In recent years, I have been deeply touched by visiting patients in bed, both young and old, and perceiving how awful it can be to be confined near one neighbor, so I have instituted dance of the fingers where possible, or just of the nose, with someone holding a mirror. Other mirrors, carefully placed can help a patient to dance hands and "converse" with someone far down the ward.

## 10   SECONDARY GIRLS

The Secondary Modern Girls' School was in a tough area, and the work chosen was done with regard to what I myself felt was needed. We played scenes about wicked motorists running over pedestrians. Then, "Who would like to be a judge?" One person said she would, so we had a court scene. A number of people became policemen and jury, and the rest of the girls in the class were the public.

The scene played through very nicely, and there were some splendid remarks in it. Self: "Do you know what happens when the judge comes in?" "Yes," said one of the girls, "everyone stands up." "All right," I said, "let's do it again, and let's have everyone

standing up this time. The other thing that occurred to me was
that the judge directed the jury rather a lot, and I think in a case
of this kind the jury would make up their own minds. What do
they do? Does anyone know?" Answer from one or two children:
"They go out and decide about it and then come back." Self:
"Yes, that's quite right. We'll do that bit again, too."

It was quite quickly done, and a splendid short argument took
place where the jury were at first undecided but finally wanted
their lunch and came back and gave a verdict of "guilty." Self:
"What would you feel like if you were judged guilty?" A girl
answered: "I'd want to hit the judge." So I suggested that they
should all think of themselves as a prisoner and it was grand to be
able to have the opportunity of lashing out at someone, even if
you didn't hit him. I suggested that they should think they were
hitting the judge because of his sentence, and we all did the most
terrific and stylized bashing to the D minor *Toccata and Fugue* by
Bach.

At the end of the lesson I discussed with them a number of
things about the drama they had done, and led their minds back
to their inability to speak with confidence at the beginning of the
lesson, and the improvement of their language-flow during the
"judge scene." But I reminded them that because of the needs of
other people, and because of their own behavior, we have to learn
to be quiet at the right moment and not just hit people at any
time it pleases us. The hitting of an imagined hated person in this
way is part of a process that I call "experience without sin." In
other words, there are plenty of ways in which one can arrange a
lawful situation for unlawful acts. Many young people, and most
delinquents, are desperately alone and searching because they are
filled with desire for dramatic unlawful acts, but nobody provides
the place or situation where they may lawfully blow off steam.
Until there are many centers which provide this training, it is
largely our fault if there are so many young people causing trouble today.

## 11　SECONDARY BOYS

Some of these lads were very backward in work and wore strained expressions. The skin under their eyes looked odd, and there was a veil over their eyes – clear indications of emotional distrubance. I was allowed to advise. We took them off all normal work for two terms, and I and other teachers suggested being shopkeepers, buying and selling. As they were very quiet, I would line them up against the wall in two groups and get them to shout at each other, for help, in annoyance, asking the way. We did a lot of athletic dance to drums and leaping after fruit in high trees; then into fantasy leaping for the stars; then back more into reality, saving goals at soccer. We mimed football matches to hot jazz. Children always seem to know where the ball is, which interests me. Then they worked in groups of about six and made up their own stories.

As usual with disturbed people, regression was evident and the gang stories approximated to what I have called "the main cathartic years" between ages seven and nine. This drama work, for about two sessions a day of one hour or less, as long as they could concentrate, was supported by painting, some craft work, physical education and outings.

Finally we tried a polished improvisation created with the whole group. By this time the skin had changed under their eyes, there was a sparkle. Behind their eyes the candles of hope had been lit, and I said it was time for them to start lessons again.

My feeling is that, after all the long words used, in all of us there is a sort of psychic bank account. Too many failures, or supposed ones, give us an overdraft. A lot of activity in drama, where even only imagined successes take place, can bring in dividends. When enough dividends come, in lots of different ways and from lots of different quarters, one is a hero again and the bank account is satisfactory. If children fail in the projected realm (i.e. 3R's) they need a great amount of success in personal play: it is nature's therapy.

## 12 FINAL COMMENT

This is a considerable shortening of a progressive method and developmental philosophy based partly on reinforced education and behaviorism. Depth psychology deals with causes and reasons for behavior and suffering. I think I deal more directly with behavior itself because this is concerned with the immediate unhappiness of the patient and his unacceptance by society. It is not easy to say what one should do, as so much of this work is intuitive. But I believe that in each handicapped or abnormal person there is a level of functioning to be discovered or a candle of normality to be lit. It is up to us to find it.

I do not use theatre in any of this treatment as such. I am more concerned with the Greek *drao*, I do, I struggle. It is drama, the doing of life, by which man may experience many situations, thus moving towards maturity, and assume various roles until he discovers more nearly the best of who or what he really is.

## FOOTNOTES

1. Peter Slade, *Child Drama* (London: University of London Press, 1954).
2. Peter Slade, *Experience of Spontaneity* (London: Longman, 1968).
3. Peter Slade, *Natural Dance* (London: Hodder & Stoughton, 1977).
4. Phyllis Lutley, "Teaching with a Purpose," E.D.A. Pamphlet (Bromley, Kent, England: Stacey, n.d.); Ian Petrie, "Drama and Handicapped Children," E.D.A. Pamphlet (Bromley, Kent, England: Stacey, n.d.).
5. Peter Slade, Eileen Lafitte, and R. J. Stanley, "Drama with Subnormal Adults," E.D.A. Pamphlet (Bromley, Kent, England: Stacey, n.d.).

MARIAN R. LINDKVIST is founder and honorary director of Sesame (movement and drama in therapy), London. Originator of Britain's first full-time training in movement and drama therapy, she lectures and tutors throughout Europe and the United States.

*Chapter 5*

# MOVEMENT AND DRAMA WITH AUTISTIC CHILDREN

Marian R. Lindkvist

## 1   ASPECTS OF AUTISM

Before attempting to introduce the subject of movement and drama with autistic children, it is necessary to look briefly at some of the problems related to the illness.

Out of about every three thousand children born, one or two may be autistic. The number of autistic boys is considerably higher than the number of girls suffering from this condition. Although it has been suggested that children can be born with this syndrome, this has not been clinically validated. Few parents are aware of its presence until the child is at least a year old. Sometimes the condition is recognized when a child is between two and four, and the symptoms may be very marked.

No child is like another, so it follows that no two autistic children are the same. Incidentally, some manifest behavior which may be observed in the "normal" child at times. A normal child, for example, may and often does enjoy tapping or scratching an object. An autistic child is likely to tap or scratch obsessively for long periods of time, oblivious to his surroundings, voices calling him, food being placed before him and other stimulating events. On the other hand, a normal child may also be seen rocking, playing obsessively and ritualistically, listening to a noise, having a temper tantrum, repeating words and phrases — indeed, the latter is the manner in which most children learn to speak. So it

95

would be quite erroneous to assume that such transitory behavior should cause any concern whatsoever. The difference with the behavior patterns of the autistic lies in the fact that they are prolonged and persistent rather than a passing phase.

Autism, or Kanner's syndrome, is characterized by many difficulties. One is the inability to comprehend language either partially or fully. Many autistic children have no speech, and some do not react to the spoken word — although they may exhibit significant levels of comprehension. Some have a little speech, and this is likely to improve with age. A common phenomenon is the repetition of words and sentences, these often being reproduced in precisely the tone of voice used by the first speaker. This echolalia sometimes occurs several days after the original sentence has been heard. It may be, and often is, used repetitively and inappropriately.

Rituals are extremely important, and some children become very upset if objects are moved from a familiar place to another part of the room. Severe and prolonged temper tantrums can take place, particularly if a favorite object is lost or mislaid. While certain sounds can be important to a child with Kanner's syndrome, other sounds can produce screaming, tantrums and total withdrawal, often with hands over their ears. Autists can be self-destructive; for example, biting at their own hands or arms (especially when frustrated), and picking their flesh. Many do not appear to be aware of pain. Some have marked stereotyped movements, such as the rapid and repeated moving of the fingers in front of the eyes, or the continuous twiddling of a piece of wool, or rocking. Inter-personal relationships are often extremely difficult, particularly those with other children.

Looking in at a group of normal children at play, one will often see them in a circle or group, in twos and threes, facing each other, touching each other and generally inter-relating. The playground of a school for autistic children is more likely to show faces turned away, children in corners, looking down, and isolated. With the symptoms described above, withdrawal and isolation are an integral part of the pattern.

The subject of autism is complex. The reason for it is not yet known. There is more than one theory as to its cause. A number of books have been written about it, of which that by Wing[1] is particularly helpful.

The autist, at such a disadvantage in so many ways, is, however, likely to be physically very beautiful. He is often musical, finding it easy to remember tunes and words of songs, even if his speech is very limited. He may develop in blocks, being backward in all those areas requiring language comprehension, and forward in such subjects as music and the tasks involving an understanding of numbers. Some autists are mentally handicapped; but many have normal or even above normal intelligence. There are many variations and complications to autistic behavior, and few children manifest all of them.

One way of helping these children to perform simple tasks, such as buttoning a coat, tying a shoelace, or wielding a knife and fork, is first to start with the final task, then to manipulate the children's hands to carry out these functions, working backwards. When this has been done a number of times and help has gradually been withdrawn, the child may well be able to complete the action himself.

Some autists deteriorate with age. Many improve greatly as they grow older. A few can be integrated into a normal school; most cannot and may, unfortunately, find themselves in large hospitals for the severely mentally handicapped where it would seem that the facilities are unlikely to bring any hope of further improvement, rather, the reverse. Before autism was defined as such, autistic children might well have been placed in hospitals for the mentally retarded at quite an early age. There they would remain, with the label "severely mentally handicapped," until the end of their lives.

## 2 HELPING THE AUTISTIC CHILD

What are the implications of autism, in terms of the loneliness, fears and frustrations accompanying the condition? If language is denied or partially denied to us, how can we relate to one another? If we do not appear to feel pain, will we feel touch? If we do, will we tolerate it? If certain sounds are threatening, what then can we hope for in terms of any kind of integration with others?

There are ways of bridging these frightening gaps and chasms. Educators and other specialists are ceaselessly exploring and discovering how much help can be given to autistic children and adolescents. One method facilitating communication and relationships is movement and drama.

From 1974 to date, I have worked consistently with fourteen autistic, or query autistic, children from a hospital in Oxfordshire, England. Many methods used were based on those developed by Audrey Wethered[2] and Veronica Sherborne, much of whose work is directly related to the principles of Rudolf Laban.[3]

From the moment of birth, and indeed before, we move. The movement of each individual is unique. It embodies what we are, and why we are what we are, at any given moment. The principles of movement can be divided into four main categories. They are: (1) *What we move*—that is, what part(s) of our body is moving; (2) *How we move*—that is, different movement qualities arising from unconscious feelings; a sudden noise, for example, could cause a sudden reaction or movement; (3) *Where we move*—that is, a high, low or medium level, and in what direction; (4) *With whom we move*—that is, in relation to others. The over-simplification of the above cannot be stressed too much. It is merely the roughest possible indication of what is a detailed and complex theory (the Laban Art of Movement), including symmetry, shapes, directions, qualities, and elements relating to qualities, to mention just a few.

If each person moves in a unique way, the autist is no exception. By careful observation of natural movement patterns, it may be possible not only to learn something of the personality of the mover, but also to relate to him in terms that can extend his movement pattern, enrich his experience of life, and help him communicate with others. Thus he may well feel and be less withdrawn and isolated. He may start to come out of himself, so to speak. This does not mean that he will cease to be autistic, but it may well contribute to his improvement.

Let us take a specific example. During a project at a large

hospital for the severely mentally handicapped, helpers visited two groups of patients once a week for two sessions, each lasting one hour. These were attended by the Principal Clinical Psychologist of the hospital. In one group, two patients were autistic. Both were non-verbal, withdrawn and isolated, and both had marked stereotypies. The young man in question was about eighteen years old. A helper noticed that he bent and stretched his legs as if about to jump with legs together. She joined in this movement and developed it into an actual jump, which was repeated a number of times. The patient responded by smiling, joining readily in the jumping. The helper introduced appropriate sounds with each jump. The patient responded by making his own sounds and laughing. This was the first contact.

In subsequent weeks the helper was able to introduce many variations: bending the body, jumping at a high and low level, fast and slow, turning in different directions and working back to back with arms linked. But the initial movement had come from the patient, not from the helper. During the second session the same patient, isolated and alone in a corner, clapped his hands. The clapping became louder and louder until it reached a climax; the man could not clap any louder. The helper joined this pattern, and then clapped more and more softly until the clapping died away. The man listened, looking directly at the helper instead of past or through her, as do so many autists. The clapping to climax required energy, so the helper first encouraged the patient to clap against her hands, and then developed the action so that she and the patient pushed against one another. She then offered her back to the patient, laughing, and saying "Push me". The patient laughingly pushed her and she responded with an over-reaction to emphasize the strength and power of the patient, by almost leaping away and returning for more. There was great pleasure and amusement in this activity and the patient finally pushed the helper all round the room. Again, this whole sequence of events started from where the patient was at that time. The staff present had never before seen such behavior from this patient.

Then, writing about him and another child, the Principal

Psychologist states:

> A particularly positive result was achieved from two of the autistic
> patients who showed a definite response to the exercises in social
> interaction, or to music and movement.[4]

When working with such a patient, one must be watchful of too
much and too sudden stimulation so that the patient does not lose
control and become unable to contain his newly found strength
and power. It is important, therefore, to work gradually towards
goals and not, in one's enthusiasm, rush into situations which can
prove dangerous to patient and helper alike. As well as progressing slowly, it is important to control movement with pauses, and
constant changes in direction and speed, and in levels. A
knowledge of the patient based on personal and clinical data is
essential.

As previously stated, autistic children vary so markedly that
group work is not likely to be as helpful as individual work.
Nevertheless, a sense of group feeling can be evoked if helpers
work sensitively together, moving from time to time from one
child to another, flowing and hovering, rather than breaking off
in the middle of a movement sequence or phrase. Thus, one
hopes and senses that all feel part of a creative activity and
atmosphere.

# 3   MOVEMENT AND DRAMA SESSIONS IN A
# HOSPITAL FOR DISTURBED AND AUTISTIC
# CHILDREN

In 1974 a research project was undertaken under scientific control. Six helpers and a leader held weekly movement sessions over
a period of six months with six disturbed/autistic children. At the
same time, six different children took part in a gymnastic session.
The children in both groups were hyper- or hypo-active, non-
verbal and withdrawn. Their ages ranged from nine to fourteen,
and all had stereotypies. Work was directed towards an endeav-
or to form relationships, to encourage giving and taking, and to

extend the ability of each child through the use of such means as touch (where possible), rhythms, such as tapping and rocking, and the use of voice. By observation of individual movement patterns it was possible to draw conclusions, albeit tentative, about some of the behavior problems relating to some of the children.

In view of the differences in the children, it seems logical to discuss some of them separately.

## Fiona

Fiona's stereotypies were the rapid moving of her fingers in front of her eyes and mouth, and the moving of her tongue up and down. She also walked on her toes, as do many autistic children. She was so occupied with these habits that she had time for little else. She would lie down, curled up, repeating these movements and rocking.

One helper curled up behind her and rocked with her, holding her as she did so. The helper did this several times and then stopped, interrupting the rhythm. Then she started again. She repeated this, never varying the stopping time. Fiona then stopped at that time herself, so the helper then changed the stopping time.

The introduction of an element of surprise can be helpful because it may arouse interest in a child who seems set in her pattern of movement. It was not very difficult to be accepted, or perhaps tolerated, by Fiona. What was difficult was persuading her to devote less time to her stereotypies.

Early in the project, children were encouraged to take off their shoes and socks. Much contact was made with feet. When a helper first introduced Fiona to foot play, she seemed so intrigued that she forgot about moving her hands and tongue. She gazed at her feet and the helper's feet and her toes, which were being waggled. This is shown clearly on film.[5]

At this stage of the project the importance of legs became very apparent. It seemed that none of these children had explored the possibilities of all that could be experienced with the legs and feet in relation to others. Much time was spent pushing partners' feet, feeling feet with feet, working feet round feet, stretching legs, foot to foot, raising and lowering legs, meeting and parting with feet and legs, while changing the position of the body.

By this time, too, all the children had made contact and seemed to have found security. It was then possible to form a circle from time to time, and move in different ways as a group.

By the end of the six months period, Fiona was using flat hands and had ceased to walk on her toes for considerable periods during sessions.

After the completion of the project she continued to attend sessions for two more years before leaving the school. From being lethargic in body and occupied with her stereotypies, she became active and ran and hopped, offering flat hands to her helper, laughing aloud, exploring hers and the helper's elbows and being very aware of her feet and legs as well as those of the helper. During those years she attended sessions with Colin, from the experimental group, and two helpers. It was possible for all four to share a mat and relate closely together, eight feet being mixed up at times. Fiona's stereotypies were practically never seen during sessions.

Three who have taken part in sessions for the past two years should be discussed. Two took part in group sessions and one in private sessions. Two of the three are still working with me.

## Eleanor

Eleanor was a beautiful and gifted child. A member of the original group, she was fourteen when she first joined the group in the movement sessions.

She spoke a little, and certainly understood most, if not all, that was said to her. When first seen on the ward, she had her legs drawn up on a chair and was rocking. In the playground she would often be pacing up and down, at intervals flinging her arms out straight to her side at chest level, bending back her wrists with hands stiff. She seemed happy on the ward and at the hospital school, sometimes producing beautiful needlecraft and art work. She could be disturbed at times and become confused.

From the moment she started movement sessions, it was apparent that she could and would be very responsive. Her shyness was quickly overcome, and soon she was revelling in the opportunity of moving her body to music. The new experience of the leg and foot work appealed especially to her, as it seemed to give great scope to her rhythmic abilities, without the same pressures which she found when she was standing upright. Her orientation in space was poor, so at first moving, particularly at any speed, caused a certain threat, as she could not relate to the time it would take to reach a certain point. Objects would, therefore, appear before her with unexpected rapidity or more slowly than she had anticipated. Lying on the floor, she could enjoy the rhythms in a very relaxed manner without the same threat.

After some weeks, she gained so much confidence that she was able to relate not only to adults, but also to other children, particularly to Bobbie. She began to initiate quite complex movement sequences and when one of Bobbie's feet became detached from hers, she calmly stopped the sequence, took Bobbie's straying foot firmly in her hand, placed it on her foot, and continued the sequence. As the weeks passed, her spatial awareness increased, as did her movement qualities, such as flow — that is a continuous flowing without pause, rather than a stopping and starting. She was also encouraged to weave and bend, rather than remain straight, as she would be in her playground pacing walk. She learned to use her body in a flexible way, and finally was filmed in a sequence with a helper where a great variety of movement flowed from her as she faced the helper, who fitted in with all that Eleanor initiated.

Towards the end of the two years, it was possible to work in simple improvisations, when Eleanor crawled round being different animals and making the appropriate animal noises. When approached by a five year old girl who had outstretched hands, Eleanor took them and skipped round in a circle with her.

Unfortunately because of her age she was moved, and is now in a large hospital for the severely mentally handicapped.

## Bobbie

When Bobbie, also a member of the original control group, first attended sessions, he was so timid that he seemed to shrink when one looked at him. He was a tall, thin, very sensitive boy of eleven years. His head shook and his posture was extremely stiff. He was so nervous that any approach from strangers, whether

physical or verbal, had to be very tentative at first, not because he
would run away, but because he seemed too afraid to do so. One
child in the same group had a habit of suddenly pushing another
child quite violently. Bobbie was petrified, and his eyes followed
her almost continuously during the first session. Helpers
deliberately guarded him from her, moving him into a less
vulnerable position when necessary, and making it clear that he
could depend on their support.

An early report suggested that Bobbie might be helped to
strengthen his ego by building up and exploring strong
movements. If he could feel his strength, he might become more
confident. The gentle and protective approach soon allayed Bobbie's fears of being touched, and within a very short time he was
relating to two or three helpers, particularly a man and an older
woman.

By the end of the first summer, Bobbie could bend his knees
and crawl under an arch made by the joining of the feet of two
group members lying on the ground. He was very much at home
during sessions, and although he did not speak, he would smile
and nod or shake his head in reply to questions. He surprised a
helper very much one day when she stood back to back with him
and leaned forward. He leaned right back on her back, flinging
his legs into the air at the same time. All she could feel was a
strange gap on the lower level and an unexpectedly heavy weight
coming from somewhere up in the air. There was much amusement on Bobbie's part when he realized how heavy he was. A nervous boy, he was beginning to take risks, to trust others and to
realize that humans have physical limitations.

During the following year, Bobbie's progress was quite
astonishing. When the man who had made the early relationship
and who was physically strong, stood with bent knees, Bobbie
could balance with his feet on the knees, holding the hands of the
man. This required considerable courage as well as confidence.
He would also be supported in a "flying angel" and would support
smaller children so that they could experience a "flying angel"
with another child.

His relationship with Eleanor blossomed both in the school and during sessions. They frequently walked hand in hand in the playground and, as has been stated, created movement patterns together week after week. After viewing a film where these incidents were shown, a member of the staff of the school (not Bobbie's teacher) said he had to ask himself who this child could be, as the Bobbie he knew bore so little resemblance to him.

## Kathleen

A lively and interesting child, now thirteen years old, Kathleen did not seem suitable for group sessions. It was, therefore, decided that she should have half an hour's private session each week; these have taken place for the past two years.

In group work either she was disruptive, or she would sit in a corner and watch. She also "watched" from corners in the ward and at school. Whenever she was approached, she would run away. She often tore her clothes, and preferred to be naked. The educational psychologist who, after the research year, was closely concerned with the program, agreed that Kathleen could and probably would gain more from movement sessions if she were allowed to remove her clothes.

The helper decided to play a completely passive role. But the best laid plans can go awry. A passive role was not possible. Kathleen would invariably start to tear up pieces of the floor, knock over valuable gym apparatus—sessions were in the gym—or do something that absolutely had to be stopped or circumnavigated. The helper was in a dilemma. Luckily a favorite occupation, intended to be disruptive, was to undo all the knots in the ropes, which had carefully been pulled to the side walls. The knots were very tight, and although Kathleen was extraordinarily strong she could not manage to undo them alone. Here was a way in. "Shall I help? Shall we do it together?" said the helper, and approached the child. Side by side, hands touching, the knots were pulled and twisted until they were undone. There were eight ropes, and eight knots to be undone. The worse the knots were, the better and longer did the physical contact last, and the more satisfying became the joint triumph and satisfaction when the knots were untied. This activity was the only positive achievement for many weeks, but it persisted, and the helper would sometimes manage to stroke part of Kathleen's arm or back while being so close to her.

The routine then consisted of going to the gym, taking off the clothes, untying the knots, doing something that had to be stopped, such as pushing over apparatus, putting on the clothes, probably tearing one or two, and going back to the ward. After a couple of months, the knots having been untied, the helper managed to get between Kathleen and the apparatus, saying, "What do you want to do with this? Do you want it down, and this way or that way? Shall we do it together?" The moving of the apparatus took a long time, and was very hard work, but it was a joint activity, and thereafter less destructive behavior took place. Moreover, there was a strong feeling of team work.

Kathleen could say short phrases and single words: "Mummy's coming tomorrow," or "Pool atta tea," which meant bathing in a swimming pool. One hot day when the ropes had been untied, and the apparatus moved, Kathleen saᵗ watching in a corner. The helper started to sing to her about her. Kathleen started singing "Mummy, Mummy" in an agitated voice. The helper picked up the rhythm and mood, moving her body to the rhythm and with the quality of the mood, which was sudden or jerky, singing "Mummy, Mummy" in reply. This conversation was continued, the helper replying in the same mood and rhythm through movement and voice for a time; then she started to vary not the rhythm, but the mood, by introducing a quality of laughter into the singing. Kathleen then introduced quite a different mood and rhythm, and the helper ended by dancing a short sequence or phrase which she accompanied with a cradle song. So ended the session.

After that, the knots were still untied, but the apparatus was left alone. The helper and Kathleen held similar conversations, and then the helper sat on the floor with her head as far away as possible from Kathleen's head but with feet near. Gradually Kathleen allowed the helper's foot to touch her foot, and then to slide or creep up her leg and back. The helper talked about what was happening: "Look, my foot is touching your foot. Now it's creeping and walking up your leg. Look, your knee is wiggling when I wobble it with my toe." The next stage was when Kathleen placed the sole of her foot firmly against the sole of the helper's foot. She started to push the other foot, and then all four feet were joined, and variations of movement were possible.

Towards the end of last year, 1976, Kathleen allowed the helper to catch her as she rolled off a bench, trusting her entire weight to the helper.[6] She would take her hand and talk in her fashion all the way back to the ward, across the school garden. The change in her behavior was noticed on the ward, and the sister in charge said, "When Kathleen is fetched from the ward, she is tense. When she returns, she is relaxed and talks more." Kathleen's tolerance of touch was also noted.

## 4 IMPROVISATION

It should be realized that it is quite possible to use the technique of improvisation with autistic children. Just as most children play out their fantasies, so some autistic or query autistic children seem able to take part in and sometimes initiate themes or subjects which can be acted out by group members. Within the group sessions, which so far have been dealt with in relation to movement, there have been children who would and did enter most fully into fantasy. The degree of involvement varied.

On one occasion a five year old boy, with very little speech but an outgoing personality, decided that a helper was a monster. With the psychologist, he approached it and poked at it with his finger, the psychologist making suitable accompanying remarks. The theme developed, and the "monster," who was exactly as "monstrous" as was required, caused delight mingled with awe. Finally several of the group decided to be monsters, and all went to sleep together in a monster nest with imaginary monster blankets and pillows.

One little girl of five with no speech, who in the early sessions was sometimes quite disturbed, seemed to catch the varying moods of the group. Even though it was unlikely that she understood the monster, her eyes sparkled with unusual delight as she came up with a helper to prod its body.

Another child, a girl of seven, talked about milk, so a cow shape was drawn in the air, and the animal was milked, then led to the stable and fed. Other animals were demanded in quick succession, and they too were drawn, led to the stable and fed. Various adventures befell the animals and the girl still, from time to time "goes to the stable" which she unfailingly places in the original position in the room.

Movement and drama are innate and can be applied for all people. It is not a question of one technique for one handicap. It is a question of studying the individual and group need at any given moment and in the long term sense.

## 5   SUMMARY & OBSERVATIONS

Although over such a short period, about eighteen hours in all, no statistical changes could be expected, certain clinical differences were noted on the ward. For example, some children came more often into the center of the room, rather than staying at the edge. In addition, children were found to be more relaxed and they looked forward to the sessions. The full Report[7] includes details regarding both the experimental and the control groups.

In work with individuals, small and larger groups, the following points should be kept in mind:

(1) Although the helper can stimulate, and offer activities, in the final analysis it is the child who sets the pace;

(2) Although planning is important, plans must be made with a readiness for changing them;

(3) It takes time to become a trained observer;

(4) The balance between supporting a child and over-indulging a child in movement and drama is very fine. The helper rather than the child must take the responsibility for deciding where the line should be drawn;

(5) The human voice makes an important contribution to the techniques described above, and it is not necessary to be able to "sing" to use it;

(6) The helper should be as close as possible to a child, both physically and mentally, but should remember that we are trying to help the child to develop his ego, not to smother him;

(7) The way in to a movement or drama session may not be through movement or drama in the accepted sense;
(8) Each child is unique. We must respect the differences.
All the above apply throughout the field — they are not exclusive to children.

## 6  CONCLUSIONS

Although it would be unrealistic to claim that drama and movement in therapy is a cure for mental and physical disorders, it seems clear that it can be used as a means of communication, for developing relationships, increasing body awareness,and for minimizing stereotypies if that is considered desirable. It can give satisfaction to the doer, and encourage verbalization as well as group awareness and a sense of sharing a creative experience. It can also increase confidence.

In the cases of the children described in this essay, it would appear that it is a welcome and permanent addition to the school and hospital curriculum.

It is hoped that studies currently taking place through qualitative assessment will show a fuller picture of the value of applied movement and drama, and that it will become a more generally accepted part of treatment programs than it is at present.

## FOOTNOTES

1. J. C. Wing, *Early Childhood Autism* (Oxford: Pergamon Press, 1967).
2. Audrey Wethered, *Drama and Movement in Therapy* (London: Macdonald & Evans, 1973).
3. Rudolf Laban, *Modern Educational Dance* (London: Macdonald & Evans, 1973); Joan Russell, *Creative Dance in the Secondary School* (London: Macdonald & Evans, 1972); Rudolf Laban and F. C. Lawrence, *Effort* (London: Macdonald & Evans, 1974).
4. Anne Scott, n.t., *Sesame News Letter* 2 (London: Sesame, 1976).
5. *The Sesame Project with Autistic Children* (1974). Film available at Concord Film Council, Nacton, Ipswich 1P10 OJZ, England.
6. *The Sesame Project* (1976). Film available at Concord Film Council.
7. *The Sesame Project* (January–July 1974). Full Report available from Sesame, 8 Ayres St., London SE1 1ES, England.

ELEANOR C. IRWIN, Ph.D., is a drama therapist at the Pittsburgh Child Guidance Center and a clinical assistant professor of child psychiatry, Department of Psychiatry, University of Pittsburgh.

*Chapter 6*

# PLAY, FANTASY, AND SYMBOLS: DRAMA WITH EMOTIONALLY DISTURBED CHILDREN

Eleanor C. Irwin

## 1 INTRODUCTION

In the past few years there has been renewed interest in the topic of play, as psychologists and educators attempt to redefine its value, not only to social and emotional growth, but to cognitive development as well.[1] One impetus was provided by the ethnologists who studied animal play and realized how play of the young led to adult competency; another was the seminal work of Piaget,[2] who viewed play as an aspect of intelligence. Research in information processing has also highlighted the importance of stimulus and arousal seeking, with attempts to delineate the variables which instigate play, such as novelty, complexity and dissonance.[3]

There is, moreover, no longer any attempt to categorize play within one narrow definition. Erikson,[4] for example, has greatly expanded the psychoanalytic view of play to include "mastery." Calling play the child's work, he suggests that there are many explanations for the "condensed bits of life" reflected in play. Among them, he suggests, may be the working through of a traumatic experience; attempts to communicate or even to confess; the exercise of growing faculties; and the mastering of complex life situations. He states: "As I would not settle for any one of these explanations alone, I would not wish to do without any one of them."[5]

Speers,[6] a psychoanalyst, takes a broad developmental view of play. He suggests that play can proceed through the following stages: primitive exploration (the baby with the rattle); imitation (of people and actions); representational play (as in drawing); dramatic play (symbolic play with a pretend plot); sociodramatic play (acted with companions, props, role assignment, verbalization); games with rules (games of skill, chance, competition, etc.); hobbies and day-dreams to adult creative activities (such as those which "play" with words, ideas, figures, symbols, etc.). Thus, play is seen as a form of activity which spans the spectrum of life, reflecting the individual's development, learnings and interests.

## 2   PLAY IN THERAPY

While educators and experimental psychologists have not always agreed on the values, definitions and purposes of play, such has not been the case with therapists. With the recognition of the difficulties of conducting verbal psychotherapy with children, clinicians have continually searched for ways of helping children to express themselves freely. Hug-Helmuth[7] and Klein[8] experimented with the use of toys in child analysis, attempting to find a way to help children to allow ideas to emerge freely, uncensored, in a manner that would be analogous to the free association of an adult. Elaborating on the psychoanalytic theory of play, Waelder[9] stated that play provided an opportunity for the child to assimilate piecemeal what, in real life, may have been too difficult to integrate in one fell swoop. By moving from a passive to an active position in play, the child attempts to control the outcome, allay anxiety and thereby (to quote Waelder) digest "the undigested meal."

Klein regarded the child's play as a kind of symbolic representation of unconscious fantasy and interpreted it as such. This was later followed by A. Freud's[10] emphasis upon the educational aspects of work with children, using play as only one aspect of the therapy within the treatment relationship.

Lowenfeld[11] and Bender and Schiller[12] broadened their study of play to include a consideration of form and configuration principles. Erickson[13] in his elucidation of the instinctual modes and configurational aspects, has richly contributed to the understanding of play, which he calls "the royal road to the understanding of the infantile ego's efforts at synthesis." At this point, play continues to be one of the chief ways of working with children in therapy, although there are many different schools of thought on theory, purpose and technique (e.g., nondirective;[14] existential;[15] relationship;[16] field approach;[17] learning theory,[18] etc.).

## 3  DRAMA IN THERAPY

Drama is a method par excellence for studying the play and fantasies of children. Stone, in discussing the relationship, comments:

> Play has several meanings, among which drama must be included and drama is fundamental for the child's development of a conception of self as an object different from but related to other objects—the development of an identity. To establish a separate identity...the child must literally get outside himself and apprehend himself from some other perspective. Drama provides a prime vehicle for this. By taking the role of another, the child gains a reflected view of himself as different from but related to that other.[19]

Through symbolization and the focus on conflict, characterization and interaction, drama provides a ready vehicle through which children can externalize and articulate their ideas, wishes, fears and feelings. Verbally as well as non-verbally, the dramatic play gives clues about the child's private thoughts and imagery. Just as the verbal messages focus and clarify the conflict, the non-verbal play also gives clues about the impulse life via bodily movements, rhythmicity, force, balance and other organizing principles. Thus, the process and action of dramatic play also serve to convey underlying thought processes and fantasies. One could say of spontaneous dramatic play, as Greenacre[20] has said of play, that one of its main functions is to aid "in delivering the unconscious fantasy and harmonizing it with the external world."

Drama therapy, as used herein, is conceptualized to be a psychotherapeutic modality in which the activity, within the therapeutic relationship, is used to help the child achieve relief from conflict and anxiety, resulting in change in personality. Drama therapy is not a form of psychodrama, although they are alike in that they are both psychotherapeutic techniques used in a planned sequential way to bring about changes in personality and behavior. The two approaches differ, however, in procedure, goals, direction and orientation. In psychodrama, the protagonist (main character) explores his conflicts in an individual drama, using other group members to portray roles as needed (i.e., they function as "auxiliary egos" for him). The director is active in leading the psychodrama, in helping the protagonist to explore his areas of difficulty, in clarifying and expressing feelings and/or in exploring alternative behaviors. While many therapists use psychodrama as a treatment modality with disturbed children, it has been this writer's experience that while some of the techniques are helpful, psychodrama as a treatment modality, per se, is not particularly effective. Psychodrama with children seems to be too direct (and directive), verbal, structured, reality and action oriented to help disturbed youngsters to truly work through their multiple conflicting feelings. Similarly, while adults might have the ego strength, psychic distance and verbal skills to confront their problems directly through psychodrama, many children do not. Rather, children seem to need the protection and disguise of unstructured fantasy play as they gain courage to confront their difficulties.

Neither is drama therapy conceived to be synonymous with play therapy, particularly of the nondirective school where interpretation is avoided and catharsis (that is, playing it out) is thought to bring about a cure. Consequently, the term "drama psychotherapy" rather than "drama therapy" may be more appropriate for the activity described herein. In this context the term drama *in* therapy is emphasized, rather than drama *as* therapy, which usually implies that the dramatic experience itself brings about change. It is a form of child psychotherapy in which the spontaneous dramatic play activity, in addition to the interventions of the therapist, is designed to help the child to express, understand and work through his conflicts, and bring about insight and change. Through the use of expressive media, such as puppets, miniature life toys, dolls and sensory material which evoke non-verbal images and schemata (such as in Lowenfeld's sand world technique[21]), disturbed children are helped to come to terms with their difficulties.

Whether in individual or group therapy, play and fantasy are essential aspects of treatment and the primary way of understanding the child and keeping track of the progress of therapy, and at times, also serve as a means of symbolic intervention.[22] To illustrate, drama therapy case material will be presented. Although the functions of these phenomena will be considered separately for the purpose of convenience, it should be understood that they are inextricably interrelated and overlap.

## 4  WISH FULFILLMENT: JAN

For many children referred for therapy, growth and development have been arrested or blocked. At times, children externalize their angry, as well as their loving wishes in play, thus ultimately making it possible for them to come to terms with reality.

Ten-year-old Jan was referred for psychotherapy because of severe depression. In spite of good intelligence, she was doing poorly in school and had marked conflict with her mother and teachers. Her past history included the sudden death of her father, which occurred when she was five. Following his death, her mother was hospitalized for six months while Jan and her sisters lived with relatives. In her initial psychiatric interview, Jan was mostly mute, volunteering little except to say that she felt like a rock. Because she had made and enjoyed puppets in school, Jan was referred for a drama diagnostic interview. She was given a variety of puppets and asked to make up and play out a story. At first slowly, then more energetically, she played out a story of a girl bitten by a bull; the girl was berated by her "witch" mother for being injured. Out of nowhere a father appeared in the story;

he defended his daughter vigorously, put the witch mother in jail and then father and daughter lived happily ever after. Among other things, the story was full of unresolved wishes and fantasies toward her father, a kind of fantasied denial of his death.

Because the symbolic disguise of drama seemed to be a way for this child to express her longings and wishes, she began in weekly drama therapy and after some months of work, she related her puzzlement about her father's death. He had had a heart attack while the family was vacationing in another city. Returning home in an airplane, the father was taken off in a stretcher — and that was the last she saw of him. Subsequently, her mother was hospitalized for six months and she was told nothing of the death of her father nor of her mother's hospitalization. She remembered seeing her aunt coming down the stairs in a black dress — "and then, from then on, I don't remember anything. It's all sort of dark," she said. In the absence of reality information, Jan began to fantasize. She speculated that her father had gone to a warm place to live (he hated the cold, she said); when she grew up, she would go to look for him in California, Florida or Hawaii. "It's funny. I know that he's dead, but I think he's alive — somewhere. It's just that I don't know where." Side by side with the knowledge that her father was dead lived the wish that he would be alive and that they would be reunited. Acceptance of reality, and denial in fantasy, co-existed in her thinking. In her dramatic play, she first expressed the wishes, then mourned and grieved over his death and later, gave vent to the anger as well as the feelings of loss. The protection, disguise and permissible outlets afforded through drama enabled her to work through her depression, become connected with others, to find pleasure in school work and creative accomplishment.

## 5   PSYCHIC INTEGRATION: STEVEN

As is well known, individuals often experience wishes and impulses as "bad" and attempt to exclude them from conscious awareness. At times the repression works; at times, repression fails and the impulses find outlets in symptomatic behavior.

Such was the case with 10-year-old Steven, who was referred for night terrors which began when he was three and had continued intermittently since that time. The family traced the beginning of the terrors to an early accident when he was struck by a car and hospitalized for six weeks. Returning home, he witnessed his mother being taken to the hospital in an ambulance, "covered with blood." The bad dreams began shortly thereafter, increased in frequency and severity until they took the form of night terrors.

In therapy, Steven began to play with puppets in a creative way. In his first puppet diagnostic interview,[23] his story was entitled "The Search for the Lost Treasure." The two main characters, a pirate and a policeman, searched for the "millions and millions of gold coins stored in a far-off mountain." They set out on a ship, fell asleep, and were beset by strange and unusual creatures who frightened them, tried to eat them, behead them and pull off their arms. They eventually encountered a witch who owned the gold. They managed to outwit her and returned home with a ship full of riches.

Interestingly, following the first puppet session, the night terrors ceased. The catharsis of the play had relieved him of his symptom; nevertheless, the task of understanding the frightening fantasies remained. As Steven played out his fantasies, first through the puppets, then through the spontaneous dramas, his conflicts were reflected in his "plots" with increasingly less disguise. In time it became clear that Steven had several "parts" to him—the pirate part (which was a "bad" part which told him to do bad things); a policeman part (which was a kind of conscience that punished him for his "bad" thoughts); a professor part (which tried to be academically successful but could not). As the puzzle pieces were put together in his play, Steven recognized that the characters in his stories were self symbols; the therapeutic task was to help him to integrate the split off parts of himself. The dramatic experience gave him an opportunity to play these multiple roles and helped him to come to terms with the conflictive aspects they represented, thus aiding the ego in the task of integration.

## 6 RE-ENACTMENT OF PAST TRAUMATIC EXPERIENCES: LILA

Through their play, children often re-enact their past life experiences, real or fantasized, attempting to allay anxiety by mastering them. Such was the case with 8-year-old Lila, who had been subject to sadistic attacks in a chaotic environment which eventually culminated in her removal from home to a foster home situation. She and her older siblings were abused by their mother and her paramours; in addition, it seems likely that she was sexually abused. After she witnessed the shooting of her mother during an argument, she was placed in a foster home where she became whiny, stubborn, accident prone, unable to work in school.

In drama therapy, her play was disorganized and fragmented. After three sessions, her anxiety abated somewhat and she began to re-enact a chaotic version of the shooting incident. Her play was a curious mixture of fact and fantasy. In her re-enactment, she insisted that the therapist be Irene, her case worker, and that she, Lila, would save Irene from being shot by "the mean witch" — who, in subsequent playings, became "the bad man." The playing, however, inevitably resulted in Lila's own death — as she pretended she was shot in the stomach, just as her mother had been. The repeated playing out, coupled with the interpretation of her therapist's understanding of the meaning of her play (i.e., her identification with her mother and her guilt in being unable to prevent her mother's tragedy), helped to relieve the anxiety and control the feelings surrounding the traumatic event. Gradually the play content changed and she assumed the role of the doctor (rather than the victim), who tried to save the "baby's" life. In so doing, she shifted from acting out (or, in Ekstein's[24] term, play action) to play acting, with subsequent gains in ego control.

Symptomatically, the bad dreams and bed wetting stopped; her passive aggressive and self-destructive behavior abated; and she showed signs of being able to take advantage of the second chance being afforded her in a loving foster home. While the drama therapy can help to resolve some of the conflicts, still, many of the scars from the past, with their long-term sequelae, cannot be erased.

# 7   TRANSFORMATION FROM PASSIVITY TO ACTIVITY: GREG

Children like Lila are often helpless victims in life experiences over which they have no control. If life becomes too painful for them at too early an age, when the ego cannot tolerate the onslaught of overwhelming anxiety, the child may retreat into psychosis. Sometimes it is possible to interrupt the process and help them to switch roles, as it were, and move from a position of passive victim to active participator, thereby regaining the control and mastery of which Waelder spoke.

Five-year-old Greg was referred to a speech clinic because he stopped talking following an accident. As his mother related the event, Greg and others were riding in a taxi, coming home from a picnic one rainy night. Leaning against the door, Greg suddenly began to fall into the street. His three-year-old brother grabbed him, but was unable to hold onto him and Greg fell into the darkness. The taxi was crowded and noisy; it had gone a full block before mother realized the child had fallen. Stopping the taxi, she ran back to find Greg unconscious in a heap, miraculously missed by the passing cars. A motorist rushed mother and child to a nearby hospital where he was detained for the weekend. Tests proved to be negative. He was released, but seemed in a daze. Taken again for testing, he was hospitalized for a week; still the results were negative. Six months later, perplexed by his persistent muteness, mother brought him for speech therapy.

Recognizing the psychodynamic components in the child's behavior, he was put in an expressive therapy group, one that encouraged the expression of feelings in play. For four weeks Greg failed to interact with others, playing alone in a corner. In the fourth weekly session, the group was playing out a fantasy in which a "bad mother" (the therapist) was jailed because she failed to "feed" her children. Suddenly, Greg stirred from his solitary position in the corner and quietly took "mother" by the hand from the jail— "No jail, mommy—no jail," he said. He led her to the housekeeping corner and "fed" her bananas and chicken—all the play food he could find.

Startled at the suddenness of the play and puzzled by its meaning, the therapists asked his mother about her understanding of it. She related that when she had been ill and was taken to the hospital on several occasions, a police ambulance had been used—and her son cried, "No jail." A more detailed social history revealed that Greg had experienced multiple separations from mother at very early ages—at one time, he was institutionalized for six months; on another occasion, he was left with relatives and abused. Retrospectively, it appeared that Greg, unable to tolerate the many separations and pain of reality, had begun to withdraw and retreat following the taxi accident. The experience gave him a chance to move from a passive position to an active one and "rescue" his mother, as he would have liked to have been rescued in the past.

Thereafter, Greg played many separation games in which he was lost and the group, especially the therapists, had to find him. Once he felt secure with the therapists he began to play with other children. One of his favorite games was that of taxi driver. Taking people to the hospital, he would help them into his makeshift taxi—carefully lock all the doors, drive to the hospital and carefully unlock the doors. In doing so, he became active instead of passive, relived the experience and supplied a different, healthier ending.

# 8   SEPARATION OF FANTASY AND REALITY: KEVIN

At times children choose a symbolic character to represent aspects of themselves and others when they are unable to handle their conflicts directly. It often seems that at some preconscious or unconscious level they understand what is happening, but they are unable to consciously recognize it. Eight-year-old Kevin, a borderline psychotic child, used the alligator puppet (named Ally) to represent his oral aggressive rage. He externalized his wishes (to eat up; to control), his fears (of being killed, mutilated, abandoned) onto the alligator. For a period of more than a year he was unable to talk about these impulses directly, nor could he tolerate any intervention from the therapist which attempted to link the play with his current or past life experiences. At times he seemed to be able to respond to interventions made within the context of the symbolism of his own stories (e.g., "Poor Ally. . .it's as though you're afraid the giant will kill you and nobody will be strong enough to help"), although, these, too, he sometimes rejected.

He seemed to portray his abusive, alcoholic father as "The Trickster" and "The Tasmanian Devil." Playing this role himself, he would upset the basket of puppets (which represented all the people in town), raging, "Where is that Ally? I'll kill him!" On several occasions the alligator was actually killed; although intensely anxious, Kevin could not tolerate any thought of resurrection. Finally, the therapist's direct message that she cared about him *and* Ally and would help him to find some way of protecting himself, seemed to "get through." Thereupon, Kevin played the role of the doctor who struggled valiantly to inject impulses into the alligator's head: "If I can just give him a brain transfusion, then maybe he can live. The trouble is that he has inherited bad blood and it's going to kill him." The outcome was that the alligator was brought back from the grasp of death, brutally injured, and was placed in an "intensive care unit" in the hospital.

On another occasion when Kevin was frightened by his father's violent rage, he resorted to having Ally devise a special pain belt. By magically pushing the button, Ally could control the intensity and duration of the "pain flow," which he administered to his enemies — principally to "the trickster" and "the giant." Ironically, Ally insisted that the pain be delivered in the heart "cause that's where it hurts the most."

After a year of such symbolic play, Kevin gradually began to be able to talk about the situation at home more directly. Following the play, he could make the translation by commenting, as he did after one episode, "The Tasmanian Devil is like my father when he's drunk. He's wild and crazy. When he calls my mother a turd and a shit, though, he is really calling himself those names. But at least I don't think anymore that I'll have to kill him." After a moment's reflection, he added sadly, "But you know what? I don't even like my father anymore. In fact, I hate him. And that's not right, cause kids shouldn't have to have a father they hate." Gradually he was more able to deal with feelings through the use of words and the unconscious playing out became more conscious, understandable, coherent and controllable. Giving "form to feeling" as Langer[25] has characterized the arts experience, Kevin was able to express, channel, identify and control his emotions.

# 9   OTHER CONSIDERATIONS

There are other functions which drama serves as well: communion with the hated or idealized parent, defense and mastery.

At times children seem to use drama as a primitive, preverbal way of communing or fusing with either an idealized or hated parent. Such dramatizations can perhaps be understood as a kind of acting out of preverbal experiences. Traumatized Lila, referred to earlier, repeatedly "became" her "bad mother" in her play and re-enacted the primitive, almost inchoate feelings as though she and her mother were one. She would begin by "bathing" her baby, but soon the gentle motions became slaps, hits and blows. She would mutter, "I hate you...I'm gonna' kill you...you bad...you gonna' kill me..." In such moments, the boundaries between self and other were blurred and she seemed unable to distinguish between fantasy and reality as she acted out her aggression on the "bad baby." Similarly, children can also find in drama, as in other play or creative experiences, a sense of fusion with a "good" idealized, omnipotent parent, as one child, Lauren, did when she became the "very nice Queen" who could do all manner of magical things. With such children, the play serves as a way of establishing a relationship which can lead to separation-individuation, neutralization of the drives and repair of the distorted ego functions.

Sometimes children use drama as a defense as did Jan, referred to earlier, in denying the death of her father, fantasizing his return and their reunion. Similarly, Jimmy's repetitive enactment of the role of a super powerful dinosaur seemed to grow out of his almost overwhelming sense of helplessness which he attempted to deny through identification with the aggressor. On a healthier note, drama may also serve as a kind of problem solving experience which can lead to mastery. Six-year-old Tommy carefully arranged the surgical instruments and attempted to operate on the boy doll, trying to figure out just what the doctors would do to his cleft lip in his forthcoming operation. The playing was an attempt to anticipate the experience and master his anxiety, reminiscent of Erikson's statement: "I propose the theory that the child's play is the infantile form of the human ability to deal with experience by creating model situations and to master reality by experiment and planning."[26]

# 10  SUMMARY

This paper has noted the developmental continuum of play and discussed its relationship to drama. The functions of drama therapy as a form of child psychotherapy have been illustrated through case material, focusing on wish fulfillment, psychic integration, reenactment of past traumatic experiences, transformation from passivity to activity, separation of fantasy and reality, fusion with the idealized or hated parent, defense and mastery. The value of drama therapy is not only in the abreaction it provides, but in the chance to articulate the fantasies through play, experience the working through of the conflicts and connect the past to the present.

# FOOTNOTES

1. S. Millar, *The Psychology of Play* (Harmondsworth: Penguin, 1968); S. Smilansky, *The Effects of Sociodramatic Play on Disadvantaged Pre-School Children* (New York: Wiley, 1968); R. E. Herron and B. Sutton-Smith, *Child's Play* (New York: Wiley, 1971); M. W. Piers, ed., *Play and Development* (New York: Norton, 1972); J. Singer, *The Child's World of Make-Believe* (New York: Academic Press, 1973); J. Bruner, A. Jolly, and K. Sylva, *Play: Its Role in Development and Evolution* (New York: Basic Books, 1976).
2. Jean Piaget, *Play, Dreams and Imitation in Childhood* (New York: Norton, 1951).
3. R. R. Collard, "Exploration and Play in Human Infants," in *Research and Thoughts about Children's Play, Leisure Today*, ed. B. Sutton-Smith (Washington, D.C.: H.E.W., 1975).
4. Erik H. Erikson, *Childhood and Society* (New York: Norton, 1963).
5. Erik H. Erikson, "Play and Actuality," in *Play and Development*, ed. M. W. Piers (New York: Norton, 1972).
6. R. Speers, "The Developmental Stages of Play" (Paper given at Carlow College, Pittsburgh, Pa., June 1975).
7. H. Hug-Hulmuth, "On the Techniques of Child Analysis," *International Journal of Psychoanalysis* 2 (1921).
8. Melanie Klein, *The Psychoanalysis of Children* (London: Hogarth Press, 1932).

9. R. Waelder, "The Psychoanalytic Theory of Play," *Psychoanalytic Quarterly* 2 (1933).

10. Anna Freud, *The Psychoanalytic Treatment of Children* (New York: International Universities Press, 1964).

11. Margaret Lowenfeld, *Play in Childhood* (London: Kegan Paul, 1935).

12. L. Bender and P. Schiller, "Form as a Principle in the Play of Children," in *Child Psychiatric Techniques*, ed. L. Bender (Springfield, Ill.: Charles C. Thomas, 1952).

13. Erikson, *Childhood and Society*, p. 209.

14. Virginia M. Axline, *Play Therapy* (Boston: Houghton Mifflin, 1947).

15. Clark Moustakas, *Children in Play Therapy* (New York: Jason Aronson, 1973).

16. Jessie Taft, *The Dynamics of Therapy* (New York: Dover, 1962).

17. H. Cohn, "A Field Theory Approach to Transference and its Particular Application to Children," *Psychiatry* 18 (1955).

18. N. E. Miller and J. Dollard, *Social Learning and Imitation* (New Haven: Yale University Press, 1941).

19. Gregory P. Stone, "The Play of Little Children," in *Child's Play*, eds. R. E. Herron and B. Sutton-Smith (New York: Wiley, 1971), pp. 9-10.

20. P. Greenacre, "Play in Relation to the Creative Imagination," *Psychoanalytic Study of the Child* (New York: International Universities Press, 1959), p. 14.

21. Margaret Lowenfeld, "The World Pictures of Children," *British Journal of Medical Psychology* 18 (1939).

22. Richard A. Gardner, *Therapeutic Communication with Children: The Mutual Storytelling Technique* (New York: Jason Aronson, 1971); E. C. Irwin, J. Rubin, and M. Shapiro, "Art and Drama: Partners in Therapy," *American Journal of Psychotherapy* 29, no. 1 (1975).

23. E. C. Irwin and M. I. Shapiro, "Puppetry as a Diagnostic and Therapeutic Technique," *Psychiatry and Art*, 4, ed. I. Jakab (New York: S. Karger, 1975).

24. Rudolf Ekstein, *Children of Time and Space, of Action and Impulse* (New York: Appleton-Century-Crofts, 1966).

25. Susanne K. Langer, *Philosophical Sketches* (New York: Mentor Books, 1962).

26. Erikson, *Childhood and Society*, p. 222.

JULIE ARDEN is president and faculty member of the White Pond Community Arts and Cultural Association, Stormville, New York. She was formerly on the faculty of New York University and the Turtle Bay Music School, New York City; creative arts consultant for B.O.C.E.S. in northern Westchester and Putnam counties, New York; and supervisor of the arts therapy program, and drama and art therapist at the Wiltwyck School for Boys, Yorktown Heights, New York. She lectures extensively.

## Chapter 7

# THE LITTLE BULL

## Julie Arden

### PART 1

I was seated on a small, round stage, not in a theatre, but in a school, the X. School For Boys. The drama was not a play, but an agonizing moment of real life recreated, not by an actor, but by an emotionally disturbed child. I, as drama therapist, was playing the role of the boy's alcoholic mother. My body was limp; my hand supported my nodding head. The boy shook my arm, his husky voice choked.

"Mother! Don't drink so much! Pray to God to help you stop!"

Through half-raised lids I peered into a pair of teary eyes, they were big and brown. Thick, dark brows raised above them forming a band of anxiety, deep furrows, contrasting sharply with wiry, chestnut curls. Anguish had contorted his fine features, but it could not erase the clear, bronze skin and pointed, dimpled chin that combined to make Alfredo Ordalgo a handsome twelve-year-old.

"Pray, Mother! Pray!" the child pleaded. "Come, Mama! I'll put you to bed." The boy was trembling; his beseeching eyes turned to our audience of one, Doctor David Schmidt, psychiatrist.

Alfredo faltered. "Then...I...hide the bottle."

The tall, slender man leaned forward in his seat and asked compassionately, "Then, do you go to bed?"

"Sometimes," answered Alfredo in a flat, depressed voice. "Sometimes, I go out in the street. I take money from her pocketbook, if she has it, and go buy a hamburger. Or I go to my aunt's house to get something to eat. Sometimes I watch television downstairs in the candy store. Sometimes I go to bed."

"Do you have your own bed now, Alfredo?" The doctor spoke casually. The boy's face abruptly turned red.

"Don't you say anything about my mother!" he bellowed. His foot crashed against a box on the stage; an untied shoe flew through the air. A stream of four letter words gave descriptive force to his tantrum.

"I didn't say anything about your mother!"

"I want to get out of this damn school!" yelled the irrational child. Then he collapsed on the floor of the stage crying, "I'm crazy! Send me to Bellevue!"

I quickly knelt beside the boy, took a role and said in a calm, comforting voice, "You are in Bellevue, Alfredo. I am your nurse."

His body relaxed. He turned his head slowly towards me and gave me a wry, fleeting smile.

"How can I help you?" I smiled back.

"No one can help me!" he moaned. His wild forelock waved from side to side as he violently tossed his head.

"Doctor Schmidt! Doctor Schmidt!" I called, "will you see this patient?"

The doctor stood on the child-sized stage, his head almost brushed the ceiling. A matter-of-fact voice directed, "Let him sit up; he will feel better."

Alfredo slumped into a chair. Then the understanding man asked him, "Why are you here?"

"Because I feel like killing people! I got a bad temper!" he mumbled.

A comforting hand slid over the lowered head as the doctor explained, "I think you can learn to control that, when you understand that you are really angry at your mother, because she can't take care of you."

With that the boy jumped from the chair, grabbed his jacket, scrambled for his shoe and bolted out the door. The doctor reached it just in time to duck a fair-sized rock.

He smiled ruefully. "Well, I guess we can count today's session a success!" He sat down and began recording in his notebook.

I sat musing. It had been a successful session, indeed! For the first time Alfredo had admitted that his mother was an alcoholic; the painful nerve of his problem had been exposed.

The stage, that six-foot circle, standing two feet off the floor, had enabled Alfredo to act out the unspeakable burden of his life. Perhaps now we could begin to treat the basic cause, as well as the results of this child's illness.

"I want to help Alfredo," said the doctor, putting down his pen. "I mean, more than just to leave W. I want to help him for his whole life."

Somewhere in this boy's background there had once been love, charm, grace, courtesy. Perhaps the grandmother in Puerto Rico, the aunt who fed him, or perhaps even Alfredo's mother, before misfortune weakened her pride and will, had given this child the foundation for a healthy life.

Alfredo carried in his small, stocky person that quality known in Spanish as *dignidad*. It was this strength we were trying to reach. If we could make it grow, this child might learn to understand that he could truly help his mother by first helping himself.

Poor Mrs. Ordalgo! She had been scarcely a woman when the pig was roasted outdoors in banana leaves and the guests sang and danced all night at her wedding. She was still in her teens when she left the green and silver mountains of Puerto Rico and made the frightening flight alone with two children to the neon-lit slums of East Harlem in New York City. Somewhere in the cold and violent city was the husband who had deserted her.

When her older, adolescent son became a narcotics addict, she sought to forget her troubles in the comforting atmosphere of the downstairs candy store where the old man made and secretly sold the never-ending supply of cheap wine, "medicine" for her "sickness." A sickness that I had been called upon to recreate with terribly accurate details described to me by this haunted child.

When Mrs. Ordalgo was sober she realized that she was not a good mother. Then, driven by guilt, she would try to show her love and care by excessively nurturing her son with food and candy. His demands became irrational and gross yet his mother could deny him nothing.

Each day the child opened his eyes to frightening inconsistency and anxiety. Would his mother be home? Would she be awake, asleep or in a stupor? Would he be fed like the favored infant whose every whim could be granted? Or would his mother be the baby who would have to be lifted out of the gutter, taken home and put to bed?

We were not too sure of what had happened to Alfredo during those traumatic times. We did not really know what acts of lust or violence had been played out before his eyes. We only surmised the quality of his premature wisdom by the anxiety and guilt that became anger as three words softly spoken, "...your own bed?" turned our stage into an arena of fury.

Could Alfredo understand that his real anger was with his mother because she could not take care of him properly? If we could help the child to come to grips with the real nature of his problems we could focus on our next aim, getting him into the halfway house maintained by the school in New York City. This residence provided a springboard for boys who were again trying community life before returning to either their own, or a foster home.

Alfredo, like many children who have been victims of adult neglect and brutality, refused to communicate when he first entered the school. No aspect of his home life could be discussed without his resorting to lies, evasion, silent hostility, invective and temper tantrums.

Then one day I saw a glimpse of a different Alfredo. He was doing a dramatic improvisation of a bullfight (his own choice of subject) in which he was both the animal and matador. I was impressed by his range of expressiveness and flair for theatrical effects. It was in brilliant contrast to his usual dull, sullen reticence.

Suddenly I saw striking aspects of the child's own problems within the symbols he had chosen to impersonate. Was he not, like the brave bull, driven to annihilating rage by the forces of his tormenting life? It made little difference who won, bull or matador. The ghastly cycle continued, kill or be killed!

These were the thoughts I expressed at the case conference on

Alfredo. Dr. Schmidt was impressed and as a result decided to try another dramatic means to bring to the surface the troubling causes of anger and guilt that were warping this child's life.

I had organized a "studio" group where creative dramatics techniques were used for a variety of therapeutic goals. Through improvisations, plays were fashioned and performed for small, invited audiences consisting largely of staff members and a few children.

Alfredo was flattered when I asked him to join. The privacy of our first session satisfied his need to be the center of attention. After all, had he not chosen to be the star of the bullring? Disarmed by the victory of gaining my complete interest he readily blurted out the play ideas that raced through his head.

We were not disappointed. Like a good playwright, Alfredo selected the elements from his own life that made for drama. To the facts he added fantasy to fulfill his needs. He briefly narrated his scenario.

He dictated the title, "The Unhappiest Boy." "This is the story of an unhappy boy. He's poor. He's a bad boy. He wants everything he feels like having, that he can get. His father don't spend much time with him. This boy is *bad* because he's *unhappy*, and he's *unhappy* because he's *bad*. His father drinks, he's a wino. He goes out with women and don't think about nis wife or son. He beats his wife when he gets drunk. The boy has a grandmother. She's the only one who cares for him. His mother, she's a wino too."

After the performance of "The Unhappiest Boy" Dr. Schmidt had his first meaningful interview with Alfredo. They talked about the boy in the play. The "real" boy's replies were diffident but definitely cooperative. The encounter was brief but it represented a milestone. The doctor was excited about the possibilities of extending the dramatics technique. The question he brought to me was challenging, "Could drama move Alfredo from fantasy to full reality?"

Time nagged and pushed us in our task. Our institution was geared for the needs of pre-adolescent children. Alfredo, who had been with us for two years, had chronologically outgrown us. His future soon had to be decided. Two tough problems remained to challenge us: a foster home for Alfredo, and his willingness to accept it.

I will never forget that first session! Alfredo bounced into the room, sprang onto the stage and smiled. Bowing with the elegant flourishes of a matador, he said with slightly accented speech, "Ladies and genemen! I now present the greatest actor in the world, Alfredo Ordalgo!" He blew up his chest (the triumphant matador) and again strutted and bowed some more. Then he collapsed on the floor of the stage in a crumpled heap of laughter, or was it tears?

He rolled over, face down, and kicked the stage with the wild abandon of a three-year-old's tantrum. We watched silently for a moment. Then Doctor Schmidt said, "What are you so angry about?"

Alfredo twisted and turned. He stared at the ceiling as his face became a contorted mask of pain and rage. He jumped to his feet shouting the refrain we were to hear over and over again for the next few months: "When am I going to get out of this damn place?"

"Where will you go?" asked the doctor.

"To my home, my street," rejoined a sulky Alfredo.

"Let us see your street," I invited. "Let's make it here on the stage."

"O.K.," he said, accepting my bait.

Then he began arranging the boxes on the stage. They became buildings designated by Alfredo as, "the candy store, my aunt's house—that's five blocks away," and on down the list of crumbling slums and stores that serviced the needs of the block's struggling inhabitants.

Rapidly chattering as he shifted his scenery, Alfredo vividly described the bar, the storefront church and the funeral parlor that completed the setting for his drama.

"Who will you be?" I asked.

"I'm a man!"

"Let's find some clothes for this man," I suggested, as the young actor followed me into the closet where we kept theatrical paraphenalia. I left him alone to choose.

He quickly reappeared with a strutting, "ditty-bop" walk. He held his shoulders and torso stiffly, propelling himself with pelvic thrusts and shuffling feet; he fingered his silk lapel, smiled and bowed with great elan as he lifted his derby. He put on his gloves, then ran back to the closet and then back to the stage where, with mock secretiveness, he pretended to hide a gun in his pocket. He lit a make-believe cigarette and began to stroll on the stage that he had turned into Spanish Harlem.

A running commentary accompanied his actions as with great speed and constant activity he made doorways out of boxes and then became the drunks and "heads" that sprawled and moaned in their shadows. With a leap he was upright, the cop on the beat, urging the unfortunates to move on as he prodded them with his night stick, or arrested them and with a fierce struggle shoved them into the paddy wagon.

His character quickly shifted as he stole and stabbed, playing both the robber and the robbed, the attacker and the writhing victim.

On the round stage, ever circling and darting, he created apparitions of fear and desire. He sat at a lunch counter gorging himself with hamburgers and french fries. He ordered Puerto Rican specialties.

He created a girl friend, changed his voice and manner, took off his derby and played the part. With a few deft gestures he again became the man and then, putting his jacket on backwards, the priest in the marriage scene that soon followed.

More stealing came as the aftermath of the wedding. Now Alfredo was a boy again. He lowered his voice to become the detective that arrested the boy and sent him to Youth House. There, again the child, he relived the terrors of his nightmares.

The exhausting phantasmagoria of the barrio came to an end as Alfredo dashed to the blackboard and drew. First a "devil-face," as he named it, appeared and then a hideous double-featured mask which he explained as the "witch woman."

Now, just three short weeks later, he had invited me to play that very witch woman, his drunken mother. Now it was all out in the open.

Doctor Schmidt closed his notebook and tapped his teeth with his pen.

"Do you think we're going too fast?" I asked.

"I don't know," he answered.

"I'll tell you this," I went on, "when he lifted me out of the gutter, he almost got angry. He was a great deal more impatient when I resisted, he was almost mad."

"That's important!" nodded the doctor. "If we can get him to put his anger in the right place maybe he'll stop beating up the world." Then he laughed, "Julie, we're not going too fast for him, he's going too fast for us! He's ready to face his problem or he wouldn't have created this scene today. Are we ready to face his guilty anger? Will the rest of the staff be prepared to cope with what's coming?"

At our next case conference on Alfredo we learned that The Little Bull was going to be even angrier. He would not be permitted a regular "home visit."

His social worker, Ted Donovan, reported that although Mrs. Ordalgo had been given money by the Welfare Department to purchase a bed for Alfredo she would not permit Ted to come into the apartment to check the sleeping arrangements. She would neither deny nor confirm that Alfredo would still be sleeping with her if he came home to visit or whether he would have any place at all to lay his head.

There was one hope in the future for Alfredo and that was an aunt and uncle with children of their own who seemed friendly and warm towards the boy. Ted planned another visit with them to explore the possibilities of a foster home situation. But Alfredo's tantrums and destructive threats and actions would have to diminish and finally disappear before that happy solution could be realized.

Special trips to nearby places of interest and stores would be substituted for the off-campus trip that the "Unhappiest Boy" would miss now that his home visits would be curtailed.

Questions arose concerning drama therapy as the clinical treatment recommended by Doctor Schmidt.

An uneasy counselor raised his hand.

"Wouldn't baseball be more 'manly' and just as therapeutic?"

"It seems to me," said the Head Counselor, "this drama therapy stirs Alfredo up. Isn't it going to make him more explosive, more difficult to handle?"

Doctor Schmidt acknowledged the "manliness" of baseball and agreed that drama therapy stirred things up. Then he tried to explain that the technique also acted as a safety valve to siphon off emotions in a controlled situation and provide a means of expressing the thoughts and feelings that dared not be communicated in any other way.

He regretted the lack of a two-way mirror—others might have had the opportunity to observe our sessions, and closed the meeting with the statement that Alfredo's improvisations would continue.

## PART 2

Alfredo slouched in. He began the session with what had become a standard opening scene. It began as he threw himself prone on the stage and then jack-knifed into a foetal position. That day he lay quite still in an almost dream-like trance.

"You feel calmer, don't you?" asked Doctor Schmidt.

"I'm sleepy!" Alfredo shouted back.

Doctor Schmidt chuckled, "You sound very wide awake to me!"

"You shut up!" yelled Alfredo. "You don't know nothing! You're stupid!" The challenging boy rolled over and pretended to snore very loudly.

I saw a cue and took it. "Alfredo must be tired. He's sleeping deeply. I wonder what he's dreaming?" I mused audibly but very softly.

Alfredo's response began as a low moan, a strangling sound that heralded the nightmares of a disturbed child.

The embryonic form on the stage released itself, as the boy screamed, "Help! Help! He's going to kill me! I'll kill him first! I'll kill him! Kill! Kill!"

"What does he look like?" I asked quietly while the doctor listened and watched.

Suddenly Alfredo jumped up and dashed to the costume closet. Wearing a long, black robe and a gruesome mask, Alfredo emerged and strode to the stage. A sword dragged on the floor from its loosely held position in the belt of the flapping costume. The mask rattled. It had been made out of a brown paper bag by another child. From behind its grinning teeth, scarred face, and big, red eyes, came the sound of panting; it brought to my mind once again that tortured bull.

Stumbling over the long robe that trailed behind him the young actor stalked the stage, his plastic sword ratcheting against the metal chairs.

"I am Alfredo," I whispered as I stepped up and stretched out on the boxes. I half-closed my eyes as I pretended to sleep. I saw him draw the sword and lurch towards me.

"I'm going to cut out your tongue!" His voice hissed against the paper mouth. "I'm going to chop off your head!"

Abruptly following his irrational whims, he pulled off the mask and dropped the sword. As it slithered across the floor he threw back his head and laughed wildly. His mood changed. He moved slowly, carefully, his eyes shifting from side to side in apprehension. He removed the long, dark cloak with great deliberation; swirling the length of it around his head he circled the stage panting and crying, "They're after me! They're after me!"

The monsters of the ghetto were real. Violence and crime, rats and junkies, pimps, prostitutes, drunks, and child molesters peopled the waking and sleeping hours of Alfredo.

The black cloak was lined in red. With the robe turned inside out, grandiosity took the place of fear. Alfredo, the brave matador charged the imaginary animal, the twirled velvet slapped my face as I stepped off the stage.

Completely concentrated on his attacker, the child danced, turning and twisting, charging and retreating. He broke into an intense sweat.

Dr. Schmidt queried perceptively, "Is there really a bull there? Did you dream this? Are you making it up?"

Alfredo dropped the robe and stood with his arms akimbo, eyeing us with a disdainful glare. "I was putting you on and you didn't even know it!" he sneered contemptuously. "Man! You think I'm crazy, don't you?"

"Do you think you're crazy?" asked the doctor.

"Sometimes", murmured Alfredo, "when I'm mad." He began
to pile the stage boxes into a barricade. As he banged them into
place he went on talking.

"I did have this dream. This gang was after me..." He assumed
a menacing position and began singing. The Jets' song from
"West Side Story" was his overture. Then he hid behind the boxes
and began again that hard breathing accompanied by a broken
monologue.

"They're after me! If any one comes near me, I'll kill him! I got
my knife right here! I'll cut out his tongue! I'll cut off his head!
There they are now!"

With a wild yell, like the Indians in a TV western, he jumped
from his crouching position to one of attack. One after another he
took on his assailants in a mock gang fight with knives.

The frightful panting began again as he lunged for the kill. In
one movement he became both the killer and the slain. He died
the prolonged, agonizing finale of an old-time actor, calling to his
mother and God to help him.

Again on his feet he peered at us over his hunched shoulders;
now he was the hunted, haunted criminal. Once more behind the
boxes he cried out, "Please, God! Forgive me! I was nervous. I
didn't know what I was doing!"

He whimpered softly then whispered to an imaginary passerby.
"Hey, lady! Hi, baby! She's gone away. I'm all alone. I did
wrong...wrong...wrong. Everybody's wrong! Mama, I didn't do
the right thing!"

He crawled on his hands and knees until he came to the spot
where he had left the robe. He got up, put it on, and rearranged
the boxes. He spoke so softly we could hardly hear him. "The
man in black is in a coffin." Then he laid himself out with his
fingers folded and pressed tightly against his chest.

"I don't think that man is dead," I whispered back. "He's very
sick. How did he get to be so sick?" I stepped on the stage and sat
beside him; he lay rigid, his eyes tightly shut. I raised his head,
propped him against my shoulder, held him in my arms.

"What made him sick?" I asked.

Slowly, Alfredo opened his eyes and rolled them way up until only the whites showed. "The vampire woman sucked his blood!" he moaned.

I tried to muster a matter-of-fact voice as I said, "We'll have to give him a blood transfusion then."

The room was very quiet, the only sound, the rustle of looseleaf pages as the doctor rapidly made notes. He raised his head, our eyes met and he nodded rapidly.

"What's a blood whateveryoucallit?" asked the reviving Alfredo.

We had never been that close before. I saw the number of scars that marred his forehead, cheeks and chin. Fights? Beatings? Accidents? The boy, now relaxed, nestled against me. As I explained to him he stared intently at my face. What did he see? What did he feel?

He felt better; the blood transfusion had worked! He jumped up, tore off the robe and threw it at me. He whipped out his comb and rushed to the mirror, smiling at himself as he ran the broken teeth through his matted curls. Then he turned and looked at me with a distinct leer and said, "Hi, baby!" He gave one more admiring glance at himself in the mirror, then swung out of the room with that strutting ditty-bop walk. After he slammed the door we could hear his whistle echoing in the distance.

## PART 3

Alfredo talked to me as we trudged up the hill to the small building that housed our dramatics studio. "I had a happy dream last night," he reported soberly as he picked up a handy rock and hurled it at a tree. He rushed into the building and we entered the room with the small, round stage. He flung himself face down as usual.

The room was colder than outdoors. I called the maintenance department and reported the heat failure.

"Do you want to act today?" I asked, cautiously adding, "Doctor Schmidt is on vacation, he won't be here."

"I don't want to act. It's too cold," complained Alfredo.

"Let's have some hot tea first," I offered. "By the time we're finished perhaps the heat will be up. Maybe then you will be in the mood."

"What does that mean, be in the *mood?*" he asked as he watched me plug in the electric kettle. I reached into my desk drawer for a bag of cookies. He smiled and rubbed his hands together in expectation.

"Well," I answered, "you're in the mood to eat cookies right now."

"Ah!" he smiled broadly, "in the mood! That means you feel like you want to do something." His eyes gleamed proudly at his quick understanding.

Soon we were sipping our hot tea. Alfredo held his cup with the delicacy of a Spanish don. "This is like my dream," he confided in a whisper. "I was home with my mother. She was giving me good things to eat." He suddenly broke his reverie and asked in a loud practical voice for more cookies.

There were no more cookies, unfortunately. At his suggestion I agreed to bring more next week. Then he nodded agreeably saying, "That's the way it is at home. My mother gets me anything I ask for."

He jumped up, picked up our empty paper cups, threw them in the wastebasket and brushed the crumbs from his hands. As he tightened his belt he ambled over to the mirror. Whipping out his comb, he slid it admiringly through his hair, saying slowly, "I'm in the mood now. I want to act my dream."

"This is the table and chairs," explained the boy as he arranged the boxes. "I'm at the table, you're my mother, you're at the stove."

"What am I cooking?"

"Bacon and eggs first!" ordered the ever-hungry child.

"How many eggs do you want, son?" I asked, trying to approximate the rhythm of a Spanish-speaking woman without resorting to an accent. How I wished I could remember more of my high school Spanish! A couple of words came back.

"*Cuantos huevos, hijo?*"

"*Seis!*" he commanded, smiling but approving my halting and poorly accented words.

"*Demasiado, Alfredo!*" I exclaimed.

"It's not too much!" he replied in English. "My mother gives me as much as I want, and she doesn't call me Alfredo!"

"What does she call you?" I questioned as I pretended to serve him.

He looked down at the imaginary plate, his head cocked wistfully as he murmured, "Bebé! Call me Bebé!"

"Bebé," I whispered; for a brief instant I let my hand rest lightly on his head thinking to myself that no twelve-year-old I knew would ever wish to be called baby. But Alfredo was appealing to me as a much younger child. "Careful!" I admonished myself, then continued as the boy's mother.

"How big you've grown, *hijo!*"

"Yes," he proudly agreed. "I need a new pair of pants!"

"I don't have the money, Bebé."

"Borrow it from my godfather," directed the practical Alfredo.

Stepping out of my role as Dolores Ordalgo I asked, "Who is that, Alfredo?"

"The old man who owns the candy store. I call him my godfather. Now we'll go to my aunt's house," directed the boy.

The next set merely shifted to another table around which now clustered the imaginary aunt and uncle and cousins. More food was consumed! From there we went to the movies; the important aspect of this event seemed to be the popcorn and soda.

He must, I felt, be brought back to reality.

"I'm glad you had such a nice dream, Alfredo. Does your mother really let you eat all that stuff?"

Premature lines once again ridged the young actor's brow. "Yes." The stocky body began to stiffen. "My mother gives me everything I want."

"Always?" I asked casually as I began to shift the stage boxes.

"Yes! No! Sometimes!" The words jumped out as Alfredo rushed to help me move the stage furniture.

"Thank you. You're a gentleman, Mr. Ordalgo." The cavalier of the future smiled.

"Who taught you your good manners?" I inquired as we continued to straighten out the room.

"My mother—my aunt," he confessed proudly.

Our time together was coming to an end. I had fifteen more minutes in which to try and bring Alfredo closer to an acceptance of his problem. It didn't seem right to let him leave that stage still wrapped in daydreams.

"Is there anything else you'd like to do? We have a little time left."

Suddenly he shouted at me, "I want to eat more cookies! I want more cookies!"

My voice raised, too, in genuinely shocked surprise. "Alfredo! You know there aren't any more cookies."

He was acting, to be sure, but the fury was real as this child picked up one of the play boxes and hurled it across the room; the performance was the very essence of displaced anger. The rage he felt for his inadequate mother was now irrationally flung at me.

He lunged towards me; his finger pointed like a gun. "You're hiding more cookies! I'm going to get them even if I have to shoot you!"

"Acting is over for today," I answered quietly.

The finger that had a minute before been a gun now got shoved into a slightly drooling mouth, the menacing voice began to whine, "More cookies!"

The moment had arrived for me to make my point. "Alfredo," I commanded, "look at yourself in the mirror!"

Without changing his posture he slunk towards the glass.

"How old is the boy you see?"

He studied the unflattering image. The finger was withdrawn from the mouth and shoved in his pocket. He murmured as his head drooped, "Five years old."

"Is that how old you feel when your mother calls you Bebé?" I asked.

"Don't say anything about my mother!" he scowled, picking up his coat as he prepared to leave.

"I'm not talking about your mother. I'm talking about *you*."

I stood between the angry boy and the door, not planning to detain him physically, but playing for a little more time. He did not put on his coat. He was listening. I continued.

"Most boys who are twelve years old, almost thirteen, do not want their mothers to call them baby. They want to be grown up and independent of home and mother."

Angry tears glistened in his eyes. "My mother can call me anything she wants to." Now he struggled into his jacket, bounding towards me and the door. Furious words tumbled out in an incoherent rage as the charging bull tried to push me aside.

"I'm not coming here any more. You don't help me! Gimme some cookies! My mother gives me all the cookies I want! All the cookies in the world!"

"Please sit down!" I urged the agitated child, who was now circling the stage in that familiar rampage like a caged animal. I touched his shoulder. He shrank from me but suddenly stopped circling and did as I asked. I sat beside him.

I counseled softly, "Alfredo, I know you miss your mother, and at times she probably misses you."

"She's all alone!" The tears rushed with his words. "My brother is in prison! She's all alone in the house! She needs me!" He flung himself from the chair to the wall where his thumping fists accented his words. "I want to get out of this lousy school!"

"Alfredo!" I raised my voice. My mind quickly grasped an idea. "Why don't you write a letter to your mother?"

He stopped pounding. I hurried on. "Dictate to me. I'll type it for you. I'll be your secretary."

He stood for a minute in sulky silence. Then he abruptly turned, brushed the tears from his eyes and in a very businesslike way said, "O.K., I'll dictate."

He seated himself on the opposite side of my desk, for all the world, in look and manner, the important executive. What an actor!

"Take a letter, Miss Arden!" he ordered, in the fashion he had undoubtedly seen many times on TV or in the movies.

I put the paper in my typewriter and said, "I'm ready, Mr. Ordalgo." How he loved to be addressed as mister!

He smiled warmly and began dictating quite professionally.

"Dear Mother, I am doing fine. I wish I were with you." His voice faltered, his whole body slumped until his head and folded arms rested on the desk. He continued to dictate, his voice now a hoarse whisper.

"I love you, Mother. I feel sorry you're by yourself. I wish I didn't get into trouble. I try not to get mad. Don't drink no more. Can't you stop, darling? I know its hard for you. I feel sorry. I love you, Mother, but you get drunk. You can't take care of me right. God help us! Pray to God! Pray!"

He stopped talking. Only the noise of the typewriter keys filled the silence as I rushed to keep up with the words that now blurred before me.

I could feel the corners of my eyes prickling, my nose burning and the proverbial lump in my throat—most unprofessional. Alfredo's head was still on the desk. His eyes were closed. I swallowed, cleared my throat and said, "We'll all pray. Alfredo, we'll all try and help you both as much as we can."

The now infinitely aged child sighed and nodded. He picked up the empty cookie box and walked out licking the last few crumbs from the bottom of the box. "See you next week," he carelessly threw at me as he left.

## PART 4

For a few weeks Alfredo seemed to be turning a crucial corner. His counselors reported fewer fights and tantrums, he fulfilled his personal and group tasks, and his school work was excellent. It seemed that The Little Bull was finding his real strength.

But when another boy in his group left for the school's Half-Way House before he did, all controls vanished and overnight Alfredo gave vent to his frustration and anger in one irrational tantrum after another.

He even begged Dr. Schmidt to send him to Bellevue. But the perceptive doctor made him admit that the hospital would not find him crazy and then would send him home to his mother.

Home was where he wanted to be and all his fights and tantrums were part of his plan to get there via Bellevue. When this ploy did not work Alfredo took things in his own hands and, with another boy, ran away from the school.

He gave all of us a terribly anxious twenty-four hours and then appeared voluntarily, extremely agitated, at the school's New York City office.

He told of hitching a ride to the railroad station and skillfully avoiding the conductors by hiding in wash rooms. But when he reached home, the terrible blow fell. His mother would not let him in.

Perhaps in a stupor she had not heard or understood the wild, insistent pounding on the door. Maybe she was frightened and confused. She may have realized that the boy had done something wrong and felt inadequate to cope with his rage or to face the consequences of his action. Whatever the motivation, it was now shatteringly clear to Alfredo that he had been completely rejected. He could no longer find the excuses he needed to rationalize his abandonment.

The next case conference on Alfredo brought some good news. Alfredo's aunt and uncle were willing to be foster parents if, after a stay at our halfway house, their nephew proved himself ready to return to the community.

In the family there were two younger children, girls, and a baby boy. Alfredo would be the big brother, the older son, with a position of status that would fill his need for a responsible role. His uncle worked in a restaurant and would try and get his nephew an after school or Saturday job. He would, in short, become a contributing member of a family which in return would give him food, clothing, shelter and most important, love and appreciation.

The news was something of a miracle! But there still remained Alfredo. Would the knowledge, so painfully gained, of his mother's rejection, now keep him from those fantasies that could never be fulfilled? Could he now stop hating and fighting?

In the weeks that followed his improvisations were filled with images of wounded animals, deep depression and murderous or suicidal fantasies.

Then one day, flourishing a knife filched from the dining room, Alfredo threatened to kill Dr. Schmidt. Suddenly he dropped the knife on the floor and stammered, "I—I—don't want to kill you!" He fell into the doctor's arms.

"I could kill myself," he sobbed. "I want to die! If I die—I die. . . ." His voice and the sobs trailed away to a choked silence.

The deeply touched man grabbed the brown curls and roughly

yet tenderly raised the child's head. With a quick, fatherly squeeze and a pat on the shoulder, he helped the boy to a chair.

"We don't want you to die, Alfredo. You have many friends who want you to live, friends who love you," comforted the doctor. The child sat bent over, elbows on knees with his head in his hands. Gradually he raised his wet cheek to the doctor and listened while he heard the plans for his departure to the halfway house.

## PART 5

Two months went by and the fights and temper tantrums had ceased. Even if Alfredo was purposely "being good" to enhance his chances of leaving, Dr. Schmidt did not believe that this act could be sustained for such a long period of time.

We started our last session with tea and cookies and small talk about school grades. Alfredo was shy, formal, charming and polite. What a contrast to the wild scenes of the past! When the cookies had disappeared the doctor asked, "Is there anything you'd like to act today?"

It did not surprise me when Alfredo said no.

Through drama we had given this boy an insight into the truth, believing it would better enable him to face reality. It helped him conquer his despair and anger.

Alfredo had strength, he had faith enough to respond to the help that we and his counselors were giving him. This strength together with his natural dramatic flair had formed the basis of our belief in the technique we used, this and the confidence the doctor and I had in each other's skill and understanding.

I had been a partner in this six months' drama and I wanted a final scene. "Perhaps you'll act something for me," I ventured. "I'd like Doctor Schmidt to play the part of Alfredo Ordalgo and I'd like you to play Doctor Schmidt." I explained, "Doctor Schmidt as Alfredo can make up any scene he wants to and you as Doctor Schmidt will be there to help and advise him. If you need me I'll be here to play whatever you like."

"O.K.!" smiled our willing hero. "I get it! *I'm* the doctor!" The look of authority immediately suffused his face and stance.

Doctor Schmidt took off his jacket. Obligingly he took on the character of the careless boy, pulling out his shirt tail and ruffling his hair. He slouched in a chair and kicked a box across the stage.

Alfredo grinned as he recognized his former attitude and behavior.

"When am I going to the halfway house? I'm getting tired of this lousy school!" whined the doctor, playing Alfredo to the hilt.

The real Alfredo, not to be outdone, walked over and picked up the doctor's notebook, then he sat down alongside the stage Alfredo.

"If you behave like this you will never be able to get along in the community. Tuck in your shirt," he ordered. "Comb your hair!" he commanded, handing his own comb to the playing doctor. "You get mad too easily," he continued smoothly in an admonishing voice. "Just because *other boys have mothers who want them is no reason to get angry at them.*"

The doctor took his cue. Now he whined just like Alfredo had a few months earlier. The words were slightly different, though. "My mother doesn't want me but I think she needs me just the same!"

The stage doctor cleared his throat. He pulled his chair around to face his patient who now sat slouched, head in hands, elbows on knees.

"Listen!" said the doctor's dramatic counterpart, "Let me talk to you man to man! Grow up! Get an education! Get a job! Maybe then you can help your mother!"

All at once the "play" doctor turned into the painfully moved child that he was. He got up and snapped his fingers. "I do have something I want to act. I want to act my interview with Doctor McCann at Half-Way House. Can I do that? Suppose he doesn't accept me. I'm nervous about my interview." Alfredo wanted to be through with the past. A good sign!

We were glad to carry him on into the future. I directed: "You're Dr. McCann, Alfredo. Dr. Schmidt, you're still Alfredo."

"No," said the doctor, turning to me, "this time you're Alfredo."

We all laughed. Then I did a ditty-bop walk to the mirror and pretended to be Alfredo combing his hair and studying himself, fixing his tie, shining his shoes. Then I took a seat, nervously waiting.

Alfredo directed the doctor. "You be my secretary, O.K.?" In a deep and important voice he ordered, "Call in Alfredo Ordalgo, please!"

I entered with my head down. Alfredo said very kindly, but firmly, "Lift up your head, don't be nervous. I only want to ask you a few questions. I'm not going to hurt you or stick needles in you."

I complied, but still played the part of a boy trying to gain composure.

"How old are you?"

"Twelve! Twelve and a half," I added.

"You'll be thirteen soon," corrected the "doctor." "Tell me, do you have nightmares? What do you dream?"

"I have good dreams," I answered.

"Like what?"

"Oh, that I'm at Half-Way House." We all stepped out of character and laughed again.

"Do you think you hear voices?" inquired Alfredo, as he again assumed his professional role. "Do you think people are following you?"

"Not any more!"

Alfredo nodded. "Good! Do you get mad and have fights?"

I swallowed hard. "I'm trying not to, I'm trying like anything."

"Good! Well," said the beaming Doctor McCann, "you can be proud! I accept you!"

Doctor Schmidt stepped forward. "Alfredo," he said, "you have nothing to be nervous about. Not only do you have all the answers. You even have the questions!"

The tension was over and we laughed long and loud. Then it was the end. Alfredo bowed a few times on the stage. We applauded. He made Doctor Schmidt and me take a bow while he clapped. Then with a smile and the merest word of thanks he sailed out.

One day, a month later, Alfredo poked his head in and said, "I'm leaving on Friday." He was rather timid as I invited him in to tell him how glad I was that he was going, and how much I would miss him.

"I'll miss everybody, too!" he offered gallantly.

He walked into the closet and in turn picked up and put down the derby, the fake money, the black robe, the terrifying mask and sword, the rubber knives and toy pistols that had been his stock in trade. Finally he singled out a dog mask. With an embarassed laugh he slipped it on.

I took my cue. I patted the head. "Good dog!" I said. The plastic tongue brushed my hand, again and again. The foolish, plastic face was smiling. The boy pulled off the mask and he was smiling too. He dropped the mask on a chair and jumped up on the stage, reaching up to touch the low ceiling.

"This is an awful low ceiling!" He stood and looked around the room. "You know, this is a *small* room! This is a *very small* stage! Funny, I never noticed how little it was before."

"The room hasn't changed, it's you, Alfredo. You're bigger. You're more grown up."

He nodded and then put the mask back in the closet. He seemed reluctant to leave, but didn't quite know what he wanted to say or do. I watched, as I had done for so long, waiting for my cue.

A big leap brought him to the center of the stage once more. "Ladies and genemen! I present Alfredo Ordalgo! The greatest . . . the greatest . . ." He wavered, and grandiosity drifted away. "I present . . . Ladies and genemen . . . I present . . . I present myself!"

It was a handsome-looking self. The wild curls were combed and a new hair cut had given him a manly look. His chinos were clean and pressed; a red plaid shirt flashed against his bronze skin. Once more he finished his presentation with the old, grand flourish of the matador, and bowed and bowed again. I applauded.

Then he was gone from the small round stage, and out the door.

---

*This narrative has been distilled by the author from a longer and more detailed account of actual experiences; the names of the child and doctor involved have been changed in the interests of privacy.— ED.

SUE MARTIN, Ph.D., is an associate professor at the School of Dramatic Art, University of Windsor, Windsor, Ont., Canada; and producer of the Henry K. Martin Theatre for Children and the Actor's Trunk Company, Toronto. She has also published numerous articles on developing creativity, storytelling, and developmental drama with brain-damaged children.

*Chapter 8*

# DEVELOPMENTAL DRAMA FOR BRAIN-DAMAGED CHILDREN

Sue Martin

## 1   INTRODUCTION

This chapter is concerned with a series of recommendations for using developmental drama with brain-damaged children. Based upon two years of informal play, it discusses the organization of the play room, environment, leaders, and play group; the execution of play via sensory awareness games, movement-mime projects and story dramatizations; and the evaluation of the play via the utilization of videotape.

## 2   BACKGROUND

There are general characteristics of brain-damaged children that greatly challenge developmental drama, playmaking for the sake of the personal development and growth of each participant rather than for the sake of entertaining an audience. Some of these children are hyperactive, have short attention spans, and have sensorial systems that register incorrect information. Others are aggressive, hostile, and negative. Most have personalities that are very unpredictable depending on medication, the weather, and the type of experiences they pass through on any given day. They have difficulty with visualization and abstract thinking and have a hard time creating on their own. Furthermore, depending

151

upon their specific learning disability, they may have problems
affecting such functions as memory, body coordination, and
speech.

With these characteristics in mind, our purpose in using developmental drama with brain-damaged children became five-fold.
First, we hoped to make each child more aware of his environment.
Our second goal was to help each child develop a longer attention
span. Third, we wanted to raise each child's ability to visualize
and create. Developing team spirit in order to help each child to
socially interact more successfully in a group was our fourth objective. And fifth, we wanted to enhance each child's self-esteem.

## 3  PREPARATION

The developmental drama program will accomplish very little if
attention is not given to preparing the room, the environment,
the leaders and the children for play. The play group room must
be empty. This is especially necessary in the first few sessions so
that nothing will steal the attention of the children away from the
creative leaders.

The room should also be checked out for all possible ways of
climbing the walls. Michael, an agile child in our play group,
utilized a small light switch box no bigger than his hand to boost
himself up the wall in reach of theatrical lighting cable hanging
from the ceiling. We were shocked when we discovered him in the
rafters some fourteen feet off the ground!

Doors must be secured or the children will make use of them to
escape the fun. Constant interruptions from flashes of dark can
be controlled by putting the light switches out of reach or off
limits. Drinking fountains must also be off limits or inoperable
due to the hyper effect water has on these children.

Carpeting is ideal for physical comfort and psychological
warmth. It is useful when working with the tactile sense to make
sure the walls, floors, and doors all have different textures for
touching and feeling. Another ideal item is an observation room
with a two-way mirror. It is, in fact, necessary if therapists, colleagues and others want to view the children at spontaneous play.
If these children see strange faces watching them, they will often
refuse to participate.

A play group of brain-damaged children needs much more discipline than does a play group of normal children. Where normal children need less structure in order to free themselves to investigate the world, brain-damaged children need more structure in order to keep them in touch with the real world long enough to investigate it. Without this structure only chaos reigns.

Psychologically, as in all play groups, the environment needs to be warm, safe, and free from ridicule. Each child must be allowed to progress at his own speed. We had one little boy who sat inside a large speaker's podium for seven consecutive sessions before he was ready to venture out into the room.

The environment, once it has been established, should be kept as stable as possible. Brain-damaged children react radically to abrupt change. Even the weather outside can influence the environment inside the room via the children themselves. Rainy days and high humidity affect the children greatly—the water concentration in the air seems to heighten their hyperactivity and displace their concentration.

Scheduling the best time for the play group sessions is very important. The type of activity preceding the play session is more significant than the time of day. For instance, we had much greater difficulty getting their attention at play when the children came to us directly from swimming than when they came from quieter activity. All the moisture and the exercise seemed to make them either superactive or overfatigued. The best situations would be to schedule the play group session just following individualized work which is not physically demanding or mentally frustrating.

It is important to be aware of the fact that not all teachers, leaders, therapists and parents can work successfully with brain-damaged children in drama. Although a thorough understanding of the basics of developmental drama is certainly needed, there are a number of other requirements that are equally essential for every creative leader working with these children.

A great amount of physical stamina is very necessary. When the leader is not taking part in the play in order to generate confidence in the group, he is breaking up a fist fight between two of the older boys, while at the same time making sure Nicki does not kick a hole in the wall, Michael does not repeat his climbing feat, and Greg does not lose interest in the play and start shooting the paper clips he has hidden in his pocket!

The creative leader must also have considerable imaginative flexibility. Often in our planning meetings two days prior to the play session, an idea would seem good to the ear and look good on paper to the eye. However, in the play group the execution of the idea would not live up to these expectations. Consequently we would all have to quickly make a ninety degree turn and change our whole course of action. These circumstances require creative leaders who can think on their feet, go with a new idea immediately and see a possibility in an impossible situation.

Frustration is another problem the creative leaders face when working with brain-damaged children. Certain personalities cannot cope with the mental fatigue caused by going back over regressive territory. During a play session a child may take a giant step forward only to come to the next play session three steps behind. One time a child may relate to you and the next time he may ignore you. In fact, in many cases, especially if there had been a change in the child's medication, the child would be a totally different personality. Adjusting to these changes is difficult for some leaders and impossible for others.

Since more boys than girls suffering from brain-damage are put into special classes, there are usually more boys in the play group. It is very important to encourage male leaders to work with these children along with females. A male image is especially important if most of the other therapists and teachers the children come in contact with are women. Richard, a boy who insisted on watching from the sidelines, could never once be urged to join the group until a male leader was added.

The ratio of creative leaders to children should be approximately one to three. This allows every three children to get close attention and permits every leader to take personal responsibility for the progress of three children.

Ideally, the play group should be made up of between nine and twelve children. The creative leaders assigned to the play group should be a versatile combination of personalities. For instance, in our play group of twelve young children between the ages of four and seven, the creative leaders were distinctly different in personality and approach. Emer, a quiet, sweet girl with beautiful soft green eyes, worked especially well with the extremely withdrawn, semi-autistic children; Kevin, a patient sociology major was extremely effective with the most negative children; Sue, with a zest for fun, was adopted by the children with the most lively sense of humor, and Shirley's kind manner communicated well with the children who needed a one to one relationship.

Our older play group of eleven children between eight and fifteen years of age was also manned by a versatile group of creative leaders. Claude, a strong young man of hearty French stock, was befriended by all those children who needed physical contact — a back to jump on or a fist to punch; Dan, an excellent observer who had gone through similar experiences with learning disabilities himself as a child, gave us a great deal of insight from the child's point of view; Phil, a young poet sensitive to life, worked most effectively with the children who were labelled troublemakers; and Janice, a hard-working and extremely dependable creative leader, could always be counted on to take charge of the most unglamorous but essential tasks.

Once the creative leaders start with the play group, it is imperative that they see the program through to its completion. It is very unsettling for these children to work with leaders who are sometimes there and sometimes not. Creative leaders working with brain-damaged children must be dependable and thoroughly committed.

## 4   EXECUTION

Stimulating the brain-damaged child to be more aware of his environment was our first goal. In response to this we took the children on a sensory awareness tour of the dramatic art building in which the play sessions were held. We walked through the halls, examined the classrooms, the dance and movement studio, the scene shop and even the faculty offices. We allowed them to roam freely and investigate. We encouraged them to touch costume fabrics, smell the sawdust, look at the room through colored lighting gels, examine the models of the set designs and walk up and down sets of prop stairs. They also did some things we did not encourage such as "hot rod" down the hall in a prop wheelchair, taste the pop from the coke machine, and perform acrobatics on top of the ballet bar. All in all, however, it proved to be useful in awakening them to their new environment.

We found that they performed well when we made a game out of what we were doing. Visually we played "I Spy," examined the cloud formations for pictures, and used Tana Hoban's *Look and See* book (Macmillan) to guess the identity of an object after seeing only a small portion of it.

The auditory sense work was very successful when we used sound effects records and guessed what was making the sounds. We also allowed the older group to make their own auditory tape. Half of them recorded sounds outside and the other half inside. They then listened to each others' tapes to try to identify the sounds. A variety of musical styles was used as structure for painting mental pictures but anything too fast in beat or emotion was bad for their hyperactive characteristic.

The tactile sense was a very important part of our work because so many of the children had difficulty touching or being touched. Some could not remember objects unless they touched them, and others found being touched a painful experience. In fact, one little boy could not stand the physical therapists to touch him unless they wore gloves because his body was so sensitive to their body chemicals. Consequently, we first encouraged the children to explore the play session room by touching it. The carpet felt warm but coarse in texture, the metal door frames were cold and smooth, the walls were rough repetitions of cement block. Next, we blindfolded those that wanted to participate further and let them figure out where they were in the room, via their tactile sense. The others reached in a large sack to feel the size, shape, texture and temperature of objects in order to identify them. We encouraged toes and cheeks to touch objects as well as hands.

The gustatory sense is difficult to explore with these children since their diets are very restricted. We became aware of this only after nearly upsetting their sugar levels. Prior to the playing out of *The Giant Jam Sandwich* by John Lord and Janet Burroway (Houghton-Mifflin), we brought in nine different kinds of jam and fifty picnic spoons so that each child could have an opportunity to taste the difference between strawberry, blueberry, cherry, etc. Unfortunately there were too many spoons and too few leaders. The tasting got out of control. In fact, one little boy was making an entire meal out of the orange marmalade when we discovered him in the corner.

Since brain-damaged children spend so much time in movement therapy, they are as agile as Tarzan himself. It is important, then, that the movement-mime projects lead them toward imaginatively oriented movement and away from skill oriented movement. We began by using the movement of animals as a source. Dog and cat fights, circus animals in review, and farm animals waking up and moving through the barn yard, proved easy to relate to. Next, we moved into creating mechanical toys and imaginary machines. The rigid and repetitious movements of tin soldiers, robots and wind-up dolls, were contrasted by the easy liquid movements of balls rolling, flowers waving in a soft breeze and snakes dancing. Their monster-making machine, after twisting, turning, gyrating and burbling, produced very imaginatively moving Draculas, Frankensteins and Wolf Men.

Music was often employed to make the image more vivid. As a kernel of pop corn they each felt warmth of fire under their bodies and the tight pull of their skin as they prepared to explode and bounce around in the pan to the recording of *Pop Corn* by the Hot Buttered. Disneyland Records' *The Chilling Shrilling Sounds of the Haunted House* was useful in setting the mood and stimulating their creativity as they moved around as imaginative "things that go bump in the night." Vocal mimicry and sounds were always encouraged as being yet another avenue of possible creative expression.

The mime work was not as successful with these children as was the free movement. The fine points about size, shape, texture and temperature of the objects they were pretending to handle, took more concentration and controlled movement than they were able to supply. Sports oriented mimes, tugs of war, and fighting sequences were the most successful. Here again we made up a game to fit our needs. "Going on a Trip" asked each child to mime the use of an object he was going to pack in his suitcase. Each child had to mime not only the object that he was going to take but also all those objects that had already been packed by others. In this cumulative way it was an excellent vehicle not only for free mime but also for exercising the memory.

The stories best suited for dramatization with brain-damaged children were those that had a lot of physical action, vivid characters, repetitious plots and a great amount of structure. "Three Billy Goats Gruff," "The Little Engine That Could," "The Gingerbread Boy," "Caps for Sale," "How the Camel Got His Hump" and "The Three Pigs" were excellent vehicles for the younger group.

The older group found *Robin Hood, The Three Musketeers* and *The Jack Tales* to be excellent sources for dramatic play. Improvising environments such as a circus, a fair and a cemetery, and filling it with characters, however, was more exciting to the older group. This was partly caused by their feeling that stories were just for "babies." In reaction to this we began to do less and less storytelling to the older group in favor of having the creative leaders take parts and present the source material in reader's theatre style. We also began to let them view certain one-acts put on by the actors in the School and to encourage them to improvise what they saw. Seeing boys and girls older than themselves seriously involved in drama seemed to raise their respect for what they were being asked to do.

No matter what the source of the play was, both groups used up the material much faster than we had first expected. Their play has less depth and less embellishments than does the play of groups of non-brain-damaged children. Consequently, in planning our sessions we would have to have twice as many activities ready than for normal children.

Props and costumes played a more significant role in their play than is necessary or useful with other children. Their attention spans were longer and their personal discipline greater when they were fully costumed than when they were not. In other words, instead of stifling their creativity by allowing the costume and props to do all the work, the costumes acted as a personal environment encouraging each child to create within its safe boundaries.

## 5  EVALUATION

Our final developmental drama project was the playing out of a very structured version of *The Three Musketeers*. We decided to videotape the final run through as an incentive for the children's best efforts. As it turned out, videotape was both an excellent incentive and an effective tool of evaluation.

Prior to introducing the story to them, two advanced fencing students came to the play room to give the children a fencing demonstration. The children were very receptive.

Next we took the foils away from the actors and asked them to demonstrate how mime could be employed to produce all the reality of the clashing steel. They began to respond to the reality of the illusion, yelling from the sidelines and cheering their respective heroes.

Acquainted with the action of the story of D'Artagnan's rescue of the diamonds, belonging to the Queen of France, the fully caped and booted musketeers began their journey as the cameras rolled.

The children were not at all disturbed by the presence of the cameras. They rode full speed into the action of the plot. They were very much aware of the changes in their environment, especially changes in mood and in time. We felt gratified that there had been great progress with our primary goal — awareness.

We were happy with the amount of progress that had been made on our second goal, too — attention span. The children spent an hour taping the whole story in seven separate sequences. Their attention was consistently involved as the action moved from the Queen's chambers; to a resting place under some trees; to an eating sequence in an inn; to a sleeping scene in the countryside; on to the palace of the Duke of Buckingham, and back to the Queen's chamber with the diamonds. Each of the middle sequences ended with a mimed sword fight to the death between the three musketeers and the Cardinal's men.

The videotape captured all the creative energy the children were releasing. One child gave his imaginary horse an imaginary drink and then hitched it to an imaginary post. Chalices were turned sideways and used as chicken legs during the eating sequences. Characterizations blossomed and dialogue flowered as embellishment and elaboration took root. The videotape provided us with observable proof of our success in raising the children's ability to visualize and create — our third goal.

The success of our fourth goal, to help each child interact well with the group, was also graphically recorded on the videotape. They helped each other with their costumes, worked together for a common goal, and never lapsed into arguments or fist fights. In fact, in the fencing sequences the roughness never got out of hand even though physical contact was constant. They truly had learned just what "all for one and one for all" really meant.

After spending too many days being ridiculed and called dumb and stupid, by a society that does not always understand, these children were happy with themselves. They actually had made an entire videotape all by themselves — they made dialogue, the characters, the action and the fun. They wanted to see it! They wanted others to see it! They were *proud* of it! And so were we, for we had accomplished our fifth goal — self-esteem.

SUSAN AACH is expressive arts specialist at the Western Pennsylvania School for Blind Children, Pittsburgh. She has written a series of articles, taught seminars and workshops on arts with the handicapped, and serves as a consultant for the Arts-in-Special-Education-Project of the state of Pennsylvania.

*Chapter 9*

# DRAMA: A MEANS OF SELF-EXPRESSION FOR THE VISUALLY IMPAIRED CHILD

Susan Aach

## 1 INTRODUCTION

Drama can be used as a tool for helping blind children to express feelings and fantasies about their visual impairment. Excerpts from sessions conducted with one child are used in this chapter to illustrate the role of drama therapy in the dynamic process of identifying and working through feelings about visual loss, and opening the way for self-acceptance.[1]

## 2 BACKGROUND

As a specialist in expressive arts, I work with 40 children between the ages of four and 11, in both individual and group play sessions, in the areas of art, drama and movement. The primary objectives of the program are to promote the children's development of self-expression and creative skills.

Working with these children, I have noted a number of concerns that have repeatedly emerged in their storytelling and role-playing, during both the individual and group sessions. One of the most urgent concerns for both partially sighted and totally

163

blind children is *how* and *why* their vision has become impaired. Each child has his or her own unique way of expressing and playing out these feelings, but the need to acknowledge and cope with these problems is characteristic of the group as a whole. These feelings are often so intense that they interfere with the child's performance in other areas, such as academics, social relations, self-care skills, and mobility; as well as inhibiting the development of self-acceptance and self-esteem. The purpose of this paper is to share what I have learned about the effectiveness of drama as a tool for meeting some of these needs.

As an illustration, I will discuss one particular child, a ten-year-old totally blind boy whom I will call Jim. Having worked with him for a period of ten months, I feel his play sessions vividly communicate the concern about visual loss experienced by him and his peers at school.

Jim's blindness resulted during infancy when his eyes were removed because of a cancerous condition called retinoblastoma.

When he was eight years old Jim entered the Western Pennsylvania School for Blind Children, residing at the school from Monday to Friday (his parents lived far away), and going home for weekends. Jim is a bright child, yet he was doing poorly in the classroom, and had great difficulty learning mobility skills. The educational director felt psychological problems might be contributing to Jim's learning difficulties, and referred him for play sessions.

## 3 ACTING OUT FANTASIES

Jim met with me twice weekly for half-hour play sessions. In these meetings I offer the children a range of options, and move in the direction they are most comfortable with. This approach is similar to Axline's "non-directive play therapy."[2] Jim chose to use the time primarily for telling and acting out stories. My role in the sessions varied. At times I helped Jim to get started or to elaborate his play simply by "recognizing and reflecting expressed attitudes," while at other times I asked questions, helped him organize the play, or facilitated the "acting out process" through role taking and the use of space and props.

In the stories Jim told and acted out, the following were the predominant feelings relating to his blindness: wondering, wishing, mourning, raging, and finally, accepting. Though I will discuss them separately, and in the sequence mentioned above, it should be understood that they are inter-related, and were often expressed simultaneously. They also recur in the dramatic play of the other children at school, though they may express only some of them, and in different ways. Some of the children, like Jim, have received an accurate explanation about how their sight became impaired, while it has never been discussed with others. Yet experience indicates that whether or not the child has received an explanation, he still has questions, wishes, and ideas of his own. Excerpts from Jim's sessions will illustrate this, as well as the dynamic process of his identifying and working through the feelings related to his loss of vision.

During the first few months Jim played out innumerable stories about people who get injured. Many of the stories concerned Steve Austin, the fictional hero of the television series "The Six Million Dollar Man." The Steve Austin TV character was in an accident where some of his bodily parts were maimed beyond repair. In the show, he becomes the recipient of some new artificial parts, an arm, a leg and an eye, called "Bionics." Steve Austin is a particularly apt self-reference for Jim. Their situations parallel each other in a number of different ways. Each sustained substantial bodily injury, though the causes were different. Each received artificial parts to replace their original ones; Steve Austin got bionic parts, Jim got prosthetic eyes. The important difference, of course, is that in the TV series, Steve's replacements are better than the original ones, while Jim experienced only the loss.

In one session Jim played the part of Steve Austin, and pretended he was being interviewed on a TV show.

"Hi kids. I'm Mr. Steve Austin. I have some *Bionics*. Bionics are artificial parts of the body. Now as you will see I have this artifical arm — *Bionics!*

"First I had these real parts. And then this man came. He said he would kill me." You be the man. You shoot — *Puchow!*

And then a man comes, and puts Steve up, and puts a bionic eye
on Steve Austin.

The above battle was fought again and again, since Jim continued to be preoccupied with the issue of loss and its origins. As
with many other children at the school, the issue is unresolved. In
the following playlet, Jim sought an explanation for Steve's injury.

"Well, let's talk to the man who saved me....I know the reason! I
know all! I am a detective. Sherlock Holmes taught me how to
solve mysteries. You find out what he done first. This mystery was,
Number 1: Who stole the car? Now, Number 2: Why did he steal
the car?

"Mr. Johnson is the criminal. I found the door. I see some money
stolen. Mr. Johnson, where are you? There you are. I've been
waiting for you ever since. I saw some money this morning at your
house. (clenches teeth)

"Why did you steal it? I want it right now! You better tell me right
now. While I was gone, did you come to my police station and take
all my money?"

In the investigation undertaken by Sherlock Holmes he finds
that a Mr. Johnson was the crook, having come to the police station and stolen Steve's money. The image of the "robbery" is very
likely an allusion to the disease that necessitated the removal of
his eyes. Jim could understandably view the doctor who performed
the operation as a thief, and the surgery itself as a criminal act that
robbed him of something he valued.

Jim wondered often and had many ideas about how and why
people get maimed and injured. The play sessions provided a
forum for him to acknowledge, elaborate, and clarify these
"wonderings." Jim's symbolism was relatively literal, and he dealt
fairly directly with the issues that were disturbing to him, whereas
other children may need a greater measure of disguise and
possibly express additional "wonderings."

# 4   MAGICAL SOLUTIONS

For months Jim's stories ended with wounds being healed,

damage being repaired, and severed body parts being restored by real or magical solutions. Burlingham says, "It is only natural that the blind are curious about and full of envy of this foreign world, and that they develop intense wishes to possess this sense which they lack, and which obviously opens up inconceivably marvelous feelings and sensations."[3] The Steve Austin character, around which many of Jim's stories revolved, eloquently expressed this wish. Steve Austin was severely hurt and lost an eye, a leg, and an arm. However, the doctors attending him replaced the severed limbs and eyes with bionic ones. The bionic parts look real, function like real parts, and provide increased powers. Although Jim's prosthetic eyes look real, they don't really work.

Jim communicates the intensity of his wish to regain sight in other stories, like the following:

First I had an eye. The middle of the story happens when my eye falls out, and the doctor gets the eye. And my mother and dad were gonna give one of their eyes and I was very lucky. I was almost gonna die. Then make pretend you're the doctor and say,

"This is the eye you lost. Did you just pull your eye out or did it fall out?" Make pretend I say it fell out. Then I put the eye back in again. Then I can see. That's the end. You can still see with one eye.

In the following quote Jim recovers his vision in a slightly different manner.

Say, let's look in the drawer and see what's inside. Well, what have we here? *This is the eye that I have been looking for!* I had an eye and you came over to my house. You grabbed my eye and you took it out. And I was so worried about the eye. I called the police. I called everybody.

Jim's insistence on a magical restoration (i.e., finding the lost eye), shows how painful the loss was and how unrealistic his expectations are. Jim uses denial in fantasy to handle the feelings of loss. It was as though this denial was pervasive, reflected, for example, in his difficulty learning braille and mobility skills. He was so involved in wishing for sight that he rejected learning any skills that would signify an acknowledgment of his blindness. Burlingham says:

> They attempt to attain the impossible by unsuitable means, and in this process neglect their own sensory world, in favor of seemingly participating in the sighted world; (thereby) interfering with their capacity to adapt to life on the basis of their own limitations and abilities.[4]

Yet Jim, like the other children, seemed to need to go through this process of wishing before he could arrive at a realistic self-image. The play sessions provided a context in which Jim could, in fantasy, fulfill his wish to regain his sight. Through such wish fulfillment he was reunited, however momentarily, with what was lost.

## 5   REALITY AND GRIEF

Jim wished his blindness could be healed, and had a very hard time dealing with the impossibility of this hope. As Burlingham has stated, "...it is one of the tragic facts, with which the blind child has to come to terms, that the process to see is not acquired gradually through growing up, but will be lacking in his life forever."[5]

After many months, Jim began to tentatively acknowledge the irreversibility of his loss. As he gave up wishing for sight, he started to mourn for the loss of it. Some of the grief and the anger Jim felt is expressed in the following story. At this point he had received one prosthetic eye, and was scheduled for corrective surgery for a second. Acutely aware of the gaps between his hopes and the reality of his situation, he expressed his feelings in his dramatic play.

> Once upon a time there was a boy named Ritz. And Ritz said to his mother, "Can I go outside and play?"
>
> "No, cuz nobody can watch you," said his mother. Then Ritz got so mad and stomped his feet. The whole house was shaking. And then his dad came and said, "What do you seem so mad about?"
>
> "I can't go outside and play." Then Ritz said, "Oh I wish I could

have that eye." Then Ritz went to the doctor. It was the same eye Ritz had when he was born. He played and he went outside and he was so happy, and everybody knew that Ritz had an eye. They were so happy that they had an eye....Are you so sad Sue? How do you feel when you don't have eyes? Even if I had both prosthetic eyes, my mom would still have to leave me in the house.

Here, Jim leaves the world of fantasy and begins to talk about reality. Like Ritz, Jim must stay inside, whereas his sighted siblings can play outside. Jim's sighted younger brother can run with abandon and excels in competitive sports. Being in a residential school, Jim sees his family infrequently, and may well feel "shut away" from people by distance as well as by handicap. Jim has cause for sadness. Though expressing these feelings does not undo the loss or remove the limitations, it does seem to help Jim and the other children begin to cope with their problems.

## *Anger*

Jim had feelings of anger that stemmed from the loss of his eyes and the limitations his blindness imposed on him. Axline says, "These handicapped children have within themselves the same feelings and desires of all normal children. Many times the handicap is a frustrating and blocking experience that generates almost intolerable tensions within the child."[6]

Some of Jim's anger came through in the Sherlock Holmes story, where Holmes was investigating Steve Austin's injury, and uncovered a robbery. In the following lines, Steve Austin talks with the robber.

Mr. Johnson says, "Well, I didn't know it was your money." "You didn't know! That had a name on it. S-T-E-V-E! You would have checked it and you would have known it was mine."

The anger Jim felt was expressed through words and through movement. In one session, Jim acted out a fight between Steve Austin and Bigfoot, a contemporary science fiction character, using a stuffed animal for the beast role. The story started:

Bigfoot says he's going to eat Steve up. Steve says, "That's what you think. I have a 22 rifle that I got." Bigfoot says, "No one can fight me."

Steve says, "What did I hear? I'm strong. My *bionics* make me strong. And I have a lot of powers. I will count to 20, and if you don't get your hands off Mr. Parker by the count of 20, you shall be dead. 1, 2, 3-20. *PUCHOW!*"

Jim shifted the target of Bigfoot's violence from Steve Austin to Mr. Parker, a detective investigating the case. It was as if he needed more symbolic distance to act like the aggressor. At this point, having already shot "Bigfoot," Jim began to sit on, press, punch, and kick him. He continued talking:

"Now you see, now you see who's stronger? Now do you see Bigfoot? That's going to teach you a lesson. He's dead."

In fantasy, Jim was able to create a culprit responsible for or intending to do injury, and punish him. For Jim and the other children, the loss or impairment of vision creates feelings of anger that need to be expressed. Of all the feelings discussed in this paper, anger was the one expressed most frequently and intensely.

## 6   TOWARD SELF-ACCEPTANCE

Over the months, through the process of struggle and denial, Jim gradually moved toward an attitude of self-acceptance. One of the reasons Jim was referred for play sessions was because he had resisted learning mobility techniques. In a drama, Jim has a teacher scolding a student for not learning these same techniques.

"Why didn't you use that technique?...You have to learn your mobility techniques, you hear me? (Jim starts to yell.) Just because you don't have eyesight doesn't mean that you have to get lost all the time. You have a cane, and you have techniques that I taught you. *So get over here girl and use your cane!*"

A number of factors probably contributed to Jim's poor performance in mobility. By refusing to learn the techniques he could feel, in some measure, in control of himself. He was also denying the need for such skills. At the same time, however, he was over-whelmed by feelings of grief and helplessness. Being able to ex-press some of these feelings helped Jim to begin developing a more realistic attitude. Burlingham states that, "The ability to express their thoughts, fantasies, and disappointments about blindness, has a liberating effect on the children ... it increases the children's curiosity about other matters and allows them to use their intelligence to draw conclusions."[7]

At the very end of the schoolyear, Jim showed evidence of resolving some of the issues he had dealt with during his play ses-sions. This is apparent in the very last story he told, titled, "How the Bad Guy Loses His Strength." The story started out as follows:

> There was a rule. When the clock says midnight everybody was supposed to go to bed. One night it was midnight. The bad guy said, "I guess I'll stay up and see what happens." The king was angry to see the bad guy up and he had a meeting with him and said, "Listen here, what are you doin' up so late? Everybody else is in bed." He said, "The next time I see you up, you're gonna lose your strength."

In the succeeding segment of the story the "bad guy" did stay up again, and the king then took his strength away with a knife. Jim said the lesson of the story was: "If you want your privileges you have to listen to what your mother and father tells you. That kingman was his father." Jim still described injury as resulting from a "badness," like not listening to your parents. At that point, he introduced the character of a queen, who suggested that perhaps the boy did not lose his strength because of bad behavior. Rather, it was a sickness that injured the boy. Jim had the king reply:

> "That sickness could have caused a dangerous disease. That sickness made him weak. Listen, we love our son. If we don't find out something to make him strong, he'll die. We need a powerful medicine.
>
> "I know it's not the boy, the boy's not the one...that did it. But the

boy doesn't know about this. People get so weak they don't know
what's happened."

The queen then suggests that the king explain this to the boy.
The king says,

"Son, I know you're anxious to get your strength. Mom and I
agreed it wasn't no one that did it. You had a sickness, a disease
that caused it."

Here, Jim acknowledged the non-malicious origins of his injury, and expressed the belief that "the boy" was not responsible.
Though occasionally he would return to the original wish for a
magical cure, he understood that the fantasies were not real. He
had begun to accept his blindness, though at times he would still
wish and rage and mourn. Jim expressed this when he said:

"Blind people, once they find they can do things by themselves — it
makes them have a happy feeling. But there's still a teeny weeny
little sad feeling that they're blind, and can't see."

# FOOTNOTES

1. The Expressive Arts Program, which began in September 1974, was part of
   a Title I ESEA Project (P.I., 89-313, Project – 48-73007-02-959) funded
   under the auspices of the Commonwealth of Pennsylvania. The project is
   under the supervision of Dr. Janet Klineman, director of Early Education
   Programs at the Western Pennsylvania School for Blind Children. The ideas
   in the paper were developed in consultation with Judith Rubin, art
   therapist, and Dr. Eleanor Irwin, drama therapist, staff members of the
   Pittsburgh Child Guidance Center, and Dr. William Marchl, child
   psychiatrist.
2. Virginia M. Axline, *Play Therapy* (New York: Ballantine Books, 1969).
3. D. Burlingham, *Psychoanalytic Studies of the Sighted and Blind* (New
   York: International Universities Press, 1972).
4. *Ibid.*
5. *Ibid.*
6. Axline, *Play Therapy.*
7. Burlingham, *Psychoanalytic Studies of the Sighted and Blind.*

JACKSON DAVIS, Ph.D., taught college speech and theatre for
twenty years and, until his death in 1980, taught classes for the deaf in
Waycross, Georgia. The parent of a deaf child, he conducted research
on theatre for the deaf and wrote and directed plays for and with
the deaf.

*Chapter 10*

# DRAMA AND THE DEAF

Jackson Davis

## 1  INTRODUCTION

The potential of drama as a therapeutic instrument for the hearing impaired is probably as great, if not greater, than for any of the other major handicaps. But the problems associated with its use are complex. If we consider drama in its pantomimic and verbal modes as a device for self-expression, flexibility, and for synthesizing and filtering feelings; if drama is regarded as an educational tool for learning language and/or for acquiring speech; if it is seen as a method of introducing the participants to nuances of thought, verbal subtleties and distinctions, and patterns of acceptable behavior; if drama, as is implied here, is considered as conferring such benefits on the actor and the performer, then no handicapped population has more to gain from it than the deaf and hard-of-hearing.

But because drama, aside from sheer mime, is spoken and includes the three elements of actor, audience, and the dramatic vehicle, the task of employing it with the deaf becomes prodigious indeed. For the deaf, particularly those who lost their hearing at birth or very early in life, are language deprived and, in most instances, deficient in the intelligibility of their speech. The deaf, to state it more simply, cannot say the dialogue clearly enough to be understood by hearing persons in the audience. The deaf can employ sign language or fingerspelling—but how many hearing persons know either of these well enough to follow the stage

175

dialogue? Use of manual communication becomes almost mandatory for deaf performers because they cannot hear one another.

A variety of techniques are employed to involve the hearing impaired either as performers or as audience members. I was trained in theatre and became interested in theatre for the deaf because I have a deaf son. I draw upon wide and lengthy experience in writing and directing plays for both hearing and deaf performers and audiences as well as teaching the deaf. Out of this background I can draw some conclusions as to the difficulties, the present status, and the potentials of drama therapy with the deaf.

## 2    THE EFFECTS OF HEARING LOSS

### Total Personality Involvement

At one time it was popular to regard the deaf as a normal person who just happened to have a hearing loss. Now there is more recognition[1] that the loss of hearing affects the whole personality. According to Tomlinson-Keasey and Kelly:

> Several modalities are lost. He's not able to coordinate vocalizations or auditory input with any of the other senses. These modalities provide only incomplete data about his world. Consequently, he relies only on those senses which he can coordinate, and which can give him feedback about his interaction with the world. He develops cognitive structures which do not use auditory input as a central means of processing the environment. Rather, his structures rely on visual, tactile, gestural, and olfactory cues, along with those he gets from mouthing objects. He processes his world on these dimensions and he apparently does it very well.[2]

Myklebust[3] calls attention to the greater role played by vision and also insists that the deaf person's world of experience is limited:

> Because total experience is reduced, there is an imposition on the balance and equilibrium of all psychological processes. When one type of sensation is lacking, it alters the integration and function of all the others.[4]

In other words, the whole person is altered by the hearing loss. We can speak of a "deaf" personality because "sensory deprivation produces an impact which modifies behavior according to a certain pattern."[5] This personality develops because deaf children and adults are struggling to achieve "adequacy and psychological equilibrium."[6] The emotional and social behavior found in deaf children persists into adulthood.[7]

## Effects on the Personality

What is the characteristic pattern of the deaf? Myklebust found it to be one of being rigid, concrete, and socially and emotionally immature.[8] He also observed that the deaf "do not require the same biases and feelings of taboo that characterize the normal population."[9] Added to this was a personality that was not as structured, or as subtle, yet more sensorimotor in character.[10] He attributed the deaf person's difficulty in identifying with the feelings and attitudes of his peers to the problems of acquiring language: "We may hypothesize that it is more difficult to develop such feelings when the many sounds which enhance interpersonal relationships are not heard."[11] The most important impact on the deaf resulting from the loss of hearing is that of isolation: "When deafness is present, especially when it is sustained in early life, the monitoring of one's feelings, attitudes, and ideas is more difficult."[12]

## The Educational Dilemma

One cannot discuss drama for the deaf without taking into account the raging conflict between the oralists and the manualists which has tormented deaf education for the past hundred years. The latest input into the question as to whether the child should be taught manually, with sign language and fingerspelling, or taught orally, has been that of the psycholinguists. Their findings result in a new emphasis on total communication — to teach the deaf child, through the use of any means: oral, manual, natural gesture. The basic contention of the psycholinguists[13] is that manual communication does not interfere with the development of communication skills (which was fundamental to the position of the oralists). They argue further that the oral method has failed with the deaf child. But sign language is a natural gesture system because it provides a better feedback mechanism than his own speech or residual hearing. To rely on the inadequate or impaired hearing mode for processing information hinders the development of thought processes. Training in the sign language must begin early, according to these psycholinguists, so that it can become a feedback tool. It does not require speech as a basis but rather:

> These symbol systems result from the continuing organization or structure which the child imposes on his environment. Symbol systems such as language, mathematics, and American Sign Language serve the purpose of mediating between the internal cognitive structures of the child and the external environment.[14]

According to the advocates of total communication, the oral method may actually hinder the intellectual and academic development of the deaf. There are those who contend[15] that fingerspelling is more effective than the combined use of both sign language and fingerspelling. This is because fingerspelling involves making the letters of the alphabet with the fingers, which allows for more conformity with the native language structure than does sign language. However, this is minor compared to the great leap toward total communication now under way everywhere in this country. Yet the oralists have not entirely surrendered their position. There are still many schools, most of them private, which teach the auditory-oral method. Nix[16] has reviewed a number of studies supporting total communication and has criticized them as being unreliable and as having been misinterpreted. The Alexander Graham Bell Association, chief proponent of the oral approach, has compromised somewhat on its stand:

> Modern educational audiology suggests that 75% to 80% of hearing impaired children have sufficient residual hearing to develop speech communication proficiency through an auditory-oral ap-

proach... At the same time, the Board recognized that an
auditory-oral program may at times be contra-indicated and that
total communication, including its auditory-oral components,
may be a viable option for some deaf children.[17]

As for the hard of hearing, or for those persons who lost their hearing after they had acquired speech, the problems are different,
and educational methods concentrate largely on the conservation
and development of speech and language,[18] and an emphasis on
lipreading skills.[19]

We have observed that hearing loss affects the entire personality
and results often in a typical deaf personality with retarded
academic development — now attributed to faulty teaching techniques — and, one may add, tendencies toward schizophrenia.[20] It
is generally accepted that the deaf can also tend to be paranoiac,
and to be very literal in their attitudes toward religion and toward
the written word. It should be emphasized that the degree of
these problems varies from individual to individual, but results
from the loss of modalities essential to flexibility, subtlety, depth
of thought, and the ability to identify with others and to live successfully in a highly competitive society. Whether these patterns
will alter as a result of new teaching methods is not yet known.
What is at issue here is: how much can drama contribute toward
enhancing the desirable aspects of the deaf personality, and how
much can it alter those which might be considered undesirable or
harmful to the deaf individual?

# 3   PROBLEMS OF USING DRAMA WITH
THE DEAF

It must be re-emphasized that any discussion of drama therapy
with the deaf revolves around two issues. First, does one consider
the act of performance, with or without an audience, as
therapeutic in its own right? Second, is the most important
therapeutic value of drama to be gained from the interaction between the performer and an audience? There are undoubtedly
therapeutic benefits to be gained from either use of drama. But a

third question emerges: Does drama imply the use of a prepared script and the attempt of the performer to fulfill the characterization of someone in that script? The conventional view of drama suggests an affirmative answer to the third question. But the therapeutic approach may be geared to the first question.

These are not idle reflections. Drama necessitates communication and communication demands mutual understanding. Because communication is the heart of the problem of deafness, difficulties arise from techniques in offering dramatic presentations, whether they be full-length or one-act plays, skits or musicals, assembly programs or classroom dramatizations. Some of these problems were detailed in a survey[21] previously done by the writer.

## Findings of the Survey

The survey was extensive. It covered 363 schools for the deaf in the United States and Canada, with a total hearing impaired population of 32,802 students. A number of questions were asked about theatre activities covering the years 1965-1970.

Only 5% of the state residential schools did full-length plays during the five year period, but more than 45% of them did one-act productions. Practically all the performances were at the state schools or private residential schools; there were almost none given in the public schools. Of course, problems of busing, the difficulties of scheduling extra-curricular activities, and the lack of personnel trained in theatre were significant. But another great consideration was the comment often made by teachers of the deaf that there was so much in the way of language to teach the children that there was no time for theatre. This did not preclude, however, the use of improvised dramatizations in the lower grades to concretize language concepts. Neither teachers nor administrators seemed convinced of the values of presenting plays for and by the deaf students. Usually, the only play seen in most of the state schools was an oral presentation by a community group, interpreted for the students, or a production by the National Theatre of the Deaf. At the state schools, there was a gradual increase over the five year period in the number of presentations given manually, but a speaking interpreter was needed for the hearing persons in the audience. Conversely, if the play was given orally, there was no interpreter in schools committed to the oral method; but there was an interpreter for schools who did not object to the use of sign language.

A number of techniques were utilized to overcome the communication barriers. For plays, the actors sometimes talked and signed, or else mouthed the words and signed. At other schools, the performers did nothing but fingerspelling; or else they used the combined method of signing and fingerspelling. The difficulty with the oral method used alone was that the actors were often incomprehensible. But through long and careful rehearsal, they were intelligible enough to be understood by those familiar with the deaf. Naturally, hard-of-hearing students, or those with sufficient residual hearing, or who had speech because they lost their hearing after they had acquired it, were able to speak well enough to be understood. For the most part, the manual schools did their plays manually; the oral schools were basically oral in their performances.

The directors of the schools could not accept the value of drama because they had not seen adequate research to prove its benefits. Often, too, no teacher could be found with sufficient interest, not to mention training, to direct the productions. At 78% of the schools responding, for example, nobody on the staff was specifically responsible for drama. The auditoria were often inadequate, but there was a slow trend toward making them more theatre-worthy. Lighting in almost all schools was provided by wall switches or panel boards, and there was little or no attempt at building appropriate scenery. In other words, there was a lack of knowledge as to how plays should be given; a scarcity of trained personnel; problems in communication between actors and audience; lack of drama emphasis in the schools; and absence of research to justify drama as a therapeutic and entertainment tool with the deaf. But two of the most frequent recommendations heard from persons at the schools who did involve themselves with theatre were: that the stage presentations be used as a basis for language improvement; and that they be geared toward improving communication between the performers and the audience.

Another problem of significance was that of translating the plays into sign language. At its best, sign language is not an effective ideational instrument, measured by hearing standards. An interpreter for the deaf must transform the spoken word into signs that can be understood by the more literal and less language-wise deaf. The signs used in a play that was written by a hearing playwright had to be "interpreted" in the sense suggested. Often, however, the teacher of the deaf would fashion a simple script that was more easily adaptable to deaf performers.

Finally, I want to mention some of the more ingenious means employed by the schools to overcome the communication problem. In presenting musical shows, the actors would sometimes be accompanied by a signing and speaking chorus; or hard-of-hearing persons would sing while the deaf signed. In one school, charts of the songs were passed out to the audience so that they could follow the words while the deaf actors sang. At another, blind students performed while the words were interpreted for the deaf in the audience.

## 4   THE DEAF AS PERFORMERS

In my experience as a director of deaf actors, I was impressed with their bodily expression. This will not surprise anyone who has watched them use sign language. They talk with their whole bodies. There is a feeling quality about their body movements that projects itself empathically to an audience.

### Use of Sign Language

The visual parameters of sign language operate in much the same manner that pitch, melody, rate, and volume do for the speaking person. The intensity of the sign, its size, the speed with which it is made, all serve to give it attributes that project both meaning and emotion. I am not fully skilled at sign language but found that, by watching the script, I could easily follow the signs, and even make suggestions as to their appropriateness. I discovered that I had to teach some of the performers not to vocalize while they acted because these non-intelligible verbalizations interfered with the performers. I also found that I could use someone in the cast, who both knew sign language and was skilled at English syntax, to translate the written words of the script into the signs. Rehearsals, by necessity, were somewhat longer than for a hearing cast, but they could not be too long either at one setting or in terms of weeks, as they would bore the performers. Like all actors, they did best when they enjoyed what they were doing. Teachers at oral schools for the deaf often made the mistake of having an extremely long rehearsal period so as to perfect the speech of the performers, and the deaf children found this a chore rather than something they enjoyed.

The deaf like plays with physical action, and the director must be careful that the play, particularly with amateur deaf casts, is not too abstract. However, the experience of the National Theatre of the Deaf is that trained deaf actors can cope well with philosophical drama. It must be remembered that this is a professional repertory company that uses professional directors and a highly selective cast. The NTD functions on the assumption that the sign language has aesthetic value which can be enjoyed by hearing audiences. I spent several weeks with the company in Connecticut and can recall being told by its managing director that its productions were intended to take advantage of the expressiveness of the deaf in pantomime and the beauty of the signs. Incidentally, one of the hearing actors in the cast speaks the words of the play as he performs, while the deaf actors use signs only.

But it is my contention that sign language serves the same purpose for the deaf as speech does for the hearing; it is a means of communication not especially regarded by its users as having aesthetic value. Those among the deaf who want the signs made "beautifully," and who object to it when it is used colloquially or in the vernacular, are usually the ones who had speech before they lost their hearing, or who are not deaf but hard-of-hearing. Anyone attempting to direct the deaf in plays will come up against this controversy. There will be those in the cast who will want the signs made with grace and elegance. The congenitally deaf, or those who use sign language as their primary symbol system, use signs as deaf children use art — as a way of describing what they are trying to say.

## Benefits to Deaf Performers

I can only surmise what the benefits were to the deaf actors in the plays I directed.

My stress here is on the use of prepared scripts by skilled playwrights because they offer dramatic values best suited to achieve the therapeutic goals which are capable of being attained.

The action of submitting one's personality to a role, of making the effort to be someone else in both body and mind, can undoubtedly aid in reducing rigidity of the deaf personality. Even learning to use the language of another individual can provide more flexibility and bring greater subtlety in the thought process. Being in a play adds to the experience of the deaf performer. He finds himself in novel situations and must meet them in ways that may not have occurred to him. Furthermore, identifying with a character may minimize the psychological isolation that is an inherent part of deafness.

Some deaf tend to crave attention. They love to be noticed, and these tendencies can be gratified in acting. The discipline of making assigned movements and gestures, rather than the sometimes gross natural gestures occasionally used by the deaf, filters their physical behavior.

The gain in language is perhaps the greatest benefit that the deaf can achieve from participation in drama. They learn new vocabulary, understand new concepts, and arrive at new insights into the nature of the structure of the language. As a corollary, the sign language itself is performed more skillfully because the actor must use signs that best convey the meaning of the script. Drama undoubtedly would be of immense value in teaching language concepts to deaf children. And if intelligibility is not taken as the prime criterion, the effort to get the deaf children to use speech helps those who are being trained orally and those in total communication.

The very discipline of being in a play is of benefit to the deaf. Their educational systems are often too lax, too permissive. The needs for social disciplines can be met effectively through drama where the child gains the value of the experience at the same time

that he is enjoying participation, an essential key to learning.
Myklebust noted:

> Unlike the hearing child, the deaf child needs consistent train-
> ing in social maturity over a long period of time. He is in need of
> emphasis on all aspects of social maturity, but especially in Self-
> direction, Socialization, and Occupation.[22]

Where the child is taught orally, but uses sign language on the
playground or in other peer situations, acting in plays cannot
help but be a chore when he associates them with using speech. It
would seem that if the child is permitted to do the plays in that
symbol system which is an easier communication tool for him,
then the enjoyment would enhance the values he would derive
from the experience.

There is another more subtle value the deaf derive from drama
as performers. They depend heavily on visual cues such as facial
expression, bodily stance, physical relationships between people
(such as approaches and withdrawals), gestures, and all those
aspects of body language also used by the normal population but
filled in by the hearing with speech cues. I have observed my son
over a period of years watching television shows. He did not
gather the plot from lipreading. Too often, the actor's back is
turned while he is speaking. (At its best, too, lipreading is not effective for the profoundly deaf. Too many of the sounds are made
in back of the mouth, and too often the deaf individual does not
have sufficient language to fill in the gaps or to understand the
context.) But my son enjoyed the TV shows and was often able,
after he saw them, to recount the plot with some accuracy. When
I directed deaf actors, I was amazed at the way they were able to
block their own shows, as it were. They seemed almost instinctive-
ly to know what the physical relationships demanded in the way
of movement and stance. The value to the deaf child of placing
him in drama situations, where he must fulfill the feeling relationships demanded both by the character and by the nature of
the conflict, would add flexibility to his feeling repertoire and

make more creative his psychological approaches to both people
and events.

Mention has been made of the expressiveness of the deaf performer. Couple the need for physical action which the deaf possess,
with the isolation and the paranoiac tendencies, and the result is
an individual who either suppresses all external displays of feeling
or who, in the opinions of those who hear, overdoes his physical
reactions. The deaf individual must, if he is to achieve harmony
with the hearing world, learn to conform to the gestural and bodily
stereotypes of his culture. Perhaps what most puzzles, and even
frightens, hearing persons about the deaf is the exaggerated body
language the deaf display, and the extent to which they allow their
emotions to carry them. Many parents of deaf children know the
violent activity of their youngsters, the stubbornness that cannot be
controlled, even the wild actions amounting often to beatings that
the children inflict on their family and their friends. It should be
remembered, however, that this is not true of all deaf, particularly
those who have deaf parents, or who became deaf after they had
speech. But it is one of those behavioral syndromes characteristic of
many deaf about which Myklebust wrote. The problem seems to be
that the deaf do not have speech as a filtering system. Their sign
language, for the most part, is a private code familiar only to them
and a few hearing teachers and other interested individuals. Drama can serve the function of acting as such a filter. For in drama,
emotions are synthetic. The experiences would seem to function
with the deaf in the same filtering capacity as does speech in the
normal person. It would show him the extent to which he can
display outward emotions and still make those displays acceptable.
It would add to his emotional repertoire and reduce rigidity and
stereotypical responses, and it would add to his social maturity.

Moreover, the experience of reading plays, which project other
social structures and hierarchical systems than those to which he
is almost exclusively exposed in his own deaf world, would add to
his individual and cultural flexibility. Although it is probably
true, as Wilbur and Quigley suggest, that the controlled presentation of syntactic structures will reduce the frustration involved
in learning to read and help provide a more rewarding learning

experience,[23] it would not necessarily follow that the enforced simplicity of language need carry over into an enforced control of subject matter and situation. The deaf read, for the most part, no literature. Their reading is usually confined to the newspapers and simple books about factual materials. Thus, the performance in plays serves the dual function of introducing the deaf to new modes of written experience and to other kinds of relationships. The vicarious involvement in societies other than their own cannot help but prove salutary.

If these benefits are to be derived from drama by the deaf, it is important that the presentations be directed by someone acquainted with theatre. It is not enough that the person know the deaf. A familiarity with dramatic values, stage composition, the techniques of acting, and all those skills that go toward enabling someone to take the written words of a script and transform it into a live performance, are far more important in bringing to the deaf those benefits that derive from theatre than even the knowledge of sign language. Ideally, the director would have therapeutic goals toward which he was striving. But that combination of being a theatre person and of familiarity with the psychology of deafness has, to the writer's knowledge, only rarely been attained.

## 5   THE DEAF AS AUDIENCE

Emphasis on total communication will probably not increase the number of plays performed in schools for the deaf. The oral schools, now rapidly accepting the concept that sign language and oralism can jointly be used, will permit their students to sign. This will be of value to the deaf performers. But though the signing will negate the necessity of an interpreter for the deaf person in the audience, there would have to be a reverse interpreter for the hearing people who do not know signs.

It is necessary for adequate lighting to be provided on stage both so that the signs can be read and so that, when hearing actors are performing, lipreading can be done. Also, fingerspelling is very difficult to read from a stage. It is too small in scope to carry over the footlights, unless the plays are done at very close range. This means that the entire production must be done in signs, and this creates the problem of teaching English syntax through the stage presentation because there are many words not represented by signs. Efforts are being made to add word endings and tenses to signs, but to date these efforts are limited to teaching young children. The adult deaf use a sign language that does not have these syntactical features.

The usual precautions with respect to child audiences everywhere hold, of course, with the deaf. There must be a great deal of physical action, broad gestures, frontal postures, and time for the concept to be absorbed. I wrote three plays, all intended to introduce concepts to deaf children: that there can be freedom within conformity; that the nature of idioms is ambiguous; and that we must accept people with their differences. All the plays were successfully received at the many schools where they were presented. Two were done by a professional cast at Ford's Theatre in Washington, D.C. for an audience of government officials. All differed from the usual children's play in that only the barest of scenery was used: a bench represented a park; two sides of a stage, the different parts of a house; a stepladder, a mountain; and so on. In other words, the children were asked to extend their imaginations, and there seemed to be no difficulty at all in deaf audiences achieving this.

The greatest problem came with transforming the dialogue of the hearing performers for the audiences. At first, I experimented with the use of an overhead projector which put the words of the play on a screen above the front of the stage. As the actors spoke, the projector was rolled. This proved too cumbersome, and the next experiment was with a reading pacer. Again, the dialogue was projected on a screen above the heads of the performers or on the side of the stage. Some of the schools augmented this screening with an interpreter. It could not be ascertained whether the deaf children were following the dialogue or watching the action on the stage.

The answer, it seems to me, is to use rear projection for the dialogue. It would be placed above the actors so that the audience could watch both the performance and the dialogue without having to do the eye-shifting necessary with the other means. The dialogue would change as the actors spoke. This would solve the problem for the deaf people in the audience who can read. For those who cannot, there might also have to be an interpreter standing to the side.

As for hearing persons, there is no problem with hearing performers. But for the deaf in the audience, there is another alternative — to have the hearing actors sign while they speak. It is difficult to teach hearing performers enough signs to make up for the deficit of speech. And I found that when professional actors learned enough signs to accompany the spoken word, they experienced almost a schizophrenic trauma. The conflict between the two kinds of symbol systems is considerable. With hearing actors, there is always the desire to make natural gestures. But many of these gestures have a different meaning in sign language, or else cannot be understood by the deaf. One can see that to rob a hearing performer of his natural gesture system is to inhibit him greatly. The director must be very careful to blend natural gestures that can be understood with the more ideographic gestures of sign language in order to avoid misunderstandings. This is one reason why it is wise for a hearing director to have someone in the cast who knows both sign language and English syntax — someone who can speak adequately enough to be understood by the director.

The deaf as spectators derive vicariously many of the values and benefits that deaf actors gain from drama. It is very important that the situation in the play be as concrete as possible, but the effort must be made to expand the purview of the deaf into the more abstract. If dialogue is to be projected visually, it must be made simple enough to be read by the slower deaf readers and must also not move too quickly. This calls for stage action to cover the lapses in changes of projection, and for slowing down the action somewhat.

Already the National Theatre of the Deaf is using plays written especially for their deaf company of actors. But, as stated earlier, the plays appeal most to the more sophisticated and educated deaf and to hearing audiences of theatregoers. This positive response results from the magnificent physical expression of deaf performers and from the aesthetic use of the sign language. We who can speak are not aware, as we are speaking, of the beauty of our language. Unless the play is one in which the quality of the dialogue is a major factor, we are struck by the impact of the feelings and ideas, not by the nature of the words themselves.

There is a great need, particularly with deaf audiences, of more "wordless" material of mime and drama that depends basically upon body language. I know that my son and other deaf children find Charlie Chaplin and Laurel and Hardy movies irresistible.

Final mention should be made of the values for the deaf that can accrue from training in other aspects of theatre—costume and scenery design, scene building, makeup, and lighting. And the deaf, with their expressive bodies, can do fine work in dance.

# 6  CONCLUSION

There is need for more use of drama with the deaf because its derived values benefit them directly. But there is also need for pinpointing the particular difficulties and for devising kinds of dramatic experiences that will deal specifically with such handicaps as language deprivation, isolation, paranoiac tendencies, concreteness, and rigidity of personality.

It can be seen that drama in its more orthodox form has a definite role to play. But so too, undoubtedly, have psychodrama, creative dramatics, spontaneous dramatizations, and other forms of therapeutic drama.

# FOOTNOTES

1. Helmer R. Myklebust, *The Psychology of Deafness: Sensory Deprivation, Learning, and Adjustment*, 2d ed. (New York: Grune & Stratton, 1964); C. Tomlinson-Keasey and Ronald R. Kelly, "The Development of Thought Processes in Deaf Children," *American Annals of the Deaf* 19, no. 6 (1974): 693-99; Frank B. Withrow, "Current Studies of Personal Adjustment of Deaf People," *Research on Behavioral Aspects of Deafness* (Washington, D.C.: H.E.W., Vocational Rehabilitation Administration, n.d.), pp. 54-57.

2. Tomlinson-Keasey and Kelly, "The Development of Thought Processes," p. 695.

3. Myklebust, *The Psychology of Deafness*, p. 50.

4. *Ibid.*, p. 1.

5. *Ibid.*

6. *Ibid.*, p. 117.
7. *Ibid.*, p. 156.
8. *Ibid.*
9. *Ibid.*, p. 116.
10. *Ibid.*, pp. 118-19.
11. *Ibid.*, p. 117.
12. *Ibid.*, pp. 117-18.
13. Tomlinson-Keasey and Kelly, "The Development of Thought Processes," p. 695; Donald F. Moores, "Psycholinguistics and Deafness," *American Annals of the Deaf* 120, no. 5 (October 1975): 463-79; E. Meadow, "Early Manual Communication in Relation to the Deaf Child's Intellectual, Social, and Communicative Functioning," *American Annals of the Deaf* 113 (1968): 29-41; H. Babbidge, *Education of the Deaf. A Report to the Secretary of Health, Education, and Welfare by His Advisory Committee on the Education of the Deaf* (Washington, D. C.: U. S. Government Printing Office, 1965) cited in Gary W. Nix, "Total Communication: A Review of the Studies Offered in its Support," *Volta Review* 77, no. 8 (November 1975): 471-94; B. Morkovin, "Experiment in Teaching Preschool Children in the Soviet Union," *Review* 62 (1960): 260-68; Marianne Collins-Ahlgren, "Language Development of Two Deaf Children," *American Annals of the Deaf* 120, no. 6 (December 1975): 524-39.
14. Tomlinson-Keasey and Kelly, "The Development of Thought Processes," p. 694.
15. S. P. Quigley, *The Influence of Fingerspelling on the Development of Language, Communication, and Educational Achievement in Deaf Children* (Urbana, Ill.: University of Illinois, Institute for Research on Exceptional Children, 1965) cited in Nix, "Total Communication," p. 485; Morkovin, "Experiment in Teaching Preschool Children," cited in Moores, "Psycholinguistics and Deafness," p. 37.
16. Nix, "Total Communication," pp. 471-94.
17. R. A. Flint, "A. G. Bell Re-examines the Association's Purpose and Mission," *Volta Review* 77 (1975): 152-54.
18. John J. O'Neill, *The Hard of Hearing* (Englewood Cliffs, N.J.: Prentice-Hall, 1964), pp. 1-134.
19. John J. O'Neill and Herbert J. Oyer, *Visual Communication for the Hard of Hearing: History, Research and Methods* (Englewood Cliffs, N.J.: Prentice-Hall, 1961), pp. 1-155.
20. Withrow, "Current Studies of Personal Adjustment," p. 54.
21. Jackson Davis, "A Survey of Theatre Activities in American and Canadian Schools for the Deaf 1965-70," *American Annals of the Deaf* 119, no. 3 (June 1974): 331-41.
22. Myklebust, *The Psychology of Deafness*, p. 220.
23. Ronnie Bring Wilbur and Stephen P. Quigley, "Syntactic Structures in the Written Language of Deaf Children," *Volta Review* 77, no. 3 (1975): 194-203.

# Part 3
# RELATED
# TECHNIQUES

Drama is an all-inclusive medium of expression. The child who is
acting "as if" he is a bear, a policeman, a mother or a monster is
expressing his inner life with his *whole* self: his body, his voice, his
total being. In drama, the expressive medium is the total self.
Marshall McLuhan says that any medium is an extension of the
body: thus, the pen is an extension of the hand, the wheel is an
extension of the foot, while the electric circuitry of radio and
television are extensions of the brain. From his point of view,
therefore, the artistic media are extensions also: visual art is an
extension of the hand, music is an extension of the vocal cords,
and dance is an extension of the body. Drama, on the other hand,
is an extension of all these elements and more besides: the inner
human life becomes externally expressed through the total medium of the human *being*.

It is curious, therefore, that drama therapy has emerged after
the therapies of music and dance. Today, however, more and
more therapists are using the other media within the context of
drama. It is easier to move from drama therapy to other media

than vice versa. Whereas drama is "whole," the other artistic media are partial. Any partial expression—the arm movement (gesture), the hand movement (art), sound creation (music)—generically derives from drama and, at any point, helps to support it. Moreover, young children hardly acknowledge the difference between media: they can as easily express their thoughts and feelings in music as in paint, in clay as in stories, in dance as in the creation of environments. One is liable to slide into another without any feeling of anomaly. It is only later that society teaches us that one medium is appropriate for one form of expression and inappropriate for another. When we are very young, however, all is grist to the dramatic mill.

This part of the book is concerned with a variety of techniques that are related to drama. Irwin, Rubin and Shapiro examine art and drama with latency-age boys (Chapter 11). Richard A. Gardner demonstrates the relationship of drama and storytelling with clinical examples (Chapter 12). Barbara M. McIntyre considers drama as an adjunct to speech therapy (Chapter 13). Irwin M. Marcus relates costumes to dramatic play (Chapter 14). Elaine S. Portner discusses the use of the tape recorder, sandbox play and spontaneous puppetry (Chapter 15). Marrion Wells shows how her company takes theatre to handicapped children (Chapter 16).

Space has precluded the inclusion of two important media used in conjunction with drama therapy for children: dance and music.

Creative movement and dance has been referred to by other authors in this book: by Peter Slade (Chapter 4) and Brian Way (Chapter 17); by Sue Jennings with the physically disabled (Chapter 3); and by Marian R. Lindkvist with the autistic (Chapter 7).

Creative music, however, is equally important. Spontaneous sound is one of the baby's greatest enjoyments: the gurgle, the chortle, the repetitions, the blowing sounds through the lips—all are happy experimentations from which two forms grow: spontaneous vocal music and language. Unfortunately, too heavy an emphasis upon the second by parents can lead to a deprivation of the first. The need to return to creative vocal music through pure sound at any age can be seen from the enormous popularity of "gibberish" (nonsense language). The main vocal developments are given in the *Developmental Drama Check List* (Chapter 1, Appendix).

Of all the many relationships between creative music and spontaneous drama in therapy, the most popular is the interrelation of improvisation in groups. Small groups create improvised sounds into a "piece" (either with things around them, or with simple instruments); then, as one group plays its music, the other groups create dramatic improvisations. This type of work can grow in a variety of ways: for example, the development of musical structure can affect the structure of the drama and vice versa.

With older children, the development of creative language can be effective in therapy. The creation of movements to unusual words, the use of word cards to spark improvisations and, with the intelligent, the creation of original languages — all have their place for specific therapeutic needs.

But whatever the medium, it is spontaneous creativity that must be encouraged. From a dramatic base, all media can be used. Drama is so often the spark that sets off the activity in another medium and can lead to therapeutic results.

ELEANOR C. IRWIN, Ph.D., is a drama therapist at the Pittsburgh Child Guidance Center and a clinical assistant professor of child psychiatry, Department of Psychiatry, University of Pittsburgh.

JUDITH A. RUBIN, Ph.D., is an art therapist at the Pittsburgh Child Guidance Center and a clinical assistant professor of child psychiatry, Department of Psychiatry, University of Pittsburgh.

MARVIN I. SHAPIRO, M.D., is a clinical assistant professor at the Stanford University School of Medicine. A member of the San Francisco Psychoanalytic Society, he has a private practice in psychiatry and psychoanalysis in Burlingame, California.

*Chapter 11*

# ART AND DRAMA: PARTNERS IN THERAPY

Eleanor C. Irwin
Judith A. Rubin
Marvin I. Shapiro

## 1 INTRODUCTION

An art-drama therapy group for latency-age boys made possible the exploration of personal symbols and intense fantasies which resulted in a therapeutically powerful and productive experience. This chapter describes the background, rationale, and dynamic process of this group. Multimodal expressive arts therapy is supported.

## 2 BACKGROUND

For the past few years at the Pittsburgh Child Guidance Center, we have been exploring the multiple uses of art and drama in work with individuals, groups, and families. Initially we followed the more traditional pattern of utilizing the arts separately, as, for example, in a special program in which groups of children participated in art, drama, and music therapy.[1] In reviewing the literature, we found that independent treatment of the arts is usually the case whether the purpose is research,[2] education,[3] or treatment.[4] Even in those cases where the children were free to select from a variety of expressive materials, the emergent data were usually treated separately. Rarely have there been attempts to define the relationships between two or more modalities.[5] Occasionally a multimodality approach has been reported,[6] but even in these situations it seemed that one modality was usually subordinate to and distinct from the other.

Intrigued with the notion of combining art forms, impressed by the potential therapeutic benefit inherent in such a combination, we decided to share skills and co-lead an art-drama group. Such an experience, we reasoned, would not only provide a chance to learn more about another modality, but would give us an opportunity to examine, in depth, the interrelationships between the two art forms.

When referrals for the art-drama group were sought, however, colleagues asked how the proposed group would be different from the more traditional play group[7] or activity group therapy.[8] We pointed out that in the proposed group, a greater range of materials within each modality would be available. We therefore wanted to extend the age range of children who could profit from a creative arts approach in therapy, despite the common belief that "the expressive methods are most rewarding with very young children."[9] Like many others we believe that art is a later form of play; thus we hoped to provide symbolic creative opportunities for older children in a form consistent with their developmental level.

## Assessment: Diagnostic Interviews

Prior to the beginning of the group, we saw each of the six children who had been referred for individual art and drama diagnostic interviews. These sessions were unstructured, with a range of art materials or puppets available. Each child was asked to create a product or story, which was followed by discussion with the therapist. The behavioral and symbolic material from these interviews was then considered with the child psychiatrist who also supervised our work with the group. This enabled us to select a "balanced" group of nine- to eleven-year-old boys, who had sufficient ego strength to tolerate regression and who could use one or both of the art modalities as well as group therapy as a medium for growth and change. While the therapists learned much about each of the boys in these interviews, the children also learned a new and nondirective way of working in both modalities and had an opportunity to try out in private the "tools of the trade" which they were later to put into practice in the group.

## Group Sessions: Expectations and Surprises

Planning for the group was based on our prior experience with other groups, and expectations about how this particular group would react. Initially we somewhat naively planned alternate sessions, having art activities one week and drama the next. However, it quickly became apparent that the boys would not adhere to such artificial boundaries, and each session verified the children's need and willingness to express themselves freely in both modalities. This was clearly demonstrated in the very first session, and proved to be a recurring pattern in the life of the group.

In this initial meeting, for example, the boys soon verbalized their anxiety over the newness of the situation. As they finger-painted around a table, they shared stories of "witches and vampires who really suck blood," of "boats that capsize" when one is unprepared, of bombs that suddenly appear and explode without warning. At that point, Joe angrily left the group and went off into a corner to paint an "ugly picture" of the art therapist. Unable to finish, he returned a few minutes later, held out his forefinger which was covered with red paint, and said, "I need a doctor. I'm cut." As the drama therapist entered the fantasy as the doctor, he elaborated, "I was cutting open my cat and got blood all over my hands." This stimulated the others, and soon the air was ripe with dramatized fantasies of hurts and injuries. One boy (who had previously drawn a picture of himself in a coffin with a scary monster standing over him) immediately imitated Joe, and covered his hand with red paint too. That, he said, was "my brother's blood because I just killed him, and he's lying in a coffin."

It is conceivable that meeting each therapist earlier in an intense initial diagnostic session facilitated this rapid involvement in dramatic and pictorial fantasy and the high degree of trust which made it possible to share and verbalize anxieties. Perhaps, too, the alternation of picturing and wiping out possible in the regressive medium of finger paint, and the mutual discussion of fantasies, induced a state of readiness for the castration-murder-doctor drama. This first session, however, was a harbinger of future events, as the children freely used both activities. So intertwined, in fact, were the two, that it became impossible to categorically state that a session was either "pure art" or "pure drama." From that point on, therefore, materials for creation in both modalities were available every week to extend the range of possibilities for symbolic expression.

A further expectation related to the need for "planned" vs. "spontaneous" activities. We had planned, and introduced quite consciously, a number of combined art and drama techniques into the early sessions in order to help the children to articulate and elaborate upon their fantasies using both modalities. For example, we would often suggest the telling of a story about a picture. During the first session Tommy had drawn in yellow finger paint a peace symbol, representing the same conflict he was to play out a week later with two puppets he made, labeled "War" and "Peace." In associating to the picture, Tommy began to talk about the problem of aggression and his concern about war and killing. When asked what peace meant to him, he answered, "Peace means a lot to me . . . I think peace means people talking together and children playing together instead of fighting . . . fighting with their fists."

Another similarly imposed combination was exemplified during the second session, when it was suggested that Matt act out the story he had told about his tempera painting of "A French Soldier Going to an American Fort." He said that the soldier had gone to George Washington to ask for reinforcements in a battle with the Indians; but he puzzled over the outcome, explaining that General Washington "sometimes says yes, and sometimes says no." To help resolve the dilemma, Matt took the role of George Washington and acted out the story with Jimmy, who, as the French soldier, came to see the general. Matt, as Washington, finally agreed to the Frenchman's request for 200 soldiers who, he explained, would win the war using cannons against the Indians' arrows, but would, of course, be badly wounded in the process.

Another combined technique involved doing art work based upon a drama. In a later session, for example, following the spontaneous dramatization of a spy story, it was suggested that the boys picture some of their feelings about the events they had just played out. Matt quickly produced a drawing of a man attempting to shoot a woman, thus describing pictorially his impulse to attack the therapist (an impression confirmed by his comment that "that lady in the picture looks like you").

In traditional and predictable fashion, art materials were often used to make puppets, masks, costumes, and props, which the children were then encouraged to use as extensions of their fantasies in dramatizations. Johnny, for example, was quite proud of his vampire mask and stake. He later added a self-made Dracula costume and intoned: "I suck ze blood. Some blood eez better zan others!"

There was indeed, on the part of both therapists, a conscious attempt to utilize any and all avenues for creative play. Even food was often used in artistic and dramatic fashion. For example, marshmallows, provided for a snack during the discussion time following the play, were made into objects or figures. Matt created a marshmallow "airplane," happily suggesting that he, as the "bombardier," would hit all the schools so there would be no more school. Tommy's marshmallow man was described as big and mean, then was toasted and eaten. Similarly, using icing dispensers, the children created "faces" on large round cookies; these were then "puppets" who dialogued together before being eaten.

In retrospect, it was perhaps useful to introduce these rather structured and suggestive combined art and drama techniques in the early stages of the group. However, it was soon apparent that the boys were capable of creating their own combinations quite independently of the leaders. In fact, in time it became clear that the boys' creative and ingenious uses of unstructured art materials often led spontaneously into the drama, promoting a dynamic interaction. Thus a cardboard carton was not only used for the suggested "box sculpture," but also became a boat for Ben, a house for Matt, and a puppet stage for Dick. Similarly, soap crayons became "makeup" as the boys painted their faces, elaborating on their specific inner fantasies. Jack, for example, streaked his face and hands to become Frankenstein, wishing to act out the role of a monster who could catch the therapist and eat her. Cotton and yarn provided for collage also became beards, moustaches, and wigs.

A natural merging of art and drama often took place, as associations to the boys' own creations were spontaneously dramatized. Thus, using styrofoam, papers, and colorful pipe cleaners, the group members made magnificent "king" and "queen" boats. It was only natural to sail the boats, relating action-filled stories of battles, attacks, losses, and races. To extend and clarify each child's fantasy, one of the therapists "interviewed" each of the boys, as though for a television program. The same playful interviewing procedure was often used after a drama or an especially intense moment to help the child achieve ego distance from the play and to help build bridges and strengthen boundaries between reality and fantasy.

We had originally expected that each child would show a preference for one modality or the other. Although initially this was so for some children, by the end of several months it became almost impossible to clearly select a "preferred" art form for each child. Most often, a child would begin with the modality which was most comfortable to him, but as his confidence and interest increased he would explore and try out new ways of expressing himself.

Frequently issues were first explored symbolically in art and later expressed in dramatic form. Although two of the boys seemed to utilize solitary or dyadic play with puppets as a way of expressing feelings before they could comfortably make and keep artistic products, most of the group members began with art and moved to drama. In general, a dynamic interaction took place, with individuals using both modalities to express and work through conflicts.

The interweaving of art and drama described in the above story of Matt and the group occurred numerous times. In many ways the above drama and its variations were the preparation for a later hospital scene in which castration and other themes were more clearly played out by the group. Each child used the dramatic structure to enact his own conflicts. Bill, for example, was "dying of thirst," afraid of abandonment, while Pete played a wild, "crazy" patient, "falling apart inside" from his inner confusion. Matt, who by this time had worked through some of his anger and fear, was able to be a kind and helpful doctor in the hospital sequence. The boys experimented first on one of the therapists, who had her arm chopped off and sewed on, her nose cut off and repaired, her guts taken out, and even the little bone in her stomach (the fantasied phallus, perhaps) removed.

As the above excerpt indicates, within the group structure it was possible for individual members to work on their particular areas of conflict, as well as for the group to work together on shared or universal conflicts. The setting encouraged the exploration of multiple alternatives in terms of time, space, and support for the expression of conflicts as the children worked toward clarification and resolution.

Based upon the essentially "individual" nature of art and the "group" nature of drama, we had expected that the boys would work independently in art and would work together as a group in drama. Much to our surprise, and perhaps because of the simultaneous availability of materials and space for work in both modalities, it soon became apparent that individual, dyadic, and group interaction was possible in each of the two areas.

There were often times when children worked alone in art, thoroughly engrossed in their activity; there were also times when individuals engaged in solitary dramatic play, particularly with puppets. Children would frequently work in parallel or cooperative dyads in art, or in dramatic play; and at times all members of the group worked together on some cooperative productive task, like a mural or a large construction. Similarly, spontaneous or guided dramas evolved in which every group member took part in a way that was truly reflective of shared needs and concerns.

A similar range of interactions occurred with regard to the boys' use of the two therapists. Just as the boys seemed able to utilize each other as either companions, helpers, observers, or protagonists, so they were able to make use of the available adults in multiple ways. We were surprised and intrigued to find that our interactions as therapists with this group were different from our past experiences with other groups. We expected, for example, that the art therapist would function more often as an authority figure or "teacher," engaged in a series of one-to-one relationships with each child. On the other hand, a drama therapist is more often seen as a "fellow player," ready to join in and pretend by taking a role with the children in the drama, relating primarily to the group as a functional unit. Much to our surprise, we each quickly found ourselves functioning at one time in one way, and at other times in another. We each took both kinds of roles, our relationship to the children alternating with the therapeutic needs of the moment, whether it was being facilitator, participant, teacher, or observing ego.

Matt, for example, went off to work alone at the easel, painting pictures and making masks of George Washington—"the father of our country"— a fairly transparent father symbol to him. His other favored symbol was a pirate—"Black Hook" or "Bluebeard"—who represented "evil" aggressive impulses toward authority figures. Both were represented as damaged in an eye, a leg, or both. Two of Matt's first paintings, done in the art diagnostic session, were of "Valley Forge," with a quiet cannon outside, and "Black Hook's Boat." Matt then told a story in which Black Hook "almost" had his leg bitten off by a shark. In his drama diagnostic session his concerns were expressed more directly. He played out numerous stories of a very wicked witch who was punished by being put in jail and was later angrily devoured by the boy puppet. As Matt began in the group, he explored aggressive fantasies primarily in art, working alone at the easel. In the third month of the group, Matt painted a "burning church" which showed the steeple destroyed; soon after that, he painted two airplanes, a big one and a little one, locked in a fierce battle. In these products and stories, Matt's anger at his all-powerful mother, his ambivalent wish to attack and to identify with his father, as well as with his fear of his father's retaliatory super-powers were eloquently expressed.

In time, however, this conflict moved from solitary art at the

easel to more direct avenues of expression, as Matt repeatedly
symbolically attacked and destroyed the powerful parent forces.
He would tease both therapists, calling us "witches" and verbaliz-
ing his wish to make us his "slaves," taking an imperious and
authoritarian role. Gradually he gained the courage to argue with
the other boys, and one day a fight actually escalated into a
physical battle. When it was suggested that perhaps the com-
batants could fight the battle on paper, the two made a large
mural, intently drawing and painting Japanese, German, and
American planes in an air war. As they worked side by side, the
air was filled with accompanying shouts and sounds of battle.
After the mural was finished, all of the boys prepared plasticene
bombs and, yelling out their fantasied stories of the war being
fought, they let loose with a hail of bullets, directed at the mural
in barrage after barrage.

As often happened, the other boys all became involved in this
shared conflict. When the battle was over, they retired to the
refreshment table to replenish their psychic needs with food. Still
excited by the drama, the boys were interviewed as the "sole survivors" of the terrible battle. Matt, of course, identified himself as
George Washington and related his version of the conflict. Suddenly, in response to an unrelated noise outside the room, the
survivors spontaneously dived under the table for cover, yelling,
"Duck! There's one plane left and it's bombing us!" In a fantasy of retaliation for their aggression, one boy lost his leg, another
his head, and another (Matt) his arm. A therapist was pressed
into service in the play as a medic who magically restored damaged body parts. Quickly the boys returned to battle and, putting up the last few pieces of the mural, they bombed the enemy
again, saying that they "had to get that last enemy plane."
After the "war," the therapists decorated the boys with
spontaneously-made medals for their bravery in battle, as the
boys talked and shared feelings about what had just occurred.

Moreover, the nature of the group seemed to stimulate various
projections on the therapists, and the enacting of "dramatized"
transference behaviors. As the children relived past memories
and explored their feelings and impulses, they were often inclined

to dramatize the transference relationship, prolonging and further exploring the fantasy. Thus, for example, when Matt had
begun to taste the sweetness of power in dramatic play as General
Washington, he pretended to be omnipotent and ordered the
therapist about, saying, "Slave, get me the tape!" or "Come here,
missy!" Later, playing Santa Claus in a spontaneous drama, he
told the therapist she was his "doll," under his power, and must
act in whatever way he commanded.

Once the children learned to take roles and to pretend, they
often elected to relate to us in this dramatic way because it served
their needs so well. It made possible, of course, a greater flexibility
for the therapist, who could play out the assigned role and discuss
it later, or could respond therapeutically in the context of the
character (for example, "You like to boss me around, don't you?")
or as her real self ("If you could *really* be such a powerful boss,
what else would you order me to do?"). This dramatized way of
working enriched the experience for the child and offered multiple opportunities to explore emotional conflicts, as each child
turned from one form to another, from one adult to another,
"working through" in both modalities. Because there were two
therapists, it was possible for one to be involved in the play in
terms which the child dictated, while the other functioned as the
"observing ego." The one who participated did not attempt to influence the play but followed the child's lead if it seemed
therapeutically appropriate; the other was thus free to observe,
comment, or interact as necessary.

Just as the various art forms seemed to be complementary, and
just as the children seemed able to use each other and us in a
variety of ways, so the therapeutic utility of the activity was
enhanced by the postplay discussion. These concluding around-
the-table talks over refreshments were essential in helping the
children to integrate the preceding activity. While a great deal of
sharing of feelings went on during the play, roughly the last half
hour of each one-and-a-half hour session was used to help the
boys to focus on the meaning of what had occurred, and to verbalize feelings and understandings. The arts are powerful tools
which stimulate regression (the rate of which sometimes must be

controlled by the therapist) and aid in the uncovering and expressing of conflict. The postactivity discussions, therefore, were
an integral and vital part of the therapeutic process, as the
children were helped to use what they had made (art) or done
(drama), using both as a vehicle for insight, verbal communication, and change.

Thus, the making and doing which served to complement each
other as available expressive tools, were themselves enhanced by
talking. The suspension of the reality principle which occurred
during the time of artistic or dramatic creativity was replaced by
a consideration of that activity in the light of the child's current,
past, or future realities. Not only did such sharing of anxieties,
wishes, and fears help to dispel each child's delusion of uniqueness;
but the differentiation of real and fantasied actions enabled the
children to gain mastery over their impulses as they gained increasing mastery over the media and tools of the two art forms.

## 3  CONCLUSIONS

Based upon the work reported here, we have subsequently used
the same approach with a group of adolescents of both sexes with
surprisingly similar results. Experience with these groups has
taught us that a successful combination of two or more expressive
art modalities is possible, and in fact may result in extension and
enrichment for both workers and children. Each therapist learned
from the other, and the experience has permanently affected and
modified our individual ways of working, broadening our armamentarium of media, tools, techniques, and even "style."

Enlarging the range of possibilities available to the children
made possible for each individual the kind of "dynamic balance"
described by Wolff[10] between social activities like drama and a
"ripening time" like that possible in art. We facilitated the use of
different media for different expressive purposes, taking into account distinctions among the children as well as the fact that
"each nonverbal projective activity has its own advantages and
limitations."[11] In this group the children were encouraged to
move freely from one modality to another, expressing themselves
in different ways according to their inner dictates, over time

gradually externalizing and working through their difficulties. At times art was used in the service of drama, and drama in the service of art, while both art and drama were used in the service of the ego. Our experience with this group suggests that it is artificial to make distinctions, to create boundaries, and to limit experience to any one modality at all times. Rather, it seems natural and "right" to allow the children to follow their impulses for self-expression in a variety of ways.

## 4  SUMMARY

This paper discusses the background, rationale, and process of an art-drama therapy group, co-led by an art therapist and a drama therapist in a child guidance clinic. The theoretical and practical differences and similarities between this approach and traditional play therapy are noted and the expectations and surprises which resulted from the "blending" of these two expressive forms are discussed in detail.

The art-drama group, composed of six latency-age boys, met for a year. Freely using both modalities, the participants engaged in symbolic and fantasy play of an intense nature which was helpful in externalizing and working through their difficulties. The authors conclude that in making available a variety of expressive arts forms, the therapeutic possibilities are enlarged and enhanced, resulting in an enriched experience for both children and workers.

## FOOTNOTES

1. E. Marine, E. C. Irwin, and M. Addis, "Fantasy and Reality Integrated through Expressive Arts and Social Group Work" (Paper presented at the National Conference on Social Work, Chicago, Ill., 1970).

2. L. B. Murphy, *et al.*, *Personality in Young Children*, 2 vols. (New York: Basic Books, 1956); J. L. Despert, "A Method for the Study of Personality Reactions of Preschool Children by Means of Analysis of their Play," *Journal of Psychology* 9, no. 17 (1940).

3. Susan Isaacs, *Social Development in Young Children* (London: Routledge & Kegan Paul, 1933); R. Griffiths, *A Study of Imagination in Early Childhood* (London: Routledge & Kegan Paul, 1935); R. Hartley, L. Frank, and R. Goldenson, *Understanding Children's Play* (New York: Columbia University Press, 1957).

4. M. Rambert, *Children in Conflict* (New York: International Universities Press, 1949); L. Bender, ed., *Child Psychiatric Techniques* (Springfield, Ill.: Charles C. Thomas, 1952); Margaret Lowenfeld, *Play in Childhood*, 2d Science Ed. paperback (New York: Wiley, 1967).

5. R. H. Alschuler and L. W. Hattwick, *Painting and Personality*, rev. ed. (Chicago: University of Chicago Press, 1969).

6. T. R. McNaught and C. A. Goldstein, "Music, Movement and Art in the Treatment of Chronic Schizophrenia," in *Psychiatry and Art*, 1, ed. I. Jakab (New York: S. Karger, 1968), pp. 123-31; R. L. Jenkins and E. Beckh, "Finger Puppets and Mask Making as Media for Work with Children," *American Journal of Orthopsychiatry* 12 (1942): 294.

7. Virginia M. Axline, *Play Therapy* (Cambridge, Mass.: Riverside, 1947); Clark Moustakas, *Psychotherapy with Children: The Living Relationship* (New York: Ballantine, 1959).

8. Gisela Konopka, *Social Group Work: A Helping Process* (Englewood Cliffs, N.J.: Prentice-Hall, 1963).

9. A. I. Rabin and M. R. Haworth, eds., *Projective Techniques with Children* (New York: Grune & Stratton, 1960), p. 10; J. A. Rubin, "A Diagnostic Art Interview," *International Journal of Art Psychotherapy* 1 (1973): 31; E. C. Irwin and M. Shapiro, "Puppetry as a Diagnostic and Therapeutic Technique," in *Psychiatry and Art*, 4, ed. I. Jakab (New York: S. Karger, 1975).

10. Werner Wolff, *The Personality of the Preschool Child* (New York: Grune & Stratton, 1946), p. 281.

11. A. G. Woltmann, "Diagnostic and Therapeutic Considerations of Nonverbal Projective Activities with Children," in *Child Psychotherapy*, ed. M. R. Haworth (New York: Basic Books, 1964), p. 330.

RICHARD A. GARDNER, M.D., is an associate clinical professor of child psychiatry at Columbia University's College of Physicians and Surgeons. A member of the faculty at the William A. White Psychoanalytic Institute, New York City, he has authored many articles, tapes, and books, including *Therapeutic Communication with Children: The Mutual Storytelling Technique.*

*Chapter 12*

# DRAMATIZED STORYTELLING IN CHILD PSYCHOTHERAPY

Richard A. Gardner

## 1 THE MUTUAL STORYTELLING TECHNIQUE

Eliciting stories is a time-honored practice in child psychotherapy. From the stories children tell, the therapist is able to gain invaluable insights into the child's inner conflicts, frustrations, and defenses.

A child's stories are generally less difficult to analyze than dreams, free associations, and other productions of the adult. His fundamental difficulties are exhibited clearly to the therapist, with less of the obscurity, distortion, and misrepresentation that are characteristic of the adult's presentation. The essential problem for the child's therapist has been how to use his insights therapeutically.

The techniques described in the current literature on child psychotherapy and psychoanalysis are, for the most part, attempts to solve this problem. Some are based on the assumption, borrowed from the adult psychoanalytic model, that making the unconscious conscious can itself be therapeutic. My own experience has been that few children are interested in gaining conscious awareness of their unconscious processes, let alone utilizing such insights

211

therapeutically. Children do, however, enjoy both telling stories and listening to them. Since storytelling is one of the child's favorite modes of communication, I wondered whether communicating with him in the same mode might not be useful in child therapy. The efficacy of the storytelling approach for the imparting and transmission of values and insights is proved by the ancient and universal appeal of fable, myth, and legend.

It was from these observations and considerations that I developed the Mutual Storytelling Technique, a proposed solution to the question of how to utilize the child's stories therapeutically. In this method the child first tells a story; the therapist surmises its psychodynamic meaning and then tells one of his own. The therapist's story contains the same characters in a similar setting, but he introduces healthier adaptations and resolutions of the conflicts that have been exhibited in the child's story. Since he speaks in the child's own language, the therapist has a good chance of "being heard." One could almost say that here the therapist's interpretations bypass the conscious and are received directly by the unconscious. The child is not burdened with psychoanalytic interpretations which are alien to him. Direct, anxiety-provoking confrontations, so reminiscent of the child's experience with parents and teachers, are avoided. Lastly, the introduction of humor and drama enhances the child's interest and pleasure and, therefore, his receptivity. As a therapeutic tool, the method is useful for children who will tell stories, but who have little interest in analyzing them. It is not a therapy per se, but rather one technique in the therapist's armamentarium.

## Basic Mechanics of the Method

Although drawings, dolls, puppets, and other toys are the modalities around which stories are traditionally told in child therapy, these often restrict the child's storytelling or channel it in highly specific directions. The tape recorder (either video or audio) does not have these disadvantages; with it, the visual field remains free from contaminating and distracting stimuli. Eliciting a story with it is like obtaining a dream on demand. The same method, however, can be employed—with some modifications—with dolls, blocks, drawings, and other play material.

I begin by asking the child if he would like to be guest of honor on a make-believe television program on which stories are told. If he agrees — and few decline the honor — the recorder is turned on and I begin:

> Good morning, boys and girls. I'd like to welcome you once again to Dr. Gardner's Make-Up-a-Story Television Program. As you all know, we invite children to our program to see how good they are at making up stories. Naturally, the more adventure or excitement a story has, the more interesting it is to the people who are watching at their television sets. Now, it's against the rules to tell stories about things you've read or have seen in the movies or on television, or about things that really happened to you or anyone you know.
>
> Like all stories, your story should have a beginning, a middle, and an end. After you've made up a story, you'll tell us the moral of the story. We all know that every good story has a moral.
>
> Then after you've told your story, Dr. Gardner will make up a story too. He'll try to tell one that's interesting and unusual, and then he'll tell the moral of his story.
>
> And now, without further delay, let me introduce to you a boy (girl) who is with us today for the first time. Can you tell us your name, young man?

I then ask the child a series of brief questions that can be answered by single words or brief phrases, such as his age, address, school grade, and teacher. These "easy" questions diminish the child's anxiety and tend to make him less tense about the more unstructured themes involved in "making up a story." Anxiety is further lessened when he hears his own voice at this point by playback, something which most children enjoy. He is then told:

> Now that we've heard a few things about you, we're all interested in hearing the story *you* have for us today.

At this point most children plunge right into their story,

although some may feel the need for "time to think." I may offer this pause; if it is asked for by the child, it is readily granted. There are some children for whom this pause is not enough, but nevertheless still want to try. In such instances the child is told:

> Some children, especially when it's their first time on this pro-
> gram, have a little trouble thinking of a story, but with some help
> from me they're able to do so. Most children don't realize that
> there are *millions* of stories in their heads they don't know about.
> And I know a way to help get out some of them. Would you like
> me to help you get out one of them?

Most children assent to this. I then continue:

> Fine. Here's how it works. I'll start the story and, when I point
> my finger at you, you say exactly what comes into your mind at
> that time. You'll then see how easy it is to make up a story. Okay.
> Let's start. Once upon a time—a long, long time ago—in a distant
> land—far, far away—way beyond the mountains—way beyond the
> deserts—way beyond the oceans—there lived a—

I then point my finger, and it is a rare child who does not offer some fill-in word at this point. If the word is *dog,* for example, I then say, "And *that dog*—" and once again point to the patient. I follow the statement provided by the child with "And then—" or "The next thing that happened was—." Every statement the child makes is followed by some introductory connective and an indica-tion to the child to supply the next statement—that and no more. The introduction of specific phrases or words would defeat the therapist's purpose of catalyzing the youngster's production of his *own* created material and of sustaining, as needed, its continuity.

This approach is sufficient to get most children over whatever hurdles there are for them in telling a story. If this is not enough, however, it is best to drop the activity in a completely casual and nonreproachful manner, such as: "Well, today doesn't seem to be your good day for storytelling. Perhaps we'll try again some other time." While the child is engaged in telling his story, I jot down notes, which not only help in analyzing the child's story but also serve as a basis for my own. At the end of the child's story and his statement of its moral, I may ask questions about specific items in the story. The purpose here is to obtain additional details, which are often of help in understanding the story. Typical questions might be: "Was the fish in your story a man or a lady?" "Why was the fox so mad at the goat?" or "Why did the bear do that?" If the child hesitates to tell the moral of his story or indicates that there is none, I usually reply: "What, a story without a moral? Every good story has some lesson or moral!" The moral that this comment usually does succeed in eliciting from the child is often significantly revealing of the fundamental psychodynamics of the story. For younger children the word *lesson* or *title* may be substituted for moral. Or the child might be asked: "What can we learn from your story?"

Then I usually say: "That was a very good (unusual, exciting) story." Or to the child who was hesitant: "And you thought you weren't very good at telling stories!"

I then turn off the tape recorder and prepare my story. Although the child's story is generally simpler to understand than the adult's dream, the analysis of both follows similar principles.

## Fundamentals of Story Analysis

I first attempt to determine which figure or figures in the child's story represent the child himself, and which stand for significant people in his environment. It is important to appreciate that two or more figures may represent various facets of the same person's personality. There may, for example, be a "good dog" and a "bad cat" in the same story, which are best understood as conflicting forces within the same child. A horde of figures, all similar, may symbolize powerful elements in a single person. A hostile father, for example, may be represented by a stampede of bulls. Swarms of small creatures, such as insects, worms, or mice, often symbolize unacceptable repressed complexes. Malevolent figures can represent the child's own repressed hostility projected outward, or they may be a symbolic statement about the hostility of a significant figure. Sometimes both of these mechanisms operate simultaneously. A threatening lion in one child's story stood for his hostile father, and he was made more frightening by the child's own hostility, repressed and projected onto the lion. This example illustrates one of the reasons why many children see their parents as being more malevolent than they are.

Besides clarifying the symbolic significance of each figure, it is also important to get a general overall "feel" for the atmosphere and setting of the story. Is the ambience pleasant, neutral, or horrifying? Stories that take place in the frozen tundra or on isolated space stations suggest something very different from those which occur in the child's own home. The child's emotional reactions when telling the story are also of significance in understanding its meaning. An eleven-year-old child who tells me, in an emotionless tone, about the death fall of a mountain climber reveals not only his hostility but also his repression of his feelings. The atypical must be separated from the stereotyped, age-appropriate elements in the story. The former may be very revealing, whereas the latter rarely are. Battles between cowboys and Indians rarely give meaningful data, but when the chief sacrifices his son to Indian gods in a prayer for victory over the white man, something has been learned about the child's relationship with his father.

Lastly, the story may lend itself to a number of different psychodynamic interpretations. In selecting the theme that will be most pertinent for the child *at that particular time,* I am greatly assisted by the child's own "moral" or "title."

After asking myself, "What would be a healthier resolution or a more mature adaptation than the one used by the child?" I create a story of my own. My story involves the same characters, setting, and initial situation as the child's story, but it has a more appropriate or salutary resolution of the most important conflicts. In creating my story, I attempt to provide the child with more *alternatives.* The communication that the child need not be enslaved by his neurotic behavior patterns is vital. Therapy must open new avenues not considered in the child's scheme of things. It must help the child become aware of the multiplicity of options which are available to replace the narrow self-defeating ones he has chosen. My moral or morals are an attempt to emphasize further the healthier adaptations I have included in my story. If, while I am telling my story the child exhibits deep interest or reveals marked anxiety, which may manifest itself by jitteriness or hyperactivity, then I know that my story is "hitting home." Such clear-cut indications of how relevant one's story is are not, of course, always forthcoming.

After the moral to my story, I stop the recorder and ask the child whether he would like to hear (and see when the videotape recorder is used) the program. Playing the program makes possible a second exposure to the messages that the therapist wishes to impart.

The therapist's attitude has a subtle, but nevertheless significant, influence on the child's ability to tell a story. Ideally this attitude should be one of pleasurable anticipation that a story will be forthcoming and surprised disappointment when the child will not or cannot tell one. The child wants to be accepted by those who are meaningful to him, and, if a productive therapeutic relationship has been established, he will try to comply with what is expected of him. Peer group influence is also important. When the child gets the general feeling that storytelling is what everybody does when he visits the therapist, he is more likely to play the game. The last factor, and probably the most important one in determining whether the child will voluntarily involve himself, is his appreciation at some level that the therapist's communications are meaningful and useful to him. If the therapist's responding communications are frequently "on target," that is, if they are most often relevant to the child's problems and situation, the child is likely to become engrossed in the game. (I say *frequently* relevant because it is unreasonable to expect that the therapist will *always* accurately understand the child's story.)

# 2   DRAMATIZATION OF THE THERAPEUTIC COMMUNICATIONS

Just as the Mutual Storytelling Technique was developed from the observation that children naturally enjoy both telling and listening to stories, the idea of dramatizing them arose from the observation that children would often automatically (and at times without conscious awareness) gesticulate, impersonate, intone, and enact in other ways while telling their stories. I found that when I introduced such theatrics myself the child became more involved in my stories and receptive to their messages. Whereas originally I introduced the dramatic elements *en passant*, that is, in the process of telling my story (just as the children tended to do), I subsequently formalized the process by inviting the child to reenact our stories as plays following our telling them: "I've got a great idea! Let's make up plays about our stories. Who do you want to be? The wolf or the fox?" At times I would invite the mother and even siblings to join us. (We often face the problem of having a shortage of available actors.) We see here another way in which mothers can be useful in the child's treatment. (A little encouragement may be necessary at times to help some mothers overcome their "stage fright.") Of course the therapist himself must be free enough to involve himself in the various antics that are required for a successful "performance." He must have the freedom to roll on the floor, imitate various animals, "ham it up," etc. He has to be able to be director, choreographer, writer, and actor — practically all at the same time. He may have to assume a number of different roles in the same play, and quickly shift from part to part. Such roles shifts do not seem to bother most children nor reduce their involvement or enjoyment. Nor do they seem to be bothered by the therapist's "stage whispers," so often necessary to keep the play running smoothly.

The therapist who can create with the child such performances has a very valuable tool at his disposal. The enjoyment the child may derive from such plays can be immense. Accordingly, they can serve to entrench the child's involvement in treatment. In addition, such dramatizations enrich the therapeutic communications. One is not only transmitting the message verbally; rather one is adding a host of nonverbal stimuli (physical, kinesthetic, visual, tactile, and at times even olfactory and gustatory). Such multisensory exposure increases vastly the chances of the therapist's "being heard." And they help immensely in getting his messages to "sink in."

## 3  CLINICAL EXAMPLES

### George

George was an eight-and-a-half-year-old boy with minimal brain dysfunction. Although he could read and write at the third grade level, he was socially functioning at about the five-to-six-year level. Coordination deficits were present and he was markedly hyperactive and dysinhibited. An organic speech defect was also present. His attention span was extremely short and he tended to be disruptive in the classroom and at home. His immaturity was enhanced by his mother's overprotectiveness. From the beginning of treatment, he exhibited persistent magic-cure expectations.

Near the end of his second month of treatment, George told a story about a boy who was changed into a duck. With quacking sounds the duck seeks a fairy godmother who would change him back into a boy with her magic wand. Suddenly he changes into a horse who similarly neighs for a fairy godmother. After a period of hiding from the fairy godmother, during which he changes back and forth from a horse to a duck, he finally is transformed back to a boy. Throughout the telling of his story, George gesticulated frequently and even created little songs depicting the animals' quacking and neighing while seeking the fairy godmother.

George's depicting himself as a duck related, I believe, to his speech defect as well as his low opinion of himself. His story provides him with a magic transformation to the more estimable status of a human being and an attendant removal of the undesirable speech. The horse serves a purpose similar to the duck in that it is also a lower animal with primitive communications. I did not completely understand the somewhat confusing horse-duck transformations and the hiding from the fairy godmother. I was, however, quite clear about the magic-cure element in the story and so I focused on that in my responding story.

In my story the duck similarly searches for a fairy godmother with a magic wand. Like in George's story he sings in duck-like fashion: "Quack, quack. I wish I saw a fairy godmother." George joined me as we looked around the room calling out for a fairy godmother. But she never responds. Finally, an old lady appears who believes she has magic powers. In response to the duck's request to be changed into a boy, she (played by me) takes a stick and waves it over the duck's (played by George) head. I dramatically incanted: "Magic, magic—duck, duck—quack three times and I'll change you into a person." However, George's responding quacks do not work and he still remains a duck. The old lady then encourages the duck (George) to quack louder (which George enthusiastically did); but even this does not result in the desired transformation. In her frustration the old lady curses the magic wand and repeatedly beats it against the ground (again, I dramatically act this out). But further tries still do not effect the desired change.

The old lady then, in a fit of rage, breaks the magic wand over her knee and tries another. But even this new wand does not work. Finally, another incantation is tried: "Abracadabraca, hokus, pokus, turn this duck into a person." With wild antics of frustration, the old lady again breaks the wand in two and discards it in a rage as it once again fails to change the duck into a boy.

At this point a man comes along and inquires into the cause of all the commotion. In the ensuing discussion he confirms to the duck that there is no such thing as magic and that his and the old lady's endeavors are futile. He asks the duck why he wants to change and the latter describes his difficulty in speaking clearly. The man advises a more practical alternative: speech lessons and hard practice over a long period of time. The program is instituted and, after a long period of arduous dedication, the duck is successful in achieving his goal of clear speech.

The purpose of my responding story is obvious. I attempted to impart the notion that there are no such things as magic cures and that a more practical and predictably effective course toward the overcoming of one's handicaps is that of constructive action.

A problem that I faced in formulating this story was of what to do with the duck. As described, the duck well lent itself as a symbol of the patient because of his speech problem. However, to portray the patient as a duck in my story might entrench this pathological personification and might thereby be anti-therapeutic. But to depict the patient as a boy would then rob me of the opportunity to deal with the magic transformation issue in a manner that was close to the patient's representation of the problem. If the therapist's story gets too remote from the patient's it becomes less therapeutically effective. I decided, therefore, that the advantages of maintaining the duck outweighed its disadvantages. In addition, the child's ability to create a fantasy that most efficiently and effectively synthesizes the various symbols is far greater than that of the therapist. I believe that we not only lack the ingenuity of our child-patient's unconscious, but of our own unconscious as well. We ourselves cannot create a dream as rich and as efficient as that which can be created by our own unconscious. The efficiency and ingenuity of our unconscious processes to utilize simile, metaphor, allegory, and efficient and innovative symbol fusion far surpasses that of our conscious mind. Therefore, I do not try to reconcile all elements of my story nor do I strive for 100% consistency. In this case I chose to be a little inconsistent (and even possibly a little anti-therapeutic) in order to preserve the duck symbol for the more important purposes of my story, that is, to present a story that focused on the patient's magic cure delusion.

Nine days later, instead of only the patient and his mother coming for the session, his father and two younger siblings (his six-year-old brother and four-year-old sister) also appeared in the waiting room. The father was about to take the younger siblings out for a walk while the patient and his mother were in session with me. I invited the father to bring the children in because of my previous experience that siblings' participation might be useful. The children were quite enthusiastic about the idea because they had heard from their brother such wonderful tales about the exciting things that go on in my office. Also they had listened to some of the audio tapes that were made during their brother's sessions and had enjoyed what they had heard. George's father, however, was somewhat hesitant to come in because he felt the younger children would be disruptive. Accordingly, I told the younger children that they could come into the room as long as they behaved themselves and that if they did so they might be allowed to participate in some of the games that George and I played, but I could not promise with certainty that they would be invited to join us. The children were quite cooperative and did not interrupt George when he told his story on the television program.

In his story George told about two groups of animals: one group that could talk and one that couldn't. Early in the story the non-talking animals seek the help of a magic fairy—but they are unsuccessful in finding one. As had occurred in my story told nine days previously, the search proved to be futile. The non-speaking animals then find a speech therapist and after a long period of training learn to speak.

Although the story clearly repeats my theme and demonstrates that George remembered what I had previously said, one cannot say that it proves that George had given up his magic cure fantasies. If the problems were truly worked out, he would not be including fairy godmothers at all. Doing and undoing is not the same as nothing ever having happened at all. In addition, one might argue that the story was told in the service of ingratiating himself to me. I believe that this is probably true. But I believe also that a certain amount of this goes on in all therapy (regardless of the age of the patient) and that it is a first step toward more meaningful change. Hopefully, the behavioral patterns that a patient first tries out in compliance with the therapist's wishes (either overt or covert) and in the need to ingratiate himself to the therapist will ultimately be found useful for their own sake by the patient. I believe also, however, that George repeated my story because of his appreciation, at some level, that it had validity and that it offered him more promise for improvement than a fairy godmother.

In an attempt to further entrench the healthy elements in George's story, I congratulated him on his story and told him that it was so good that I thought it would make an excellent play in which his brother and sister might want to join us. The siblings served as willing recruits in a story in which there were two groups of animals: one that could talk and one that could not. I (playing the roles of script writer, director, choreographer, and actor) first asked the children to act the parts of animals who could talk. I too chose one, and all of us together joined in making various animal sounds. The children readily joined in and wholeheartedly enjoyed what we were doing. Then we switched to portray the animals who couldn't talk. Here the children were encouraged to enact the parts of animals who were struggling to utter words but were intensely frustrated by their inability to do so. Straining and grunting we tried to speak; but to no avail. Words would just not come out. Then came the search for the fairy godmother who would wave her magic wand and thereby give us the power of speech. We wandered around the room—searching here, looking there, up and down, even out the window—all the while calling out for the fairy godmother. Intermittently I asked if anyone had heard her respond or had seen any evidence of her; but they all agreed that there was no evidence that she was anywhere around. Louder and louder we yelled; more and more ardently we searched; but still no fairy godmother appeared.

Finally, we admitted that our search had been in vain, and I then asked the children what could be done. Inevitably George suggested the speech teacher. I then suggested he play the role of the speech teacher and the play ended with his successfully teaching us how to speak; only, however, after a somewhat difficult and arduous course.

Within a month, magic-cure themes were completely absent from George's productions in treatment. They neither appeared in his stories nor in his other therapeutic productions. And even material dealing with its *absence* (which for reasons described above is not as healthy as no concerns at all) was not present. But more important was the clinical situation in which he was dedicating himself more arduously to his academic work as well as taking a more practical approach to his other presenting problems.

The efficacy of a therapeutic approach—no matter how reasonable it may appear—ultimately rests on whether it can produce clinical change. In George's case, I believe that there was a cause and effect relationship between the dramatized storytelling experiences he had in my office and the altered behavior he manifested both in the classroom and in my office. Of course, George's treatment continued because there was still much work to be done. Other therapeutic approaches were utilized as well; but for George the dramatized storytelling continued to be an important part of the therapeutic approach to his problems.

## Sally

Sally, a six-and-a-half-year-old girl with minimal brain dysfunction, was asked to discontinue dance lessons because of her hyperactivity, distractibility, and interference with the learning of the other students. She was very restless in the dance class and would not attend to the teacher. Instead, she ran around the class, bumped into other children, and exhibited other disruptive antics. A few months later the class gave a recital and, of course, Sally was not a participant. However, because her five-year-old sister was in the recital she was invited to see it.

Sally was transfixed throughout the dance recital and for weeks afterward sang fragments of the songs that were presented and imitated segments of the dances. It was during this period that she presented material in her play that clearly related to her feelings about her dance lessons and the recital. She began with the dolls and the dollhouse and told a story about a robber which I will omit because it is not directly relevant to the issues I wish to focus on here. Her transcription starts at the point where she introduced the dancing school experience.

PATIENT: Then when the robber was gone they had to go to dancing school. And then the biggest girl — the biggest girl was gonna be the assistant.

THERAPIST: Hh hmm.

PATIENT: There's only one dancing teacher and the biggest one is the assistant.

THERAPIST: All right. Go ahead. Then what happened?

PATIENT: (fidgets in chair).

THERAPIST: What happened there?

PATIENT: (just staring into space, swinging legs).

THERAPIST: Huh. What happened?

PATIENT: Then they left and the assistant, the older child, walked in and all the other children. Then you know what? Then there was (moves doll figures around on table in front of her) a boy there who wanted to be this boy's friend and he let go of it. He wanted to be the girl's friend. And this boy has to be the dancing teacher's friend — I mean the dancing assistant. And there was a girl (moves girl figure toward playhouse on table) and she jumped around (bangs figure on table) and pushes in between the children (still moving figures around).

THERAPIST: Hh hmm.

PATIENT: And then the teacher — and then the assistant put her

out the door (moves figure outside of playhouse). Then later
on in the year when the recital came, the Daddy said, "Could
I use this child for the recital?" And so he said — and so all the
children and the dancing assistant (moving figures around as
she is talking) said, "No."

THERAPIST: Why? Why did the dancing assistant say no?

PATIENT (continually moving figures around on table): Because
she jumped around.

THERAPIST: What happened then?

PATIENT: Then she had to sit in the audience.

THERAPIST: Uh huh. And how did she feel in the audience?

PATIENT (still moving figures around): Sad.

THERAPIST: Then what happened?

PATIENT (moving figures around): Then — then when the recital
was over, then the girl — then the girl tried tumbling school.

THERAPIST: All right. What happened in tumbling school?

PATIENT (intensely concentrating on moving other figures about
on table): All the other children from dancing school were
there.

THERAPIST: Uh huh. Okay.

PATIENT (still moving figures about): And even the assistant was
there.

THERAPIST: Okay. And what happened there in tumbling
school?

PATIENT (waving arms up and down): They tumbled and the girl
didn't even run around.

THERAPIST: She didn't!

PATIENT (still waving arms up and down): So later in the
week — year — when the recital came they — this one be a
leader.

THERAPIST: She became a leader! Oh boy!

PATIENT (excitedly singing): And threw her hat up into the air!

THERAPIST: Uh huh! Oh boy! And what else?

PATIENT: And then the other children — the other children didn't
want to be a leader. Then they were in the class and then she
was all finished (moving figure around) with
her. . .(mumbles). . .

THERAPIST: She was all finished with what?

PATIENT: Her leader act.

THERAPIST: Her leader act. Okay.

PATIENT (moving figures): And then—then—and then big clowns—and then the assistant baby wanted to be—so (concentrates on taking figures out of playhouse) they came out—they came—they came out—and got a—(waves arms back and forth) and got a trophy. And they sang (sings while moving arms alternately up and down and moving body from side to side), "Every show must have an end, have an end, have an end. Every show must have an end. Every show must have an end, have an end, have an end. Every show must have an end, da la de da."

THERAPIST: Okay, is that it? Is that it?

PATIENT: Yeah.

The sequence clearly makes reference to the patient's disruptive behavior in the dance class. The experience of being asked to leave the room was an actual one. In fact, this was a frequent occurrence prior to the teacher's asking the mother to take Sally out completely. The idea of transferring to a tumbling school was clearly a healthy adaptation on Sally's part. There, her hyperactivity would be less noticeable and she could channel her energies into more constructive directions. The sung sequences ("And threw her hat up into the air," "Every show must have an end...") were taken directly from the recital and reflect the patient's deep response to the performance. Although she saw it only once, she remembered verbatim significant segments.

In accordance with the above understanding of Sally's story, I responded.

THERAPIST: Do you want to make a play out of that story you just made? Do you want to make a play out of it?

PATIENT: What is a play?

THERAPIST: A play. A play is, you know, we'll act it out. We'll take the different parts. Okay?

PATIENT: Okay.

THERAPIST: All right. Who do you want to be now? Do you want to be the girl and I'll be the teacher or shall I be the girl and you'll be the teacher? What part do you want to be?

PATIENT (as she gets up from the chair): The girl.

THERAPIST: You want to be the girl? Okay.

PATIENT (excitedly jumps up and down, moves arms up and down, and has smile on face as she goes midway across the room to the couch and then sits on it).

THERAPIST (getting up from chair by table): Okay, I'll tell you what. I'll be the teacher. Come over here.

PATIENT (starts to move across room toward therapist).

THERAPIST: Okay, let's make believe that this is the dancing class first. Okay?

PATIENT (stands facing him about three feet away and nods head affirmatively).

THERAPIST: Okay. Come over here. Come closer (motioning to patient to come nearer to him). "Everybody dance and you mustn't run around or annoy the other children or else I'm going to have to send you outside the room Okay? Okay, everybody, let's see you dance."

PATIENT (puts hands on waist and twists body all around while standing in place; has back toward camera).

THERAPIST: Okay. I'll tell you what. (walks over to patient and switches places with her so that she is facing camera and therapist is semi-facing camera). Why don't you stand over here like this and I'll be the teacher over here? "Now let's see you dance."

PATIENT (practically repeats same dance motion of putting hands on waist and twisting body all around while standing in place as she did previously).

THERAPIST: Okay. "Are you going to bother the other children?"

PATIENT (lifts arms up and down): No.

THERAPIST: "Good." Shall I make believe I'm a girl bothering other children?

PATIENT (excitedly): Yes.

THERAPIST: Okay. (walks over to patient and stands by her side). Let's say I'm next to you in that class and you're trying to dance. Go ahead, you try to dance.

PATIENT (dances in place, lifting arms and legs).

THERAPIST: And I'm going to go around (bumping into patient and running around her), ha, ha, ha. I'm going to run around and I'm going to bother her. "Get out of my way." (dances all around patient who is laughing happily and amused by the whole thing). I run around and I bother all the children. And then the teacher says to me — she says (in stern tone), "You are very bad. You have to go out of this room because you're bothering everybody!"

PATIENT (excitedly jumping up and down, giggling and laughing).

THERAPIST: So I go (moves toward door and in crying, pleading voice). "Please don't send me out of the room. Oh, please."

PATIENT (so engrossed and amused that she is jumping up and down and laughing).

THERAPIST (changes position with back toward camera and switches back to stern tone of teacher): "You're very bad because you're running around and you're not listening to what I am saying!" So what happens?

PATIENT (excitedly makes a suggestion): She sends you out.

THERAPIST (goes to door, has left hand on doorknob, back toward camera and patient, pretending he is crying): "Oh, I don't want to go out. (opens door and goes halfway out). Oh, I don't want to go out (making crying, pleading, begging sounds). Please let me come back in." (closes door).

PATIENT (all the time thinking the situation is hilarious and continuously laughing and jumping up and down in place even after therapist leaves room).

PATIENT'S MOTHER (watching play from chair out of camera range): Go let Dr. Gardner back in the room.

PATIENT (who has stopped all action for a moment): Okay.

THERAPIST (knocking on the door from the outside; voice is still pleading): "Please let me come back in the room. (more knocks and in begging tone). Please let me come back. I promise I'll be good."

PATIENT (jumping excitedly again up and down and laughing at the same time): Okay. (then stops action and stands in front of door closet waiting for therapist to come back in).

THERAPIST (as he comes back into room): So does the teacher let

the boy come back? Oh, first make believe I'm a girl. Does the
teacher let the girl come back?

PATIENT (hands behind back standing in front of closet, in
serious tone): Yeah.

THERAPIST (standing next to patient): So what happens when the
girl comes back? Let's say the girl is back. What does she do?

PATIENT: I don't know.

THERAPIST: Is she good? Does she run around and bother the
other children? Does she listen to the teacher or what?

PATIENT: I don't know.

THERAPIST: Well, what happens is. . . Well, this child, this little
girl didn't listen. Once she came back into the class—let's say
you're starting to dance again (motions to patient to dance).
Go ahead, you start to dance.

PATIENT (following instructions, dances in place lifting one leg at
a time and has arms crossed in front of her).

THERAPIST: Well, instead of dancing like she was supposed to,
she starts running around the room again (immediately runs
gleefully around the patient and makes loud sounds) and she
didn't listen to the teacher and she just pushed around
(bumping into the patient who has begun to laugh excitedly
again) and wouldn't let anybody dance. And so what did the
teacher do?

PATIENT (excitedly): Send her out.

THERAPIST: The teacher said what?

PATIENT (jumping up and down and laughing): You try to go out.

THERAPIST (pretending he's crying and in mournful voice): "Oh,
I'll have to go out of the room again. (opens door and as he's
leaving) Oh, my goodness. . . I'll have to go out of the room
again."

PATIENT (still very excited and thoroughly engrossed—laughing
all the time and jumping up and down in place).

THERAPIST (knocks on door and begs to be allowed to come back
into room): "Please let me come back in. Please, please."

PATIENT (after hesitating a moment to see what was going to
happen next): Okay.

THERAPIST (entering room again): Well, what happened was

that the teacher said that she can't stand the class anymore and this girl couldn't stay in the class. And that was it. Now, what happened at the end of the year when they had the big recital?

PATIENT (staring into space).

THERAPIST: Where was this girl? Was she on the stage in the recital?

PATIENT: Yeah.

THERAPIST: No. Where was she?

PATIENT (jumping up and down): In the audience.

THERAPIST (as he moves toward chairs in front of table where session first began): Let's make believe she's sitting in the audience. All right? She is sitting in the audience. (sits down on chair).

PATIENT (has excitedly crossed the room midway, jumping and hopping around away from where therapist is sitting).

THERAPIST: She is sitting in the audience. Am I the girl sitting in the audience?

PATIENT (stops action for a moment and looks at therapist): Yeah.

THERAPIST: And are you on the stage?

PATIENT (dancing in place): Yeah.

THERAPIST: Were you the good girl?

PATIENT (still dancing in place): Yeah.

THERAPIST: And I'm the bad girl. Right? I'm the one who wouldn't listen to the teacher. So you're in the recital. Okay? (motions to patient) Come over here. Over here. (Phone rings and while therapist answers it, patient is singing, clapping, and dancing in place. Then she goes around in a circle, jumps down on the floor and does a half-somersault. Therapist finishes short conversation over phone and directs attention to patient.) All right, come on. We have the recital now. There's a recital. You're on the stage. Okay?

PATIENT (nods while dancing around).

THERAPIST (starting to cry): And I'm the girl sitting here in the audience.

PATIENT (dancing and jumping around in a circle and making gleeful sounds).

THERAPIST (crying louder): "Look at all those kids having fun and I have to sit here. Oh my."

PATIENT (getting further carried away and swept up with play; laughing and jumping around).

THERAPIST: What are you doing? Are you dancing on the stage?

PATIENT (drops to floor and tries to do a somersault, which is only half-successful; gets up and jumps around, making her own music).

THERAPIST: What are you doing? Are you dancing on the stage?

PATIENT (seems to be too caught up "performing" to answer therapist's questions).

THERAPIST: Okay, what am I doing here—the girl in the audience?

PATIENT (finally walks over to couch, which is located a few feet from therapist's chair, and sits down): Sitting.

THERAPIST: And how do I feel? (motions to patient)...Come over here.

PATIENT (bouncing up and down on couch from sitting position, oblivious to therapist's instructions): Sad.

THERAPIST: And how do I feel?

PATIENT: Sad.

THERAPIST: And what am I thinking?

PATIENT: You were in the. . .(mumbles). . .

THERAPIST: Am I thinking what? What am I thinking? (motions again to patient)...Come over here.

PATIENT (still bouncing up and down on couch): You were thinking you were in the recital.

THERAPIST: I am thinking that I was in the recital?

PATIENT: Yeah.

THERAPIST: But am I in the recital?

PATIENT (still bouncing on couch): No.

THERAPIST (beginning to pretend he's crying): "No, I'm sitting here very sad. Oh, I wish I could be in that recital."

PATIENT (gets up from couch and dances around in circle, humming or singing a tune).

THERAPIST (watches for a few seconds): Come here. I want to ask you a question.

PATIENT (heads toward therapist and looks at him for a moment and then heads for couch but doesn't sit down).

THERAPIST: "What can I do so that I can be in the recital next year?"

PATIENT (walking and dancing around): Try tumbling school.

THERAPIST: Tumbling school? What do I have to do there?

PATIENT (still moving around): Tumble.

THERAPIST: Uh huh. All right. Let's make believe it's tumbling school. Okay?

PATIENT (nods while moving around).

THERAPIST: Okay, here I am (getting up from chair) in tumbling school. Do you want to be in tumbling school? (motions to patient to come to him) Okay, come on, we're both in tumbling school. (patient stands by therapist's side) The teacher is teaching us how to tumble. Okay?

PATIENT (waiting to be told what to do).

THERAPIST: Okay, let's do some tumbles. Go ahead. Do a tumble.

PATIENT (lifts arms up above head and positions body as if she is about to do a cartwheel).

THERAPIST (imitates patient's stance and looks like he's about to do a cartwheel too): Go ahead.

PATIENT (runs forward instead of tumbling): Pretend you're doing it.

THERAPIST: Okay, I'll pretend I'm doing it. Like that (goes forward as if about to tumble). Okay, you over here.

PATIENT (gets back into position as if about to tumble again, but this time she does a half-cartwheel).

THERAPIST (pretends he tumbles but he spins body around; makes whirling sound; motions to patient): Okay, now come on over here. Now the teacher says (in stern voice), "Now everybody listen and be quiet." Now what do I do? What do I do?

PATIENT (moving up and down in place): I don't know.

THERAPIST: Am I quiet? Do I listen to the teacher or do I run around and bother the other children?

PATIENT: Run around.

THERAPIST: Well, this year I think I've learned my lesson. Last year I couldn't be in the dance recital so this year I'm going to be very careful to listen to the teacher so whenever she

says anything I'm not going to run around and bother the
other children, and I'm going to listen to what she says. All
right.

PATIENT (in low voice): All right.

THERAPIST: So what happens at the end of the year?

PATIENT: A recital (starts to walk away from therapist).

THERAPIST: Am I in the recital?

PATIENT (faces therapist): Yeah.

THERAPIST: Okay, let's make believe that this is the recital. Okay?

PATIENT (walks back and stands by therapist's side).

THERAPIST: Okay. "Here I am (gleefully takes a step to the side,
still facing patient) in the recital. Oh boy! I'm in the recital!
It's so much fun! Am I glad that I didn't run around."

PATIENT (jumping up and down excitedly in the middle of the
room).

THERAPIST: "Am I glad that I listened to the teacher. (motions to
patient) Come here. Let's be in the recital together."

PATIENT (eagerly runs over to therapist and stands by his side,
singing merrily).

THERAPIST: Okay. What should we do in the recital now?

PATIENT (singing and puts hand on head): Throw your head up
in the air (throws hand in air as if waving a hat and then jumps
up and down excitedly).

THERAPIST (copies patient's motion of pretending she's throwing
head up in the air while singing): "Throw your head up in
the air." Okay. Now what?

PATIENT (thinks for a second and then positions herself again as
if about to do a cartwheel with hands outstretched above her
head and one foot forward): Now.

THERAPIST (imitates patient's motion as if he is about to do a
cartwheel too): Like that. Okay.

PATIENT (as she does an actual cartwheel): Pretend to do this.

THERAPIST: Okay, I'll pretend to do this. (pretends to cartwheel,
spinning body around) "Oooh, it's hard! Wow! This is a fun
recital!"

PATIENT (jumps excitedly around, making her way to therapist's
side).

THERAPIST: "Am I glad I was good last year. Am I glad that I

didn't run around among the other children. Am I glad I
listened to the teacher. This recital is fun!" Okay, it's the end
of the recital. Shall we say good-bye?
PATIENT (has walked over to couch and sits down with a bounce):
    Yeah.
THERAPIST (motioning to patient to return by his side): Come on.
    Let's say good-bye.
PATIENT (walks over to therapist and half-facing camera and
    therapist, waves left hand): Good-bye.
THERAPIST: Do you want to watch this program on television?
PATIENT (as she makes her way to couch, which she bounces on):
    Yeah.
THERAPIST (walking out of camera range): Okay.

Although I have tried to include all the actions taking place,
the transcript cannot truly communicate the dramatizations.
Most prominent was the patient's excitement and its associated
hyperactivity. Although my story was designed to help the patient
reduce her hyperactivity, the very excitement of the dramatization tended to enhance it. However, the jumping up and down
was related to the excitement of making the play and similar
agitation would be seen with nonhyperactive children in similar
circumstances. Actually, I introduced nothing new in my play;
rather, I tried to reinforce the healthy messages exhibited in
Sally's story. There was no question that the playacting modality
is very attractive to children and messages communicated in this
way are certainly attended to and, I believe, incorporated into
the child's psychic structure.

# 4   CONCLUSION

The author summarizes the Mutual Storytelling Technique that
he has found useful in the treatment of a wide variety of
psychiatric disorders of children. In this method a story is first
elicited from the child. The therapist surmises its psychodynamic
meaning and then creates a story of his own—using the same
characters in a similar setting, but introducing what he considers
to be healthier adaptations than those revealed in the child's

story. More recently, he has found that dramatizing the story with the child enhances the therapeutic efficacy of the technique. In this article, the basic method is reviewed, the value of dramatization of the stories discussed, and illustrative case material is presented.

The reader who is interested in further information on the dramatization of mutually told stories may wish to refer to previous publications describing this technique.[1,2] Those interested in actually hearing therapist-patient dramatized sequences taken from audio and videotapes (with my comments and analyses) may wish to refer to my audio tape series.[3]

# FOOTNOTES

1. Richard A. Gardner, *Therapeutic Communication with Children: The Mutual Storytelling Technique* (New York: Jason Aronson, 1971).
2. Richard A. Gardner, "The Mutual Storytelling Technique," twelve one-hour tapes (New York: Jason Aronson, 1973).
3. Richard A. Gardner, *Psychotherapeutic Approaches to the Resistant Child* (New York: Jason Aronson, 1975).

BARBARA M. McINTYRE, Ph.D., is a professor and chairman of theatre at the University of Victoria, Victoria, B.C., Canada. From 1967 to 1969 she was director of the Children's Theatre Conference of the American Theatre Association, and has published widely on creative dramatics with specific reference to exceptional children. Her books include *Creative Drama in the Elementary School.*

*Chapter 13*

# DRAMA AS AN ADJUNCT TO SPEECH THERAPY FOR CHILDREN

Barbara M. McIntyre

## 1 INTRODUCTION

Man's ability to communicate his ideas and feelings through articulate speech is one of the basic ways in which he differs from other mammals. This ability provides a profitable and successful avenue of communication for the majority of people. For some, however, communication through speech is exceedingly difficult and often painful. Speech is to them a problem. They are the speech and hearing handicapped.

According to generally accepted surveys, approximately six percent of the elementary and secondary school population in North America have speech deficiencies sufficiently serious to be classed as speech defectives. This indicates that children with speech and hearing problems form one of the largest groups classed as handicapped.

Charles Van Riper, a pioneer in the field of speech and hearing disorders, writes:

> Speech is defective when it deviates so far from the speech of other people that it calls attention to itself, interferes with communication or causes its possessor to be maladjusted.[1]

Speech pathologists must evaluate the speech of each client individually in order to understand the specifics of the problem. The diagnosis must

237

reflect the reality of the situation, the etiology of the problem and provide a focus for therapy.

> Diagnosis is an empty exercise in test administration, data collection and client evaluation if it fails to provide logical suggestions for therapy.[2]

Only a certified speech pathologist is qualified to accurately assess the situation and prescribe speech therapy.

Following the diagnosis of the child's speech problem, the speech pathologist recommends the necessary treatment. When direct speech therapy is indicated, it must be conducted by a speech pathologist or a clinician. The clinician may use many dramatic techniques, such as role playing and puppetry. These are conducted on an individual basis and directed toward the specific remediation of the child's speech difficulty. There may be occasions, however, when a clinician in conjunction with a child guidance counselor, a pediatrician, a teacher, or another professional may suggest that the child pursue some artistic or humanistic group activity such as creative drama as a therapeutic measure.

> Speech therapy shares with other fields of human relations the goal of helping each individual to change behavior in interpersonal relationships to the extent that he can function in such relationships with greater relative adequacy in terms of satisfaction and security.[3]

According to leaders in the speech and hearing profession, therapy goals must focus on a learning atmosphere. In addition to an opportunity to learn speech skills, therapy needs to provide emotional and intellectual security. To some extent these broad humanistic goals parallel the stated goals for child participation in drama therapy. Drama leaders such as Ward,[4] Siks,[5] McCaslin[6] and Courtney[7] in North America, and Way[8] and Heathcote[9] in England, claim that participation in creative drama provides opportunities for the children to grow personally, socially, emotionally and intellectually. Although scientific documented research into the effects of participation in creative drama is slight, there is a great deal of philosophical and observational evidence to support such claims.

Ludwig[10] reported that a group of kindergarten children who participated in a twelve week program of creative drama with emphasis on listening made a significantly greater improvement in articulation than did their controls. I found in a related study with preadolescents[11] that the participating children significantly reduced the number of articulation errors during a six week summer program of creative activities of which drama was one. It should be noted that in both these studies factors other than the dramatic activities were obviously operating. In both instances group activity was emphasized and children with normal speech interacted with the experimental groups. It would appear, then, that group activity which has as one of its goals the personal, intellectual and emotional development of the participants, and includes handicapped and non-handicapped children, could be an excellent adjunct to speech therapy. Such an activity is creative drama.

As an adjunct to speech therapy, drama may be utilized as diagnostic observation, therapeutic experience and as an active part of a speech improvement program in the schools.

## 2  THE DRAMATIC PROCESS

There are many ways of conducting creative drama. The variations depend largely on the personality, background and training of the leader involved. The five-step dramatic process I have outlined[12] is similar to the approach advocated by many drama specialists. Because of the author's training and experience in speech pathology, however, the process is particularly appropriate when drama is utilized as an adjunct to speech therapy. It includes five steps: (1) sense awareness; (2) movement; (3) characterization; (4) improvisation; and (5) dramatization.

Introductory sessions in drama stress the development of the senses — in particular, listening, seeing and feeling. Simple sensory games are planned and played, and every child is involved. The first games center on general listening and seeing activities. Gradually gross listening and looking gives way to conscious isolation and identification of specific sounds and sights and feelings. Sound instruments, sound effects recordings, tape recorders, slides, films and pictures may be used to help stimulate the children's imagination and interest in their senses. All activities

are conducted in an open space and involve freedom of movement. At one time a group of children may imagine that they are
pirates being led on a journey by night sounds. At another time
they may imagine themselves as space men listening and reacting
to ground control. A picture, an artifact, or music might
stimulate an exciting journey through a storm-torn desert. Whatever
the activity, the teacher's goal at this point will be the isolation and
identification of sense impressions and their coordination in active
dramatic play.

Correlated with sense awareness and incorporated into all activities is the development of the next step — non-verbal communication
through bodily movement. Starting with the concepts presented
by Boorman,[13] the children are encouraged to explore the space
around them. They use a variety of body shapes — curved,
angular and straight — at different levels — high, medium and
low, executed with contrasting efforts — sustained, sudden and
relaxed. These explorations are linked to an understanding of the
relationship between physical movement and the expression of
ideas and emotions.

These movement explorations lead naturally into characterization. With the guidance of the teacher, the children develop
experiences and take on the roles of differing characters. They
discuss and create characters and try them on to see how it feels.
With increased awareness of their senses and the relationship between physical action and feeling, they are able to become the
wicked witch, the happy space man, the benevolent mayor, or the
frightened child. Within an imagined environment in a forest, a
launching site, a busy street or a playground, they show through
movement and speech how these characters feel and react to one
another in an exciting situation — a storm, an accident, a parade,
or a ball game. Many variations in character are possible as the
children experiment with different roles in a variety of environments. They gain skill in showing who they are, where they
are, what they are doing, why they are doing it and how they feel
about it.

The improvisational step in the dramatic process encourages
the development of speech communication between characters.

Here the participants develop original dramatic incidents without scripts. The ideas for the setting, characters and conflict are organized with the help of the teacher into an improvised play. The resolution of the conflict, however, is usually not spelled out prior to the playing. An improvisation may deal with a situation of immediate interest such as a conflict between teacher and child or an imaginary problem such as the situation of two boys being on a camping trip and losing radio communication. Whatever the situation involved or the characters projected, emphasis is on the solving of the problem or completing the task through verbal communication.

The dramatization step is the culmination of the four previous ones. Here the children play out stories, poems, news events, historical incidents and social situations based on their understanding of ideas, frequently originated by others. Utilizing the skills developed previously, they informally play out a sequence of events which has a beginning, a middle and an end. Here the children's pre-planning and sequencing become very important and a new element of individual and group evaluation is introduced. Starting generally with the process suggested by Siks,[14] the teacher sets the mood, assists in the selection of material, guides in the planning, the playing and in the evaluation.

Although these five steps can be isolated and observed they form no rigid format. Understanding of the free flow of ideas across and within the steps is very important. Children with speech problems need help in developing sense awareness; particularly listening, understanding, and experiencing the expressive use of their bodies, playing different roles with their peers, using spontaneous verbal communication and developing the sequencing of their thoughts and ideas. They further need to consciously evaluate their progress in verbal communication. A skilled drama teacher or drama therapist, armed with a loosely constructed plan, but with the clear objective of providing opportunities for children's physical, emotional, intellectual and creative growth, may find this five-step process beneficial for all children, but particularly so for those with problems in verbal and non-verbal communication.

## 3   DRAMA AND DIAGNOSTIC OBSERVATION

Traditional speech evaluations are conducted on an individual basis in surroundings frequently strange to the child and by persons with whom he is unfamiliar. A variety of tests and diagnostic techniques are carried out. At times they may include some dramatic activity such as role playing or puppetry, but information concerning the child's behavior and interaction with his peers is not readily obtained. The opportunity to observe the child in a familiar setting working with other children may prove profitable, particularly if there is some confusion concerning the diagnosis or treatment of the problem. In such cases it may be very helpful to observe the child participating in a drama group. Demonstration classes of creative drama connected with university and college programs often provide such opportunities. At other times a school or community drama program may be available. The following example may serve to illustrate the value of such observation.

John was a bright eight-year-old boy who was referred to a university speech clinic for a stuttering problem. During the diagnostic interview, although some nonfluency was observed, it did not appear to be serious. Both parents and teacher, however, were very concerned. After the examination, it was decided that John should report to the clinic once a month and join the creative drama class which was held weekly at the university. John attended the class and appeared to enjoy the sessions. He cooperated well with both teacher and the rest of the children. One day the children were dramatizing the story of King Midas and the Golden Touch. John volunteered to play King Midas. The role of King Midas had previously been played as a grumpy old man. John's Midas was completely different. He yelled and screamed and ordered servants around and almost forgot the plot of the story. The rest of the children were impressed with John's idea of the king and an excited discussion followed. They questioned the meanness of the king and asked John why he played him this way.

"He was a mean man," John said. "Anyone who is mean enough to let his little girl turn into gold is as mean as my teacher."

The incident was reported to the speech pathologist. During her next session with John she asked him about his teacher. John admitted that he heartily disliked her. He said that she kept "bugging him" about his speech and didn't let him "read out loud like the other kids" and consistently told him to "slow down." When asked why he hadn't said something about it before, John said he didn't want to make any trouble. The incident was reported to the parents and the teacher. John was quietly moved to another class, continued the drama sessions and gradually decreased his stuttering.

Diagnostic observation of speech defective children within a creative drama class is also available in some schools. The following is such an example.

Mary was a pretty, apparently well-behaved ten-year-old with a severe articulation problem. The speech clinician assigned to the school was concerned at the lack of progress she was making. In spite of weekly therapy sessions, there appeared to be no improvement in Mary's speech. The clinician talked with Mary's teacher, but with little success. The teacher reported that Mary had few friends.

"It is hard to explain," she said. "She is quiet and unobtrusive, but she seems continually in the way. I sympathize with the children. She is a child very hard to love."

"Her mother feels that the children do not like her because of her speech," the clinician continued.

"I don't think that is the reason," the teacher replied. "I can't figure it out."

Shortly after this conversation, an extracurricular class of creative drama was organized. The speech clinician suggested that Mary join the group. The class was conducted by an eager graduate student, whose purpose was to promote more drama in the schools. In order to create interest, she invited the teachers to observe the classes. The speech clinician took advantage of the offer and began attending regularly.

On the surface the classes appeared to be progressing very well. The children played sense awareness and movement games with enthusiasm and excitement. There did, however, appear to be a "ganging up" against Mary. The clinician noted that she was left out frequently. At a conference with Mary's mother, the speech clinician heard the same complaint. "It is because of her speech that the children don't like her. If this keeps up, I'm going to withdraw her from the class."

The next creative drama class attended by the clinician emphasized characterization. Both the speech clinician and Mary's teacher attended and took careful notes on the proceedings. They noticed that none of the children appeared to have much difficulty in understanding what Mary said. The clinician observed, however, that immediately following every playing, Mary rushed to the teacher's side with comments concerning other children.

"Don't you think David's giant was too big and loud? Connie really didn't look like a ballet dancer. Jeff kept whispering to John instead of concentrating on his character."

As the playing out of the characters proceeded, Mary quietly but skillfully twisted the action and roles of the other children and pointed up their deficiencies to the inexperienced teacher.

"That's what she does all the time," the classroom teacher whispered. "It is very easy to see during drama. Mary is continually playing the role of the good little tattletale."

In the weeks that followed, the speech clinician held a conference with the classroom teacher, the drama teacher and Mary's mother. These four adults had observed Mary's unconscious bid for attention. They worked out a strategy founded on a different attitude toward Mary. As their attitudes changed, so did the attitudes of the participating children. Gradually Mary's behavior changed and the children included her more readily in their activities. Speech progress continued to be slow, but it was steady.

"I believe it was something within the dynamics of the dramatic process that allowed us to see Mary's interpersonal problem," the speech clinician reported to her supervisor.

At any rate, the observation made during this drama class was a very successful adjunct to Mary's speech therapy.

# 4 DRAMA AS A THERAPEUTIC EXPERIENCE

In the previously discussed examples more than diagnostic observation can be noted. In each case something triggered the release and expression of strong emotion which, when observed by a speech specialist, resulted in a better understanding of the child and his problem. Although the creative drama classes were not designed to effect specific behavioral changes, therapeutic results were noted. The following example illustrates the long, slow, progressive therapeutic effect of drama as an adjunct to therapy.

Eddie had a repaired cleft palate and the speech nasality that usually accompanies this physical defect. He was nearly eight years old when he first came for evaluation. His speech, though nasal, was easily understood, but Eddie was a silent child. He spoke when absolutely necessary and then in monosyllables. His mother reported that he was extremely self-conscious about his mouth and his speech. Speech therapy was indicated and a weekly program was set up. In conjunction with the therapy, it was suggested that he register for a drama group that met weekly. Eddie did not want to join the class. His mother, however, overruled him, and he appeared at class on the opening day. At first he refused to participate and sat at the side of the room. It took more than a month's time before he quietly joined in the dramatic play.

From the moment Eddie began to participate it was obvious that he possessed an unusually graceful body. His ability to change from a "slithering" snake to an "alert" ostrich won the admiration of his classmates. At first he spoke very little, but his concentration on an idea and his use of pantomimic action were very effective. Gradually he began to participate more actively and slowly he used more speech. He expressed his ideas with a minimum of words and a maximum of physical action. An imaginary journey through a steaming jungle, with Eddie as leader, took class members through a maze of trees and swamps full of strange sounds and dangerous animals. Eddie made all the animal sounds and reacted accordingly.

"I could almost feel that lion's breath," said one of the children. "Eddie's such a good leader!"

Eddie's speech therapy sessions were discontinued by the time his second year of drama began.

"I'm coming to the creative drama class just the same," he told the teacher. "I'll be there to help with the new kids," he assured her. Over the course of that year he changed from being a physically active member of the class to the verbally proficient, unquestioned leader. He seemed to forget that his speech was somewhat nasal and volunteered to play as many roles as possible. His mother was pleased with his progress, but she was disappointed when his classroom teacher reported that he remained silent in the school classroom.

When registration for a third year of creative drama was discussed, Eddie was not too enthusiastic.

"We'll get mostly new kids in the group, and we'll have to start back at the beginning," he protested. "Maybe I'll just come over once in a while to help you out," he told the teacher. "I'm pretty busy with the scouts."

About a month later the speech pathologist and drama teacher met with Eddie's mother.

"I wanted to tell you both," she said, "that I'm not as worried about him now. His speech isn't going to hold him back."

The realization of this had come to her when she attended a scout meeting at which the boys were to receive badges. She had known in advance that Eddie was to receive an award. What she did not know was that he had been chosen by the boys to make a presentation to the retiring scout master. With simple assurance and acceptable speech, Eddie thanked the leader and presented the gift before an audience of nearly one hundred persons.

"No one seemed to notice the nasality," his mother said. "Everyone commented on what he said and the poise with which he said it. I want you to know Eddie's explanation for his success."

"It was easy," he had explained. "It was just like creative drama. You have something to say, so you say it."

Eddie's speech had not changed greatly over the period of years. It was his attitude toward his speech that had changed. He was the beneficiary of the therapeutic effects of creative drama as an adjunct to speech therapy.

# 5 DRAMA AND SPEECH IMPROVEMENT

The speech improvement program in schools is the responsibility of both the classroom teacher and the speech pathologist or clinician. According to Eisenson and Ogilvie, the aims of the curricula involved are threefold:

> (1) to correct any speech difficulty that calls attention to itself, causes the child undue concern or detracts seriously from his communicative ability; (2) to help him eliminate minor articulation and voice difficulties and non-standard pronunciations if he and the teacher elect this option; and (3) to assist him to become an effective speaker and listener.[15]

The first aim is the responsibility of the speech pathologist. It is accomplished by direct speech therapy conducted outside the classroom. The second and third aims are the responsibility of the classroom teacher with the supervised support of the speech pathologist. Only a small number of children are involved in the accomplishment of the first aim, but the total classroom population is involved with the accomplishment of the second and third.

The speech improvement program takes place within the classroom, most frequently as a part of the language and speech arts.

> It consists of systematic instruction in oral communication which has as its purpose the development of articulation, voice and language abilities that enable all children to communicate their ideas effectively. Speech improvement is not concerned with the work of the speech clinician with speech and hearing handicapped children outside the regular classroom.[16]

This systematic instruction must be developed by the classroom teacher and take into consideration the age, experience and needs of the children in the class. The total class, including those children receiving direct therapy outside of the classroom, should participate. A broad comprehensive program in speech improvement will aim to develop the following skills through participation in the suggested activities:

(1) Development of listening skills. Listening experiences and games for gaining information, enjoyment and solutions to problems are important. However, exercise and ideas for the isolation, identification and discrimination of speech sounds are vital.

Recorded programs such as *Listening with Mr. Bunny Big Ears*[17] and *Count Down for Listening*[18] were developed specifically for this purpose and may be helpful, as are listening and speech drills.

(2) Development of non-verbal communication skills. Exercises in bodily movement, gesture and pantomime may encourage relaxation and understanding of the relationship between language and movement. Here Boorman's *Dance and Language Experience*[19] may prove exciting for the younger children.

(3) Development of individual verbal communication skills. Individual and small group activities which include role playing, spontaneous and planned conversations, introductions, problem solving discussions, as well as regular speech articulation games and drills stimulate interest in improving speech. Opportunities to present speeches to entertain, to inform or convince also help the children use their skills creatively. Suggestions by Logan, Logan and Paterson[20] are very helpful.

(4) Development of verbal group communication skills. Here group experiences and activities which include improvisations, debate, parliamentary procedure, radio and television discussions, and play reading provide excellent stimulation for the development of group communication skills.

(5) Development of the ability to logically organize and clearly express ideas, thoughts and concepts. Experiences which culminate in the use of all the communication skills are recommended. These include the formal and informal dramatization of stories, poems and plays, participation in simulated conferences, debates and group discussions.

To a great extent the five sets of suggested activities for the development of speech improvement parallel the five steps in the previously discussed dramatic process. It is in this manner that creative drama can be seen as an adjunct to speech improvement programs.

## FOOTNOTES

1. C. Van Riper, *Speech Correction, Principles and Methods* (Englewood Cliffs, N.J.: Prentice-Hall, 1963).

2. Lon T. Emerick and John T. Hatten, *Diagnosis and Evaluation in Speech Pathology* (Englewood Cliffs, N.J.: Prentice-Hall, 1974), p. 8.
3. O. Backus and J. Beasley, *Speech Therapy with Children* (New York: Houghton Mifflin, 1951).
4. Winifred Ward, *Playmaking with Children* (New York: Appleton-Century-Crofts, 1957).
5. Geraldine Siks, *Creative Dramatics: An Art for Children* (New York: Harper & Row, 1958).
6. Nellie McCaslin, *Creative Dramatics in the Classroom* (New York: David McKay, 1968).
7. Richard Courtney, *Teaching Drama* (London: Cassell, 1965).
8. Brian Way, *Development through Drama* (London: Longman, 1968).
9. Dorothy Heathcote, "Drama as Education," in *Children and Drama,* ed. Nellie McCaslin (New York: David McKay, 1975).
10. C. Ludwig, *The Effects of Creative Dramatics Activities upon the Articulation Skills of Kindergarten Children,"* (Master's thesis, University of Pittsburgh, 1955).
11. Barbara McIntyre, "The Effect of a Program of Creative Activities upon the Articulation Skills of Children with Speech Disorders," *Speech Monographs* 25 (1958): 42-48.
12. Barbara McIntyre, *Creative Drama in the Elementary School* (Itasca, Ill.: F. E. Peacock, 1974).
13. Joyce Boorman, *Creative Dance in Grades Four to Six* (Don Mills, Ontario: Longman, 1971).
14. Siks, *Creative Dramatics.*
15. Jon Eisenson and Maidel Ogilvie, *Speech Correction in the Schools* (New York: Macmillan, 1971).
16. Geraldine Garrison, "Speech Improvement,"*Journal of Speech and Hearing Disorders,* Monograph Supplement 8 (July 1961).
17. "Listening with Mr. Bunny Big Ears," *Language Development and Speech Improvement through Dramatic Play for Primary Age Children: A Series of Twenty-four Lessons* (Freeport, N.Y.: Educational Activities, 1965).
18. "Count Down for Listening," *Speech Improvement Series of Twenty-four Lessons for Intermediate Grades* (Freeport, N.Y.: Educational Activities, 1969).
19. Joyce Boorman, *Dance and Language Experience with Children* (Don Mills, Ontario: Longman, 1973).
20. Lillian M. Logan, Virgil G. Logan, and Leona Paterson, *Creative Communication: Teaching the Language Arts* (Toronto: McGraw Hill Ryerson, 1972).

IRWIN M. MARCUS, M.D., is a clinical professor of psychiatry at Louisiana State University Medical School, New Orleans, and an adjunct professor at Tulane University's School of Social Work. He is also a supervising and training analyst in adult and child analysis, and chairman of the child/adolescent division of the New Orleans Psychoanalytic Institute.

*Chapter 14*

# DRAMA THERAPY IN COSTUME

Irwin M. Marcus

## 1  INTRODUCTION

Play patterns of the younger child allow vivid communication and the participation of others, but the grade school child prefers props to support his role in the fantasy. Therefore, costumes are provided in abundance for the purpose of setting the stage for dramatic play. In turn, this reopens an avenue that was once so pleasurable and useful for expressing emotional and conflicting experiences. Thus, the costume technique is designed to combine the advantages of the situational method and free play. Children who are disturbed because they have had to endure traumatic experiences can work toward mastery through playful repetition of more digestible portions of these events. By changing roles, children who were passive victims can become active aggressors. Their feelings of painful helplessness can be re-experienced with a happier, stronger, and successful conclusion. Although play is usually not complete abandon, there is sufficient relief from both reality and the conscience to allow for a display of the child's fantasies about himself and others. Play enables the ego to deal with the external pressures of reality and with the intrapsychic impact of impulses and conscience. With more complete emotional involvement in the fantasies of play, the child has a greater outlet for his anxiety and can experience the pleasure of wish fulfillment.

During the years of development and maturation, there are

251

changes in the child's motivations, dynamics, and methods of play. A number of excellent papers have been concerned with various aspects of the theory of play; among them are those of Sigmund Freud,[1] Anna Freud,[2] Erikson,[3] Waelder,[4] Ernst Kris,[5] Piaget,[6] and Peller.[7]

Fantasy life underlies all human activities and retains its basic themes, although during the course of healthy development reality issues will have a stronger influence upon the individual. Whereas the younger child can express his fantasies spontaneously with whatever material is available, the older child is less free in this respect. The latter may show initiative and creativity on an independent basis, yet he tends to require the cooperation of others for role playing and support in his more formalized imaginative games. Thus, the older child prefers real materials and more true to life situations, or stories he has seen or experienced in other ways. The limitations placed upon the type of communication an older child will permit, either in play or directly, is a reflection of his defenses and his fears of the fantasy content.

Experienced and skillful therapists are able to work with the various disguised manifestations of underlying mother-child or child-father and sibling relationships and conflicts. The transformations are seen in the child's sports, hobbies, secret clubs, and his intense feelings over winning and losing the great variety of structured popular games. Play behavior in the latency period is characterized by defenses that veer toward games which lack spontaneity, and tends to be conventional and competitive, with relatively little emotional content. The older child is gradually moving away from the disappointments and frustrations of his earlier dependency upon his family. With developmental changes, he is ready to seek the pleasures and security of new object relations through identifications with peer group and parentlike figures. The desire of an older child to play the usual games considered appropriate for his age, helps his defense against his earlier family conflicts by clinging to impersonal activity and shifting his competitive feelings toward his peers. However, this quality of ego development can be a real barrier to communication between a child and therapist, when the child dedicates himself to concealing his feeling and is ashamed of his daydreams. Furthermore, the latency period is the time when adults expect the child to conform, to accept limitations, to develop good learning and study habits, skills, and group behavior. Thus, his anxieties are often met with reassurance, logical arguments, or ridicule which fosters the child's defenses against communication of his fantasies.

Utilizing the knowledge of play theory, drama therapy in costume deliberately stimulates a more spontaneous play pattern in older children. The intent is to revive the imaginative play of the earlier years in a manner that would diminish the defensive embarrassment frequently produced by the usual play materials. Although "dress-up" games are part of Oedipal period play, its Anlage may be seen in the early imitation and identification activities, when the child experiences the pleasure of closeness with mother and father through clumping around the house in their shoes and decorating himself with any other item of apparel he can snatch from the household. The popularity of the box of old hats, sometimes included in a nursery school setting, is an example of the natural attraction of children to "dress-up" games. It is an activity which is permissible at times in all ages, and thus resistance to this play is less likely to occur. The mutual pleasure of costume play enhances the likelihood of the child's returning to the same materials for more consistent "working through" of disturbed feelings and conflicts. In contrast, the anxiety or hostility displayed in activities of play where there is less pleasure, and the therapist's role is more vague in the child's mind, may contribute to the disruption of play.

## 2  RATIONALE

Anyone who wishes to relate to children must know how to play or converse with them. Therapists are at times "kept in the dark," and at a considerable distance in the relationship, because a child may reject playing with dolls or puppets, would rather play a game or color a picture than paint freely or play with clay. Costumes are natural equipment within the current experiences of both the child and the therapist. The therapist at varying times throughout his life will "dress-up" for costume parties or events,

DRAMA IN THERAPY: VOL. I

as a not infrequent experience in social "fun" activities. The basic premise of this paper is easily observed among adults in New Orleans during Mardi Gras.

I analyzed a married woman who had a frigidity problem. She reported that prior to therapy she dressed as a "baby," her regression from the Oedipal conflicts. In a later phase, she spontaneously selected the role of a "flapper." A patient who had to fashion a costume for his "date" at a party created a "nun's outfit" for her, and in analysis recalled he once heard someone say she was promiscuous, but he rejected the idea because of his affection for her. Another woman, with sexual frustration as one of her problems, repeatedly dressed in skin-tight leotards as a "devil." A homosexual man once dressed as a "bum," but with a very large nose, whereas another homosexual patient could never decide what he wanted to wear, reflecting his identity problem. Finally, there are always a number of adults who dress as the opposite sex whenever costumes are permitted for an occasion, an obvious revelation of unresolved conflicts.

In drama therapy in costume, the therapist does not dress up nor, in my experience, does the child require this. The costumes are for the patients. The therapist remains an adult with his responses geared to the reality of therapy, and he should not slip into acting out his own unresolved or revived conflicts. However, the ability of a therapist to be an adult who can understand and still be with the child in his fantasy play is a unique and essential quality of child therapy. The basic principles are no different with this form of drama therapy. The child's need for the therapist to accept a role is more dependent upon the therapist's response than the latter's appearance in a costume. The therapist's anxiety about "what does this mean?" when viewing certain other play activities is diminished and replaced with the increased security of feeling a sense of mastery through improved contact and communication with the child.

A striking aspect of drama therapy in costume is the ease with which older children can act out vital unconscious material without sufficient awareness to intensify anxiety and, thereby, resistance. The complementary role assigned to the therapist by the child allows the therapist to engage in meaningful responses, which promotes further communication and fosters problem solving. If the child is suffering from a neurotic illness, the interpretive possibilities open to the therapist are well known to those with experience in the field. The fantasy play may be linked with the significant episodes and figures in the child's real life; or the therapist may call attention to resemblances between play situations and the real relationships in a manner that allows the defenses to be worked upon. Metaphoric interpretation may be used when the assessment of the child's ego strength suggests that a distance must be maintained between the fantasy and the conscious awareness of the child — although, of course, the therapist must eventually bring the known conflicts into consciousness. When regressions are already present or easily evoked, as in the borderline and psychotic states, tenuous object relations can at least be maintained by confining interpretations to the patient's own regressed language, as Ekstein and Wallerstein show.[8] Repetitious play on the regressed level, as long as the contact remains, provides a foundation for later, more mature identifications and the emergence of secondary-process thinking.

In therapy, the traumatic experience, conflict, and anxiety must be externalized and brought into the child-therapist relationship. As Anna Freud[9] noted, fruitful work in child therapy requires a "positive attachment." Since the specific play roles become the chief avenue for communication, the context of the emotion is more readily recognized and handled, thus permitting the therapist to sustain his position as the child's ally. A trusting and meaningful relationship evolves from friendly playful activities as such. This form of play therapy allows the therapist to communicate with the child on whatever level the child presents. "Playing out" fantasies, feelings, and traumatizing situations through "make-believe," emphasizes the demarcation between reality and fantasy, while bridging the gap with communication and understanding. Thus, the therapeutic nature of the dramatic play is promoted through sharing the disguised experience and mood, through closeness, mutuality, good communication, and understanding of the specific anxieties which accompany the fantasies.

In all the techniques of play therapy, varying roles are explicitly or, more often, implicitly assigned to the therapist and assumed by the patient, depending upon the child's needs at the time. However, part of the difficulty in practicing and teaching play therapy is precisely the problem of understanding the child's communications through play. Unfortunately, this factor may impart in the minds of parents, student therapists, and others a mystical and esoteric quality to the direct treatment of children. Costumes as a stimulus for imaginative play clarify the explicit nature of the role and utilize the child's need for motility, activity, and defensive disguise.

# 3  METHODOLOGY

What is actually done when drama therapy utilizes the costume technique which I have developed?[10] How are the procedures applied by the therapist and integrated by the patient? This is best demonstrated with an actual case, Evan, a nine-year-old boy referred to me because he was a slow learner and about two years behind in schoolwork. He seemed confused and incapable of following directions. Teachers complained of his daydreaming and inability to concentrate. He was effeminate in his mannerisms and submissive in his relationship to his twin brother. His constant and pervasive lying included serious distortions about his teachers, friends, and other adults. He stole, but accused others when objects were missing and later found to be in his possession.

In psychological testing Evan achieved an I.Q. on the Verbal Scale of 94, on Performance 92, and on the Full Scale of 92. It was difficult for the examiner to understand his stories on the Apperception Test, but one could grasp his sadness, feeling of loneliness, and fears that his mother would kill him. Both he and his brother showed ego disorganization. His schizophrenic mother had been hospitalized for several years, and since the age of two he had been in institutions and foster homes. Sessions were conducted weekly, for fifty minutes, with myself as therapist. The costumes included the following: those appropriate for a baby, mother, father, doctor, superman, witch, devil, clown, skeleton, ballerina, and three large pieces of colored cloth for a self-designed outfit.

The total length of therapy was one and a half years, with one interruption for a month of summer vacation.

Evan was shy and reluctant about selecting a costume from the many hanging in open display and denied having any memories of play with costumes. In low, hushed tones he recalled various situations in which he was deprived of a variety of toys and play materials. His actions and communications were highly inhibited and constricted. He preferred to find a chair, sit down, and stare with a blank expression—a response that frequently causes therapists to become frustrated. However, the therapist's sympathetic responses to Evan's past and present situations, and continued encouragement to try making up a play with the costumes, gradually succeeded. Evan cautiously examined each costume and finally selected the mother's outfit. He began playing the role of a teacher, asking the therapist to be the principal, and at other times the teacher's husband. He prepared large meals for the family, gave his children money for food, and in the school play he instructed the children, using a nearby blackboard, and assured them that they would pass.

The theme of a good mother who fed her children well, prevailed for many sessions. The therapist commented on Evan's great concern that the children be fed. He responded by recollecting that others had told him his mother was sick and could not take care of him, and that he longed for his mother. In time, the therapist mentioned that sometimes children are very angry about their mothers leaving them. Evan seemed to have a minimal response to this comment, but the sessions gradually shifted into a detective story. He reported a woman murdered because she murdered her children. However, the good woman who punished the bad mother would in turn be punished by the police. We talked about people being afraid to say their angry thoughts because of fear of being punished. The therapist interpreted that sometimes very sad children have very angry thoughts that frighten them, because they are afraid they will be punished by having to live away from their homes. During this phase of the play, Evan interjected thoughts about the fantasied cold weather in the play, and of how he hated to be "out in the cold."

Evan later switched into the role of the ghost of the bad mother (stimulated by his selecting the skeleton costume during this phase) who had been murdered in previous sessions. There was much anxious and excited play about coffins and a ghost seeking revenge. In the end, the ghost was defeated by the therapist, who was assigned the role of policeman. Evan began to show overt warmth toward the therapist at this stage, being reluctant to leave at the end of the sessions, hugging the therapist upon leaving and arriving, and expressing eagerness about the next visit of his social worker who would transport him. He became more responsive and communicative with her during their time together. The sessions shifted to his playing the wife in a loving marriage. During this phase, among his many comments, he exclaimed, "Darling, darling, darling, hold me in your arms." In these periods we were able to talk about his fantasies about his father (who had deserted them), his wishes to have his father back, his fears about whether his father had hurt his mother, his fears about being hurt himself, and his fantasy that the only way a boy could be loved is to be like a girl. However, he had another solution to being loved which became apparent in the following sessions when he selected, for the first time, the baby costume. In the baby role, he arranged the chairs into a bed and curled into the foetal position, made goo-goo sounds, engaged in rocking motions, and sucked his thumb. The satisfaction and regression on this level of play were so intense that, for a while, he was inaccessible to contact. However, in coming out of the baby role, he was exuberant, smiled happily, and seemed much more relaxed.

The therapist did not appear to have any specific role during the foregoing, other than to allow Evan the gratification of his longing for the fantasied pleasures of being an infant again. This time he could imagine starting life with a new parent figure, the therapist. The therapist commented on how children who are unhappy wish to be a baby again and have new parents who will take care of them: to love and be loved. Evan responded very strongly with memories of a foster home he loved before he was shifted into the institution. I commented on his disappointments in the past and concern about trusting each new person in his life, including the therapist. His costume play then vacillated between the role of baby and that of a mother, re-enacting a cruel mother who hated her baby, whom he gave his brother's name. During these sessions he expressed a great deal of hostility toward his brother, and verbalized his feeling of being hated by his mother. With self-designed costumes from the pieces of colored cloth, he became a cruel queen and captured an explorer (the therapist) who had landed on "her" planet. The explorer was tortured in many ways, whipped, shot with ray guns, and made into a weak, submissive man.

His fantasy patterns showed marked sadomasochistic features. There were many variations of his fears of being injured, his self-image of being castrated, and his desire for and fear of inflicting destruction. His castration anxiety and sense of helplessness were translated into the fears of the explorer, and the resemblance of the cruel queen to a hated and feared mother were interpreted. His image of women as castrating, vindictive, dangerous torturers of men necessitated concealing his own masculinity. In response to the therapist's query about what made the queen so mad, he replied that "her face had been burned off by old men." He later remarked about women having to be cut open to take their babies out. Periods of decreased anxiety followed as the foregoing was repeatedly worked through. In later sessions he assigned the doctor role to the therapist to repair the damaged queen.

After several months of therapy, progress reports prepared by his social worker indicated that he had become more aggressive and defended himself in a physical encounter with another boy. His effeminate behavior diminished, and he showed improved ability to tolerate frustration, to accept discipline and disappointments. He became more demonstrative in expressing affection for the worker. After a year of therapy, his academic work began to show real improvement. His intense interest in the costumes gradually diminished, his communications became more direct, and he manifested a growing interest in typical organized boys' games.

The history of Evan was one of severe neglect early in life. His instinctual life could not be combined with the pleasurable sensory stimulation of good mothering. He experienced too much real deprivation and frustration which impaired the adequate development of his ego. Combining instinctual tensions with only fragmented perceptions causes a child to produce distorted fantasy perceptions of his environment. The result is a diminished attentiveness to the outside world, greater absorption in unconscious fantasies, gratifying daydreams, and impaired reality testing. With his ego organization thus disturbed, Evan's instinctual tensions were frequently relieved through "nonsense" and "silly" talk and behavior. His energies were dissipated by these conditions, and a severe learning and behavior problem was inevitable. His hunger for a mothering relationship caused him to cling to primitive, distorted identifications with mother figures and to be submissive and dependent upon his brother and other boys.

Evan was very responsive to play opportunities provided by the costume technique. He quickly constructed a plot around a family setting, and he played the mother role. Play forms combined or merged with one another while preoedipal play, with its preoccupation with mother, was present for a prolonged period. He dramatized the role of a mother figure, his teacher, and displayed his wishes for the good mother who would be loving to her children and husband. He presented a fusion of mother and teacher, playing both roles; in addition, he demonstrated his wish to be like her, to have her with him at all times, and to replace her in order to achieve closeness with father. During his preoedipal play he was characteristically very serious. His rage and anxiety in relation to mother gradually unfolded in the murder plot, as he tried to get rid of the bad mother and retain the good mother identifications and introjects.

Guilty reactions appeared in the punishment scenes wherein the police apprehended the good woman who killed the bad one. Fantasies of the magical power of bad mothers, corpses, and ghosts who can destroy their children, reflected the delusional fear of the absent mother, and provided opportunities for the therapist to play the policeman (institute-therapist-social workers, and benevolent conscience) who will protect him and diminish his fears and guilt. His rage and guilt were also felt toward his brother and were concealed behind a submissive reaction formation, but these feelings were ventilated in the baby-mother scenes. On the baby level he gratified and expressed his dependency needs and fantasies without having to defend against them with denial or repression. By the maintenance of the therapeutic relationship through the most regressive periods of the play, the transferences became a bridge for reopening avenues of identificatory processes.

In later play, he assumed the role of the powerful omnipotent adult (queen) and happily controlled the therapist (child). During this play, he displayed his feelings about people who lied to him about his family and his own origin. On another level, he relieved his Oedipal conflict by controlling father and being (possessing) mother. His castration anxiety was an important theme throughout this phase.

As the pressures of his intrapsychic conflicts were played out, his relationship to the therapist grew more positive and new identifications occurred, his attention to reality improved, as did his ego organization, and learning again became available to him. His ability to separate from mother attachments and develop his own individuality increased gradually, and he became more assertive with his brother. Identifications with male figures became more acceptable and effeminate behavior diminished. The strengthening of the ego was also apparent in his increased tolerance for frustration and discipline.

I have found drama therapy in costume especially helpful with children who had been less verbal in their daily lives. Once into a costume, they become animated and spontaneously begin a series of verbalizations around the "safer" fantasy material. This is a distancing device, because they do not feel they are revealing their own thoughts; it becomes an excellent bridge toward comfort in communication and eventually "getting in touch" with themselves.

As a result of my work with costumes, a nursery school teacher[11] introduced costumes into two groups (four-and five-year-olds) as part of their general play materials. She used costumes of superman, devil, skeleton, angel and witch. She reported a wide range of intense emotions expressed during costume play. The children appeared freer in playing out a role when costumes are a prop, supporting the fantasy. In both classes, the costumes became their

most prized equipment. Each child displayed a definite preference
for a particular costume. She noted that some children had a strong
need to use a costume in play and rushed to obtain it, upon arrival
in the morning—"costume dashers." The superman costume was
the most popular at all times with both girls and boys. The devil and
skeleton costumes were also attractive to both sexes. The most active
motility was elicited by those wearing the superman and witch
costumes. A cluster of qualities appeared with each costume: superman (omnipotence, magical powers, benevolent father role); angel
(good, clean, passive, mother roles); witch (noisy, magical powers,
dirty, spooky, aggressive behavior); devil and skeleton (frightening,
growling, noises, scratching, aggressive roles). Children who were
previously frightened and inhibited in using the slide, were not
frightened when they first used the superman or witch costume,
dramatizing their ability and wish to move freely and quickly. One
boy who was intimidated by a bully in the class, stood up to him for
the first time while in the superman costume. In general, the
children in the nursery school experienced a feeling of confidence
and well-being while dramatizing their fantasies in costume.

## 4   CONCLUSION

Older children tend to be more defensive about their feelings and
avoid communication about fantasies and daydreams. Their play
preference is for conventional, competitive games. The costume play
is designed to deliberately stimulate an imaginative play pattern. In
earlier play patterns, the children prefer props to support their roles
in the fantasy; therefore, a variety of costumes are provided to set
the stage for spontaneous fantasy productions. Thus the costume
technique combines the advantages of the situational or structured
method, and free play. The method may be employed in certain
phases of child psychotherapy and analysis. It is conceivable that, as
a projective instrument, the method may be useful for research into
self and body imagery.

A striking aspect of this method is the intensity and pleasure experienced by the children in acting out their unconscious material
with relatively less resistance and, thereby, less interruption of play.
The complementary role assigned to the therapist by the child allows
the therapist to engage in meaningful therapeutic responses and

diminishes the amount of speculation sometimes necessary in certain other forms of less communicative play.

Costumes are enjoyed upon occasion in all ages, and are less likely to be considered too babyish by older children during therapy. Drama therapy in costume appears to be a worthwhile addition to child therapy, especially with older children who are less spontaneous in communication. The materials represent the only addition to the therapy. The therapeutic technique is essentially the same as we know it and interpretive work proceeds gradually to more mature levels. The goal likewise remains unchanged; to help the child understand reality in keeping with his developmental capacity.

# FOOTNOTES

1. Sigmund Freud, "Beyond the Pleasure Principle," *Standard Edition,* 18 (London: Hogarth Press, 1955), pp. 7-64; idem, "The Ego and the Id," *Standard Edition,* 19 (London: Hogarth Press, 1961), pp. 12-66.
2. Anna Freud, *The Ego and the Mechanisms of Defense* (New York: International Universities Press, 1946); idem, *The Psychoanalytical Treatment of Children* (New York: International Universities Press, 1959); Anna Freud and D. T. Burlingham, *Infants Without Families* (New York: International Universities Press, 1944).
3. Erik H. Erikson, "Configurations in Play: Clinical Notes," *Psychoanalytic Quarterly* 6 (1937): 139-214.
4. R. Waelder, "The Psychoanalytic Theory of Play," *Psychoanalytic Quarterly* 2 (1933): 208-24.
5. E. Kris, "The Psychology of Caricature," *Psychoanalytic Explorations in Art* (New York: International Universities Press, 1952), pp. 173-88.
6. Jean Piaget, *Play, Dreams and Imitation in Childhood* (New York: Norton, 1951).
7. L. Peller, "Libidinal Phases, Ego Development and Play," *The Psychoanalytic Study of the Child,* 9 (New York: International Universities Press, 1954), pp. 178-97.
8. R. Ekstein and J. Wallerstein, "Observations on the Psychotherapy of Borderline and Psychotic Children," *The Psychoanalytic Study of the Child,* 11 (New York: International Universities Press, 1956), pp. 303-11.
9. Anna Freud and D. T. Burlingham, *Infants Without Families.*
10. Irwin M. Marcus, "Costume Play Therapy," *Journal of the American Academy of Child Psychotherapy* 5, no. 3 (July 1966): 441-52; idem, "Newer Techniques in Child Therapy," in *Current Psychiatric Therapies,* ed. J. Masserman (New York: Grune & Stratton, 1966), pp. 42-45.
11. I am grateful to Gloria G. Wilkinson for sharing her observations with me.

ELAINE S. PORTNER, M.S.W., is an assistant professor of clinical psychiatry at the University of Pittsburgh Department of Psychiatry. She is also a family therapist at the Western Psychiatric Institute and Clinic, Pittsburgh, where she uses drama therapy in the diagnosis and treatment of young children.

*Chapter 15*

# DRAMA IN THERAPY: EXPERIENCES WITH A TEN YEAR OLD

Elaine S. Portner

## 1 INTRODUCTION AND THEORETICAL ASSUMPTIONS

The dramatic activities of children have variously been called play, pretend, fantasy, and/or make-believe. These activities reflect crucial developmental phases in the "normal" child, and have important implications for therapy.

Once a child has acquired the ability to distinguish between pretend and real (a mental achievement which Piaget has noted occurs as early as twelve months), the universal phenomenon of fantasizing serves many useful functions for emotional well-being as well as cognitive development. As an imitative experience, play helps a child to learn about his environment and to practice behaviors, resulting in pleasure and acquisition of abilities. In symbolic or make-believe play, unlike imitation, a child interprets and rearranges reality to suit himself, unencumbered by the restrictions of the real world.

Rosalind Gould[1] states that spontaneous fantasy is indispensable to optimal integration of affect and cognition. A child whose environment discourages or prevents him from free expression of spontaneous fantasy may be deprived of opportunities for such integration, which are fundamental to social-moral development and healthy ego-functioning. A child's intellectual and emotional resources are reflected in his fantasy. Flexible and free access to imagination, as well as to reality, are required for optimal development of ego functions. According to Gould: "The child's internal well-springs and external world experience intermingle or oscillate in various ways in fantasy expressions to the enrichment of both sources of knowledge. The two worlds of reality and imagination need never be as far apart as is often implied."[2]

The therapeutic aspects of play have been recognized by Freud and others who have viewed fantasy and dramatic play as *catharsis*, as expressions of needs and wishes, and as a coping mechanism to master, by repetition, an anxiety-provoking experience. Instant need gratification is the main mode of functioning "in the genesis of the psychic apparatus," observes Eckstein.[3] Mobility and motor development dominate the pre-verbal period of personality development, which the child usually experiences in an intense dependent relationship with the mother. "As the psychic apparatus develops, modes of problem solution grow richer, and impulsive action is supplemented. . . by play action." Eckstein distinguishes action from play action as follows: action is the attempt for immediate mastery of reality to make it subservient to the individual's needs; while play action is delayed in regard to reality, combining "the quasi-gratification of play with an attempt at resolution of conflict."[4] Continuing mental development leads to eventual replacement of play action by expressed fantasy and higher forms of thought.

Play action thus becomes an essential theoretical dimension of drama therapy, especially when considered in his broadest definition as ". . . a complex phenomenon. . . which includes the act, the fantasy, advanced elements of language and frequently strong aspects of reality testing."[5] Play, like the dream, may well be thought of as the royal road to the unconscious. "Whatever the patient produces, acts out, plays out, or talks out, is to be understood within the framework of psychotherapy as the communication of the unconscious conflict that has driven the patient to seek the help of the psychotherapist."[6]

Many have commented on the valuable attributes of play. Erikson states that to play it out is "the most natural autotherapeutic measure childhood affords."[7] Lowenfeld[8] distinguishes between the outer aspect of play as manifested in the overt content, and its inner or psychological aspect as represented in the symbolic meaning of the play. Similarly, Isaacs[9] comments on the "inner drama" which a child externalizes through dramatic play. As phenomena of mental life, fantasy as imaginary behavior is important to the understanding of the total personality. Murray submits that "fantasies are important *per se*, because of their relations to overt behavior, emotion, creative thought and neurotic symptoms, and because they may lead an experimenter to the discovery of the critical conditioning events of childhood."[10]

Thus, through play, children communicate unconscious conflicts. In addition, play can be viewed as "psychic work which can lead to new functions in the ego-organization...(allowing)... patients to make a new and different commitment."[11] The techniques of drama therapy provide a variety of opportunities for patients to focus on and work through areas of conflict. Particularly with children who often find it difficult to verbally express concerns, the use of symbolic play enables the child to communicate through action, gesture, movement and rhythm.

In this chapter, four examples of drama therapy techniques are reviewed as they emerged with one patient during the first few months of treatment, consisting of: (a) patient's use of tape recorder to express and cope with issues of trust and confidentiality; (b) the emergence and clarification of areas of conflict through the patient's sandbox play; (c) evidence of newly gained insight in patient's spontaneous puppet play; (d) therapist's introduction of role play to deal with timely issues.

## 2 THE REFERRAL AND THE PATIENT

Robert was a ten-year-old boy whose presenting problems included stuttering, immature behavior, and enuresis. Infantilized by his parents, he had a poor relationship with his father who was seldom available physically or emotionally as a male identification model.

During an initial drama diagnostic interview, Robert was found to be an intensely inhibited, frightened youngster who had great difficulty expressing feelings. He turned his frustrations inward and seemed to view himself as incompetent and inadequate. In his puppet play, he appeared to portray mother as controlling and castrating, and saw father as well-meaning but helpless. It was suggested that he may well also have identified himself as castrated and be expressing his frustrated oral rage through the symptom of stuttering. At the diagnostic conference, it was recommended that Robert be involved in individual expressive arts therapy.[12] Weekly individual one hour sessions were scheduled for him, while his parents participated in a parents' group.

## 3  FOUR EXAMPLES OF DRAMA THERAPY TECHNIQUES

Robert, whose stuttering problem interfered with his capacity to express himself verbally, used symbolic play to effectively communicate his conflicts. The examples which follow demonstrate a natural progression in the course of Robert's treatment. For most children, the initial weeks of therapy are difficult, and issues of trust and confidentiality are primary. Children, especially when constricted like Robert, need time to figure out what "therapy" is all about. They wonder if it is really safe to reveal their thoughts, even disguised in play. Robert chose to work with the tape recorder, one of the cleanest, most orderly of materials, involving minimal use of the body in expression. As time went by, his confidence increased as did the creative use of self and materials. In the sandbox play, Robert grew bolder, making use of miniature people and toys, in which he created a set and a saga in free, spontaneous play. Just as Lowenfeld employed the "world picture" technique,[13] Robert graphically demonstrated the underlying dynamics of his conflict. In the third month of treatment, Robert used puppets, gaining greater clarity and insights about what he was and wished to be. He responded to more direct confrontation in a method described by Irwin and Shapiro[14] and showed signs of integrating the material which had emerged in past weeks. Robert moved from indirect to more direct avenues of exploration in the role play described as the fourth drama therapy technique. New modes of behavior with his parents were rehearsed as he experimented with healthier adaptations to reality.

*Patient's use of tape recorder in beginning weeks of therapy to express and cope with issues of trust and confidentiality.*

During the first session, Robert tentatively explored the toys and the candy. Munching on a Tootsie Roll, he warmed to the idea of playing with the tape recorder. He carefully planned a performance. First, he recorded an imitation of Howard Cosell at ringside commenting on a boxing match. This was followed by a Count Dracula sequence in which he threatened to "suck ze blood." In conversation, his speech was generally dysfluent and barely audible. On tape, however, he spoke loudly and clearly, without stuttering. After hearing the re-play of his taped performance, Robert insisted on erasing the cassette. Perhaps his insistence was related both to his feelings of inadequacy that the tape was not good enough, as well as concerns that someone might listen to the tape unbeknownst to him. It is also possible that he could not tolerate his fluency and needed to destroy the evidence.

As soon as he entered the office the next week, he set up the tape recorder and organized a puppet story. In the story, a female character was afraid to go too far from home for fear of getting lost. This seemed to reflect his intense dependency needs and concerns that he could not make it on his own. Robert also seemed to identify himself as a female, a conflict that became clearer as work progressed. Although he did not erase this cassette as he had the previous one, he carefully hid it in a drawer, saying he did not want anyone to listen to it. Even I was not allowed to see where he concealed the tape, since he was not yet sure that he could trust me.

At the third session, Robert began by retrieving the tape cassette (and some candy) from the drawer. It was clear that he had thought about the session and planned the performance of a magic show. Although previously he had either played the role of a female or used a name other than his own, in this session he was Robert the Magnificent, the magician with special powers. He was better able to tolerate hearing himself on tape, neither erasing it nor hiding the cassette. For the first time, he also chose to use other toys. He played for a while with the Twirlopaint set, indicating a greater sense of comfort as he ventured away from the security of the tape recorder toward the exploration of new materials.

Gains in therapy rarely proceed in a straightforward manner. While the first few weeks represented some steps toward gaining trust in me and growing comfort with the therapy hour, the fourth session was filled with resistance. Once again the tape recorder was the symbolic focus of this issue. "Where's the mirror?" he asked as he walked in the office. "My sister said that people can watch me by looking through the mirror." He looked all around, even up on the ceiling, but there was no mirror. He continued to be agitated despite my reassurances of the confidentiality of our sessions. Next, he tested my trustworthiness another way. "Let's take the tape recorder to the waiting room and tape people without them knowing," he suggested. I explained that people would not be taped or filmed at the clinic without their knowledge and permission. Still agitated, he suddenly opened the office door and looked up and down the corridor. Attempts to interpret his suspicions or recapture the strength he had evidenced in the previous week were futile. Passively, he replayed the tape, identifying himself as a female, Margo the Magnificent, instead of Robert.

In the weekly collaboration with the parents' worker, I learned that his mother had an interview at the clinic during the same hour that week. Robert was concerned that somehow she would be able to watch or hear him. A somewhat intrusive and over-protective mother, she had sought information from him after each session. In subsequent meetings, I supported his rights to privacy, and the resistance passed. Further, I welcomed his ability to confront me with his concerns. His testing was appropriate and led to a new level of trust.

## The emergence of areas of conflict through the patient's sandbox play.

For several weeks during the second month of treatment, Robert chose to use the sandbox. At first, he compulsively smoothed the sand, creating neat rows. Then, after selecting some toy soldiers, he divided the sandbox into two halves. "It's daytime. . . warm. . . people are fighting for their freedom, but the army is collecting taxes and stuff and keeping them from being free." He gathered rubber bands and paper clips for ammunition, saying, "Now to wipe out this army." But in reality, he knocked down both the townspeople and the army; therefore, there was no victory that day in the townspeople's struggle for freedom. Although the sandbox sequence could be interpreted in many ways, the symbolic play of the oppressed and the oppressors could be seen as representative of his own struggles. He seemed to be waging his own fight for freedom via his struggle for competency, adequacy, and independence. Stifled by the part of himself he recognized as weak, there were, as well, people in his life who confirmed his weakness. During the course of the play battle, he attacked both sides equally, indicative of his own ambivalence. He had conflicts about wanting his "freedom" yet also wanting to be dominated and dependent.

During the second week of the sandbox battle, he operated in a decisive and organized manner. "Same as last week," he said, "the townspeople are fighting for their freedom, and the army is trying to defeat them." Then he confided that he wanted the townspeople to win. Using rubber bands and a big paper clip which he had brought along, he aimed alternately at the army and the townspeople. During the battle he kept up a running commentary which reflected both self-confidence and self-deprecation. "He aims; pulls back and he fires...Dumb idea...I'm cheating my people...Ha, ha, I blew him out...he's dead...(and finally to the army) I've had enough of you!" As he systematically wiped out the entire army, the rubber band occasionally snapped against his hand. "Pretty soon, I'm going to lose my hand," he said. It was as though, even in symbolic play, he felt guilty for expressing his anger and expected to be punished. At the end of the battle, there were twelve victorious townspeople left. But, as though he could not accept success, he suddenly reopened the war and downed all twelve. As he was shooting the townspeople, his speech became an infantile lisp: "Thilly, thilly, thilly." The regression to baby talk suggested his yearning for the safety of childhood and more acceptably dependent times.

Many of Robert's conflicts emerged through the sandbox battle. In day to day life, his emotional repertoire was limited; he allowed himself to be little else than "nice." His expression of aggression through the sandbox battle was met with his own feelings of guilt. A major conflict was whether or not he *wanted* to become more assertive and independent, as demonstrated by the townspeople's struggle for freedom. He had control over who won that battle, just as he had control over his own struggle — but the decision (at this time at least) was to keep the oppressed from gaining freedom. Other questions he seemed to be grappling with included: Could he aggress without losing control? Could he be assertive without loss of love? He learned that he could assert himself in therapy without endangering our relationship, but it remained a real question if his mother would be able to tolerate an age-appropriately aggressive and assertive son. Nevertheless, battle lines of his own were clearly drawn in the sandbox battles.

## Evidence of newly gained insight in patient's spontaneous puppet play.

In the spontaneous puppet play during the third month of treatment, Robert began to explore and accept parts of himself other than the non-threatening, non-aggressive nice boy. He chose four puppets: a boy and three animals (elephant, giraffe, and fish monster). He identified himself as the boy, and the animals as his brothers. "We're four twins, you know." Later, further reflecting his confusion, he called the four twins, "quadriplets." (In reality, he had no brother, just two older sisters.) He reported that the boy was nice (perhaps the bland, passive self); that the mean fish monster ate people and scared them; that the elephant was strong, sturdy and big; and that the giraffe was tall, proud, high and mighty.

When I suggested that all four of these might be looked upon as four different parts of him, this seemed to make sense and he expanded his descriptions. He said that he scared girls, just as the fish scared people. (Probably wishful thinking.) "They scream, I scream, we all scream for ice cream." As he said that, the fish monster flew up in the air; on the way down it tapped my shoulder. I suggested that the fish monster part of him could also be the joker part (a role he had often played), exploring the notion that people sometimes conceal some of their feelings, hold them back or disguise them as a joke, so no one will know. He responded that this happened with him, not at school, but at home. The elephant part of him he identified as strong, giving him "the strength to do anything." And lastly, the giraffe, tall and proud, "gives me pride, so I don't give up on things."

Through his play, he was able to work out, symbolically at first, four separate people whom he could afterward accept as four parts of himself (as he is now, or as he would like to be). His aggression as the fish monster was accompanied by a trick which served to disguise the aggression which he had difficulty expressing as an acceptable part of himself. The selection of elephant and giraffe and his symbolic descriptions of them further revealed this struggle, but also indicated a sense of hope. As the giraffe, he could stick his neck out, so to speak, and the strong part of him (elephant) gave him the confidence to carry on. The three animals were a welcome accompaniment to the otherwise nondescript boy puppet.

Inherent in this series of sessions were indications of Robert's willingness to be introspective, his ability to make use of insight oriented therapy, and a commitment on his part to do some work and accept some responsibility toward expanding and growing.

## Therapist's introduction of role play to deal with a timely issue.

Perhaps the most openly confronting and direct use of drama in therapy is through role play of a specifically articulated issue. With Robert, an example of this mode occurred four months after therapy had been initiated. From a discussion with the parents' therapists, I had learned of a conflict the family was experiencing at home. Mother wanted Robert to go to an overnight camp for three weeks in July; father was indifferent; and neither parent knew the child's preference, claiming he would not say. As a result, there had been no decision.

It was likely that Robert "would not say," but it was equally likely that he had some preferences on the subject. In the next therapy session, I explored the camp issue with him. I felt it was important to provide him with an opportunity to gain awareness of his feelings in order to help him deal more effectively with the issue at home, if and when it should arise again. I suggested that we use the camp theme to act out (and tape) the decision-making process that might go on at home. Assuming the role of director, he said he wanted us to act it, rather than use puppets or toy people. He assigned me the role of mother, while he was the father. The conversation follows:

(FATHER=PATIENT; MOTHER=THERAPIST)

Father:  Well, Sally, I think it would be a good idea for Robert to go to camp, because you know he hasn't gone to any camp, just to day camp. What's your reaction to this?

Mother:  Well, I'm glad you brought it up, because when you think of it, he never has gone to overnight camp. And he is already ten and a half years old...

Father:  Yeah, but the decision is up to Robert. What's he going to say? He probably wouldn't like to go. He might like three weeks at a YMCA camp, but we'll have to talk to him.

Mother:  Camp might be a nice change...

Father:  I agree. And, it would be a good thing for him to get away from us, because he's with us so much.

Mother:  You think it would be a good thing for Robert to get away from us?

Father:  Um hmmm. He's been with us a lot, and I think it would be a good thing for him to be alone — with other kids — and friends. So, let's go down and ask him... I'll go and talk with him.

(ROBERT=ROBERT; FATHER=THERAPIST)

Father:  Robert, your mother and I were just talking about summer, and I was wondering how you would feel about going to overnight camp for a few weeks.

Robert:  I don't want to go really.

Father:  Can you tell me what your feelings are about camp?

Robert:  (becoming dysfluent) I don't know. I just don't think I'll be... it'll be fun for me, besides if I wasn't here, I might get lonesome, even though there are kids there.

Father:  Sometimes kids get lonesome at camp. Sure, and I think kids always wonder what camp is going to be like, and if they are going to like it.

Robert: Besides, you already signed me up for little league baseball for the summer.

Father: Oh, so you'd have to miss that if you went to camp?

Robert: Yeah.

Father: Well, maybe there would be baseball at camp. We were thinking that since your sisters will be away in July, you might like to do something special in July, too.

Robert: I guess so.

Father: What do you think that something special could be?

Robert: I don't know.

Father: But you're not sure if you want the special something to be camp.

Robert: I guess not. (more stuttering) Can we talk later?

Robert picked up a whiffle ball and suggested that we play catch rather than do any more acting. This time, though, he wanted me to participate more actively instead of sitting and pitching to him while he played both teams. I began by resisting in a way analogous to his handling of the overnight camp issue. I balked at first, saying that he was the expert ballplayer, that I had never done that sort of thing. "You're asking me to try something I've never done before...I don't know how it will work out...It's hard sometimes to try out new things." Consciously mirroring his resistance and fears, I articulated the worries I imagined he had in regard to camp in the guise of the baseball game he was proposing to me. Finally, I said, "It's kind of like you and camp. But how will I know if I can do it, unless I try?" With a big grin, he went into a routine of "Try it, you'll like it." I agreed to play baseball.

Important information was elicited during the role play. Robert had clearly stated the double message of the parents. (We want you to go away to camp, but we also signed you up for little league baseball.) Robert demonstrated his wish for more interaction with his father as well as to be consulted on decision-making. ("But the decision is up to Robert.") His resistances ("I don't want to go really") and his fears ("I might get lonesome") were openly stated as he attempted to resolve the problem. His speech contained many dysfluencies, but only when he played himself attempting to express feelings...not when he played father. Having role-played those feelings in the treatment session, he was able to talk it out directly with his father, and he subsequently made the decision to go to camp.

# 4 DISCUSSION

In the four examples discussed in the preceding pages, the patient used the therapeutic situation to resolve many problems. Drama was used as a treatment modality to work toward the following goals: facilitating the awareness and expression of the conflicts; making sense of the material; helping the patient to gain new insights which were then integrated into his own expressed wishes for change; and exploring new patterns of behavior which resulted in greater satisfaction in relationships with others.

With the tape recorder Robert dealt with his (at first) unspeakable concerns related to trust and confidentiality. In the sandbox battle, he defined areas of conflict. More open confrontation led to new insight and introspection through the puppets which were seen as aspects of himself. And, finally, in the role play, he dealt with a concrete reality situation and gained experience in expressing feelings and rehearsing new modes of behavior.

Drama was of particular interest to him, though other children may favor different expressive modalities, such as art, music or movement. In the process of therapy, children often make use of various symbolic modalities. The therapist can influence the patient's choice by the availability of materials and by the unconscious communication of the therapist's own comfort or discomfort with a particular art form. Each child should be evaluated carefully to assess ego capacities as well as natural preferences for an arts modality. In neurotic children like Robert, play, acting out and play action serve valuable functions: recollection, mastery of conflict and search for identity. Robert, the subject of this paper, responded to many types of therapeutic drama techniques.

# FOOTNOTES

1. Rosalind Gould, *Child Studies through Fantasy* (New York: Quadrangle Books, 1972), p. 274.
2. *Ibid.*

3. Rudolf Ekstein, *Children of Time and Space, of Action and Impulse* (New York: Appleton-Century-Crofts, 1966), p. 170.

4. *Ibid.*

5. *Ibid.*, p. 171.

6. *Ibid.*

7. Erik H. Erikson, "Studies in the Interpretation of Play," *Genetic Psychology Monographs* 22 (1940): 561.

8. Margaret Lowenfeld, *Play in Childhood* (London: Gollancz, 1935), p. 321.

9. Susan Isaacs, *Childhood and After: Some Essays and Clinical Studies* (London: Routledge, 1948), p. 69.

10. H. A. Murray, "Techniques for a Systematic Investigation of Fantasy," *The Journal of Psychology* 3 (1936): 118.

11. Ekstein, *Children of Time and Space,* p. 283.

12. The author is grateful to expressive arts therapist, Eleanor Irwin, Ph.D., of the Pittsburgh Child Guidance Center, for invaluable consultation during the course of Robert's treatment and the preparation of this chapter.

13. Margaret Lowenfeld, "World Pictures of Children," *British Journal of Medical Psychology* 18 (1939): 65.

14. Eleanor C. Irwin and Marvin I. Shapiro, "Puppetry as a Diagnostic and Therapeutic Technique," in *Psychiatry and Art,* 4, ed. I. Jakab (New York: S. Karger, 1975), p. 89.

MARRION WELLS is an actress/musician and puppeteer. A recipient of the Dame Irene Vanbrugh Gold Medal for Stage Technique, she is director of Arion Productions in Hastings, England.

*Chapter 16*

# THEATRE FOR THE LESS FORTUNATE

## Marrion Wells

## 1 INTRODUCTION

"Theatre for the less fortunate? What do you actually *do?*"

"We visit schools for the handicapped. That is the only way most of these children see any live theatre."

"You perform a play for them?"

"They aren't exactly plays...there is music and movement and sometimes singing...and puppets...particularly for the younger ones...maybe some magic...and comedy...as well as an actual story. The children don't only watch. They take part. Some of them wear costumes and play short parts, and others form groups and are soldiers, ladies in waiting, smugglers, or the staff of the Civic Hall...we *need* them to take part to develop the story."

"Why do you do all this?"

"Why? Because we have proved that by giving them the opportunity of becoming so integrated within the performance, such an essential part of it, so swept along by the wave of enthusiasm that spontaneously, and totally, their involvement in the presentation makes them forget their disabilities, overcome their handicaps and reach, albeit only momentarily, across the barrier between 'them' and 'us.' "

## 2 ARION

Arion is a small organization of professional players who, since the late nineteen fifties, have been giving ten performances week-

279

ly for an average of forty weeks each year in schools, from the
large industrial areas of Great Britain and Ireland to remote
Welsh valleys and the rural communities of the Scottish islands.
Approximately 30 percent of these performances are to "special"
schools, mostly purpose-built one-story blocks accommodating
fewer than one hundred day pupils. These are from a wide catch-
ment area, but sometimes are made up of some day, some boarding
pupils. Those more severely disabled are housed in units attached
to hospital complexes, or converted stately homes deep in the
heart of the country where children from heavily industrial-
ized areas have the vistas of green fields, gardens to care for,
animals to tend, and (above all) space. The majority are state administered, though some are from the private sector of education.
Our services, usually financed by the Local Education Authority
as an "amenity" are available to all types of schools, physically
handicapped, hard-of-hearing, partially sighted, spastic, spina
bifida assessment units, children from problem homes or the non-
communicative. The largest proportion of our performances are
to the educationally subnormal (E.S.N.) and the more severely
disturbed, as these form the majority of the special schools in any
area.

We are storytellers with a difference. For younger audiences,
adaptations are made from both familiar and the lesser known
tales of Grimm and Andersen, of children's classics such as *Heidi*,
or ballets like *Coppelia* and *The Sleeping Princess*. Senior audiences
enjoy *The Arabian Nights*, Thackeray's *The Rose and the Ring*, or
original adventures incorporating present day situations, affording
opportunities for action without violence, and with a surprise
twist at the end. The characters portrayed are firm, decisive,
readily identifiable. In order to indicate how one person may portray a variety of parts, each performer in each presentation plays
at least two, sometimes four or five, differing roles, showing how a
change of voice, walk, stance, and/or movement can create
another person, allied to a variation of costume, wig, hat, ac-
cessories and footwear. Young audiences are quick to spot two
different characters wearing the same pair of shoes.

Each presentation is in two acts of approximately forty-five and thirty minutes' duration respectively, the exact timing depending upon the length of time taken by each audience in participation.

Towards the end of Act One, the audience is given some "task" to carry out in the short interval between the acts. They may have to *make* something, to *find* something, or to *think about* something—the end product of which will be necessary to continue the action in Act Two. Theatrical tradition is followed by having one "highlight" immediately before the end of Act One, and a climax late in Act Two, resolved by the final curtain so that everything ends happily.

The only facilities required from the venue are floor space to erect our light-alloy screen, an electric point, and whenever possible, a piano. The screen, two meters high and extending up to six-and-a-half meters wide, is dressed in curtains of bright paint-box colors—red, gold, and green—and covers our dressing space and "effects"; the center portion opens to reveal an inset of a cave, a tunnel, or whatever the story demands, to heighten the atmosphere. The final inset is always bright and sparkling. This provides a background and focal point for the action and transforms the hall from its everyday image, while the audience has a sense of "occasion" from the moment they enter. In front of the screen is the acting area, around which the children sit (all who are able) cross-legged on the floor. Two narrow aisles go from the acting area to the back corners of the room, dividing the audience into three blocks. The youngest sit in that on the actors' left, facing the senior children, who sit in the block on the actors' right. The middle age range children sit in the center block facing forwards. Sections of the participation in each story are aimed at the younger element, others at the older ones, as special schools often cater for a wide age range, for example seven to thirteen or nine to sixteen years. By seating the audience thus, the players can decide where to address a given sequence. The aisles facilitate movement of children to the acting area and of artists amid the audience, where some of the action occurs.

The equipment packs into a station wagon. Invariably we are met on arrival forty-five minutes prior to the performances by some of the older, more able pupils detailed to help with the unloading. As 80 percent of our bookings are return visits, they greet us as old friends, reminding us of what happened last time, what they did, or what we wore. This contact with us as "visitors" is considered to be part of the value of the presentation, giving these pupils some responsibility as part of their social training.

Since our early days nearly twenty years ago, our work has developed considerably, in line with principles of special education. Our primary objective has always been the involvement of the audience "in depth." In order to extend, and experiment with this, our performance is discussed in detail afterwards, with the staff, and sometimes also with the pupils, and later among ourselves. As I am a performer, as well as writer-director, this analysis means we are able to put our findings immediately into practice.

## 3   FORMS OF PARTICIPATION

Over the years we have, therefore, developed this participation into four main types:

A.  Children, usually one boy, one girl, play short but important "cameo" roles, after ten minutes of preparatory briefing.
B.  Children spontaneously come to join the players to contribute to the story development.
C.  Representatives of each age range (chosen or suggested by other members of the audience) form groups in the acting area.
D.  The entire audience is involved in word and movement, directed by one of the company.

### Type A

The children in the first category are chosen in conjunction by the head (principal) and class teacher. To retain the element of surprise, we suggest that their classmates are not told of this, and often the participating children are not themselves told beforehand. We ask that they shall not be extroverts, but children who will benefit from the experience. Often the teachers will wait to discuss their selection until we arrive, as different roles in different stories require different types of children. There is always one part that is written for a child with little speaking ability. We travel with various sets of costumes to fit every size of child, and stipulate only that those selected may be able to dress themselves in their own clothes after their part is finished. In case of doubt a teacher or helper comes backstage to help with this task at a pre-arranged signal.

We have found from experience that the optimum number of actors playing to handicapped audiences is no more than three, and so the "prepared participation" is usually limited to one boy and one girl (in the case of segregated schools, two of the same sex) as we have no more room backstage. One player takes the boy to rehearse him, another the girl. The roles portrayed are a messenger, a gypsy, a gardener, or a shop assistant, which require movement. In the ten minutes allowed for preparation, the player must assess the child's degree of mobility and adapt his/her instruction accordingly. A clear-cut demonstration by the actor will usually be imitated quickly by the child. Similarly the player must determine whether the lines of simple dialogue can be assimilated, or whether the player must "feed" the young performer so that the child may merely answer "yes" or "no." The script is so devised that a key word in the actor's line will jog the child's memory and lead to his response. Experience has taught us that repetition of this key word will prompt the same reply from the handicapped child.

The children are dressed in their costumes. Then each is given a seat backstage and told when and where to make his/her entrance. (Our setting affords the possibility of four different entrances and exits.) The first appearance is early in the story, so that there is no long period of tense waiting. A few seconds before entrance, at the recognized cue, an actor backstage gets the child ready and shows him/her the way into the acting area. In most cases the child is there already.

The child's part is designed to be interesting and amusing to those watching as well as to the child playing it. If the participant can "score" off the player, so much the better! Staff will watch in detail every movement and achievement of the child performers.

When his first sequence is finished, the actor on-stage will indicate to the child the appropriate exit where another player
waits off-stage to receive him. The child is then briefed for his
next appearance. In this way, the child's role has the appearance
of continuity without danger of his forgetting or being overcome
by the unfamiliar situation. As soon as it is finished, he changes
back into his own clothes and quietly rejoins the watching audience. The children's roles are placed in either Act One or Act
Two, not both, so that they have the chance of seeing part of the
presentation with their fellows. At the final curtain, the participating children are always thanked publicly for their help.

By thus incorporating the children we have to be prepared even
more than usual for the unexpected. In the few minutes we have
off-stage we can never relax, but there are rewarding moments by
compensation. We remember one performance of *The Wizard of
Oz* with a physically handicapped Tin Man who, when Dorothy
"oiled" his neck and arms, as directed by the script, indicated
with extra loud squeaks—with no prompting from us—that she
should oil the wheels of his chair.

## Type B

This participation depends entirely upon the rapport of each
individual actor with the audience. Our stories contain solo passages carried out by each player and although these are tightly
scripted, it is left to the person and experience of the player to
carry this through as deeply as he may. The audience is never
asked directly to help us (it is the character's lines that indicate
that he needs assistance) but the actor must be surprised and
delighted when offers of help are forthcoming. Once a child or
group of children has reached the acting area, the player relies on
his technical skill to make sure that they do not obstruct the
audience's view, positioning himself in such a way that the participating children are readily seen—and thus heard—by the
audience. He has been trained to make his voice carry, speaking
with his back to them. The children have not. His expertise
manifests itself in the apparent spontaneity of the sequence so
that even the watching staff may think the entire scene is ad lib.
At the end, he must be able to send the children contentedly back

to their places to enjoy the rest of the story as part of the audience. We are careful never to have the same child coming to the acting area more than once in each presentation.

## Type C

Some scenes call for a group of children to assist one of the actors: to bring gifts to the Queen in *The Sleeping Princess,* or to take the Scarecrow in *Oz* to see the Wizard (having no brain he is unable to go alone). These children are suggested by the audience but the player must remain in charge at all times to ensure that they come as quickly and quietly as possible to join him, and that the action is quickly resumed. Sometimes these children have to speak lines. When there is some difficulty, the player re-phrases, but does not repeat, the line so that it may be heard by the audience. He adjusts his vocabulary to the age group, but he must above all never "talk down," neither mentally nor physically bending to the participants. One aspect of our work which has always aroused comment is the dignity of our approach to the young people.

## Type D

An example of mass participation is the simulation of a storm. The youngest group will be the rain, an onomatopoeic pitter-patter allied to a "raindrops running down the windows" effect with the fingers when a staccato scale is played on the piano. The middle group will be the wind, a controlled whistling with a swaying from side to side as they sit, to a glissando accompaniment. The senior group clapping for the thunder, in tune with a series of vibrato diminished chords in the bass. The clapping first distant, nearer, louder, quicker, then dying away. The three are then put together to make the sounds of the storm. When the player says he can see a storm blowing up, as the rain starts to fall — once the notes of the "rain" are heard from the piano — the participation will readily start. It is the responsibility of the actor to see that it finishes on cue.

## 4  RESULTS

These types of involvement are successful. Over the years we have

had reports of partially sighted children whose paintings have
shown how much they have assimilated, of "difficult" children
who, to the amazement of the staff, have offered to help others in
a play situation, and of one exciting moment when a child who
had never spoken since entering this school shouted out to call the
attention of one of the characters on-stage.

We believe that the value of our presentation manifests itself in
many ways, as the headmistress of one school in greater London
indicates:

> We have frequent visits from the *Arion Theatre Company* to this
> school for mentally handicapped children. Their performances
> are the first introduction to the live theatre for many of our
> children, and each child, however handicapped, gains a great deal
> from them.[1]

## 5   CONCLUSION

Our participatory productions are an answer to those who consider
that "special" plays should be written for "special audiences." We
contend that the reverse is true.

The fact remains that we are theatrical performers using our
craft in an endeavor to bring some small magic to those who
never know life as we know it. The time taken traveling is ever-
increasing (I drive an average of 40-45,000 miles a year) and we
get tired . . . very tired. But this is forgotten with the crayoned
drawings pushed through the car window as we leave and the
whispered, "This is you in that lovely red dress;" or the sheet of
paper with some indeterminate lines across it under which the
teacher has printed: "Please come again. We love you very
much."

## FOOTNOTE

1. Mrs. J. Roper, currently at Court Meadow School, Cuckfield, Sussex,
England.

# Part 4
# EDUCATION

Traditionally, education has been concerned with "learning." However, this term has meant different things over the ages. In the Renaissance, humanist educators like Mulcaster emphasized "the whole man" and saw that the acquiring of information was merely part of a larger "whole." In the Puritan tradition and the philosophy of John Locke, "learning" became the inculcation of information. Later, when education became universal, this approach helped the industrial revolution by training generations of clerks who could write business letters and compute books of accounts.

These traditions have continued in the twentieth century, but there has been a growing movement which opposes this. It occurred in slightly different ways in Britain and America but, in both countries, it was assumed that psychological health was a necessary prerequisite for any form of learning.

In Britain, it began at the turn of the century. In the Perse School, Cambridge, Caldwell Cook introduced *The Play Way*[1] to his boys. In his English lessons, instead of reading Shakespeare round the class, he took the students out into an old house (the famous "Mummery") where they acted the plays in theatrical conditions. But it was not primarily Shakespeare that Cook was interested in: "It is not acting we teach the boys but *the value of action* . . . the natural means of study in youth is play."

From this beginning, British education came to accept that spontaneous dramatic action had value in and of itself. Over the years, it spread into many aspects of education: to "the primary method" where young children played about shops or post offices, and learnt that they *had* to read and write if their play was to continue;[2] and to "the project method" of secondary schools where students took a theme (say, oil) which usually culminated in a large improvisation.[3] This was the period of Robert G. Newton's improvisation with the unemployed during the Depression,[4] Susan Isaacs' study of child play,[5] and Margaret Lowenfeld's work in play therapy.[6]

But it was after the Second World War that this early work bore fruit in Britain.[7] Drama was not merely used to teach other things. It also became a subject in its own right — creative drama — for all students from the pre-schoolers to those leaving senior high schools. It consisted of two areas: (1) exercises for spontaneity, creativity, relaxation, speech, movement, perceptual awareness and concentration; (2) spontaneous improvisation around themes. Evaluation normally consisted of the teacher's subjective judgment as to whether each student was reaching his own personal potential. Between 1948 and 1968, creative drama became available for most children and students, and to one-third of teachers-in-training as a subject of study.

This growth was largely due to a generation of drama teachers who had begun their work before the war. They included Peter Slade and E. J. Burton. Peter Slade advocates "child drama."[8] He sees natural play as "an art form in its own right." In other words (like Stanislavsky and Caldwell Cook), for Slade dramatic action has values for itself alone. For him, its greatest value is as "a natural therapy" producing *catharsis* — "the spitting out of evil in a legal framework" — which he calls "dramatherapy." Child drama is "the child's way of thinking, proving, relaxing, working, remembering, daring, testing, creating and absorbing," and so the leader becomes a Socratic questioner rather than an imparter of knowledge and directions.

E. J. Burton[9] sees drama as a *total* activity, like life. It is always therapeutic because it involves sharing and community: "It is a process of total experience assessment and analysis." The human actor: (1) explores and relates to the environment; (2) develops and uses emotional response; (3) comes to "feel with" other people—the community; and (4) becomes self-aware in the creative response. Above all, drama develops human potential and is a "healing."

In the subsequent generation of British drama teachers, the previous value of dramatic action for psychological health has been continued. Brian Way[10] feels that creative drama has more to do with developing people than developing drama. He works more for the participants' experience than for communication between actor and audience. He sees drama as psychologically healthful in that it develops concentration, sense awareness, imagination, the body, speech, emotion and the intellect. Dorothy Heathcote[11] uses improvisations about life situations and leads students to self-discoveries within dramatic action. She "aims at surprise and discovery for the participants rather than for any onlookers," and regards both learning and therapy as *social emergents* from spontaneous drama.

Each of these British workers, together with others like Gavin Bolton, Veronica Sherbourne, Christopher Day, and John Hodgson are concerned with *all* children and students in schools of any age, and they view drama as providing *both* psychological health and the required educational learnings.

In American education, things were somewhat similar but also different. Although John Dewey's "learning by doing" altered education from the beginning of the century, his scientific position was that of behaviorism. As a result, when Winifred Ward[12] established the field of creative dramatics and children's theatre in the 1920's, based on the work of Dewey and Hughes Mearns,[13] it was different from her British counterparts. Although based upon spontaneous play, it built from parts into wholes; it also led to Dewey's "end in view" which, with Ward, became play production. Thus creative dramatics was tied to children's theatre—the performance of "good stories" by adults for children. Largely, this work ceased at the elementary level, while secondary schools turned to the study of theatre arts. Ward's work was followed by that of Isabel Burger[14] and Geraldine Brain Siks,[15] both of whom were more concerned with the art form for children than with the therapeutic value of spontaneous dramatic play.

Two later influences upon American education came to alter the emphasis. First, British methods became well known in the 1950's, and many senior teachers went across the Atlantic to study the British approach. Second, the improvisational games of Viola Spolin[16] re-emphasized that dramatic action was of value for itself alone: that improvisation not merely improved incidental skills but brought out all the qualities necessary for the psychological health of human beings, as well as for learning.

Today, there is a growing change in American education. Nellie McCaslin,[17] for example, emphasizes the therapeutic value of both spontaneous drama and theatrical presentations in schools.

This part of Volume 1 is concerned with drama therapy in education. Brian Way demonstrates the classic British position of drama as therapeutic in human development (Chapter 17). E. J. Burton presents an existential view of drama for the disadvantaged and the gifted (Chapter 18). Nellie McCaslin presents an overview of modern American practices, both in creative dramatics and theatre, and gives examples from special education (Chapter 19).

# FOOTNOTES

1. Caldwell Cook, *The Play Way* (London: Heinemann, 1917).
2. E. R. Boyce, *Play in the Infants' School* (London: Methuen, 1938).
3. Eric Newton, *Acting for Youth* (London: University of London Press, 1938).
4. Robert G. Newton, *Acting Improvised* (London: Nelson, 1937); idem, *Together in Theatre* (London: J. Garnett Miller, 1954).
5. Susan Isaacs, *Intellectual Growth in Young Children* (London: Routledge, 1930); idem, *Social Development in Young Children* (London: Routledge, 1933).
6. Margaret Lowenfeld, *Play in Childhood* (London: Gollancz, 1935).
7. For details, see: Phillip A. Coggin, *Drama in Education* (London: Thames & Hudson, 1956).
8. Coggin, chap. 4.
9. E. J. Burton, *Teaching English through Self-Expression* (London: Evans, 1949); idem, *Drama in Schools* (London: Jenkins, 1956).

10. Brian Way, *Development through Drama* (London: Longman, 1968).
11. Dorothy Heathcote, "Drama and Education: Subject or System?" in *Drama and Theatre in Education,* eds. N. Dodd and W. Hickson (London: Heinemann, 1971); Betty Jane Wagner, *Dorothy Heathcote: Drama as a Learning Medium* (Washington, D.C.: N.E.A., 1976).
12. Winifred Ward, *Creative Dramatics for the Upper Grades and Junior High School* (New York: Appleton-Century-Crofts, 1930); idem, *Stories to Dramatize* (Kentucky: Anchorage Press, 1952); idem, *Playmaking with Children,* 2nd ed. (New York: Appleton-Century-Crofts, 1957); idem *Theatre for Children* (Kentucky: Anchorage Press, 1957).
13. Hughes Mearns, *Creative Power: The Education of Youth in the Creative Arts* (New York: Dover, 1958).
14. Isabel Burger, *Creative Play Acting* (New York: Barnes, 1950); idem, "Creative Dramatics: An Educational Tool," *The Instructor* 73 (September 1963): 133-36.
15. Geraldine Siks, *Creative Dramatics: An Art for Children* (New York: Harper & Row, 1958); idem, *Children's Literature for Dramatization* (New York: Harper & Row, 1964).
16. Viola Spolin, *Improvisation for the Theater* (Evanston, Ill.: Northwestern University Press, 1963).
17. Nellie McCaslin, *Creative Dramatics in the Classroom* (New York: David McKay, 1968); idem, *Children and Drama* (New York: David McKay, 1975); idem, *Theatre for Young Audiences* (New York: Longman, 1977).

BRIAN WAY, an ex-actor with the Old Vic Theatre, was for many years director of London's Theatre Centre. The author of *Development Through Drama* and many participatory plays for children, he currently shares his time between lecturing and conducting workshops all over the world and creating pottery at home.

*Chapter 17*

# A HUNDRED PERCENT IS A HUNDRED PERCENT IS A...

Brian Way

## 1  DRAMA AND RELEASE

The natural aspiration of all human beings is to be the fullest human being they are born to be. The major negation of this aspiration is the ambition of others to mould a person into an acceptable image. Both home and school can do this. They are governed by the pervading influences of a society concerned with conformity based on a norm which has arisen from established standards.

Neither home nor school is necessarily concerned with the "real me" deep inside each individual, the "me" that may be different from the acceptable image and unable to comply with established standards. But it is, nevertheless, "the real me that is screaming to be released;" note—not moulded nor fashioned—simply *released.*

Creativity is concerned with the release of that "real me." It counterbalances other influences. Academic processes, usually geared to product, develop and change only in so far as they can achieve product more effectively and quickly. Creativity is concerned with process, at a rhythm closer to each individual. Product is important mostly to the individual creator who may arrive at a different product from that originally conceived, and almost certainly different from the conception of others. Academic education is concerned with correct answers, but there are no correct answers in creativity. Academic education is an imposed process of in-flow, whereas creativity is a natural process of out-flow. Academic education is predominantly concerned with the intellect. Emotional experience is largely a matter of reaction to the success/failure ratio for each individual, and the ambition factor from parents and school. Creativity is directly concerned with the emotional (and spiritual). If developed in an uncritical atmosphere, it provides opportunities for harmonious and unifying inner experiences. Through creativity, intellect is balanced with intuition, fact with imagination, past with future, tangible with intangible, criticism with appreciation, academic study with the self-control of emotions, and concern for personal progression with an awareness of and sensitivity to others.

Although tension and relaxation are common to both academic and creative forms of education, hypertension is almost solely the province of the academic field, particularly where this is allied to examinations and other systems of competition. When creativity takes place in an uncritical framework, with moments of total privacy and an absence of evaluation, then it will avoid creating hypertension, and help to alleviate that arising from other sources.

The inner conflict is between the intuitively perceived true self—"the me that screams to be released"—and the acceptance, with varying degrees of willingness, of the self imposed or moulded by others. In these terms, therapy can be equated with release, and with the re-creation of balances that have been upset by unnatural forces.

The most unnatural of these forces is that of compulsory education. Indeed, so unnatural is this force that the need for therapy in modern civilization will end only when education has been radically changed. It is not natural for human beings to be incarcerated in buildings—often devoid of natural light and air — for hours each day in order to be filled with knowledge of the past and abstractions of the present. The real education that takes place in the preschool child—and many major developments take place before the child comes to school — is regulated by a natural and personal rhythm. Focusing the eyes and the hearing, disengaging from the oneness of the world and self to an awareness of their separateness, the coordination of limbs, the mastery of walking and talking—these and many other intricate learnings take place without the aid of schooling. Perhaps, without schooling (at any rate of the established and traditional kind) this process of growth would continue,and lead to the kind of searching that, in one's own time and rhythm, can be answered through balanced and appropriate experiences of in-flow and out-flow.

Most of the preschool developments arise from the various activities under the generic title *play,* which is fundamental to academic discovery as well as to creativity.

In *Child Drama,* Peter Slade defines two distinct forms of play, Personal and Projected:

> Personal Play is obvious Drama; the whole Person or Self is used. It is typified by movement and characterization. We note the dance entering and the experience of being things or people.

> Projected Play is Drama, too; the whole mind is used, but the body not so fully. Treasures are used which either take on characters of the mind or become part of the place ("stage" in a theatre sense) where Drama takes place. During moments of typical Projected Play we do not see the whole body being used. The Child stands still, sits, lies prone, or squats, and may use chiefly the hands. The main action takes place outside the body, and the whole is characterized by extreme mental absorption. Strong mental projection is taking place.[1]

And again:

> In Personal Play the tendency is towards noise and physical exertion on the part of the person involved; and if noise is not employed, exertion is. In Projected Play the tendency is towards quietness and physical stillness; and if there is not quiet some physical stillness is there.

Throughout the whole life, Man is happy or unhappy in so far as
he discovers the right admixture for his life of these quite distinct
manners of using energy.[2]

Should this balance be upset, many personality problems arise,
including those of relationships with other people and society.
Academic education is perhaps mainly responsible for upsetting
the balance because it is largely concerned with projected activity.

Drama is the personal activity that can help to redress the
balance, rebuild personality and confidence in self, and reopen
the areas of sensitivity to other people. This can be as true for
adults as it is for children.

With children, lack of opportunities for drama can lead to a
loss in balance of the two ways of using energy. This results in a
loss of concentration and absorption, of sincerity, of effort and of
personal confidence. They thus become more vulnerable to the
fears of failure that accompany competitive academic education.
If many years go by without the balance of personal activity, then
these losses and resultant fears will be exacerbated by the onset of
puberty and adolescence. Problems may become engrained in attitudes and behavior, many resulting from a lack of self-respect
and/or respect for others. From this point of view, early and
continuous use of drama should be considered as a beneficial
*preventive* measure, reducing the need for much therapy. However,
to consider drama in these terms tends to overlook its positive
value in the release of the whole personality.

Relaxation, breathing, awareness, sensitivity and selectivity are
complex progressive areas of human growth. They are a natural
outcome of creativity that includes drama, and are fundamental
to the development of such basic emotional skills of living as sympathy, understanding, tolerance and compassion. These are all as
basic as the accepted skills of reading, writing and number, and
they require as much regular and continuous practice if results
are to be achieved. They go beyond preparation for a job or function in life — they are part of the essence of life itself. Drama helps
the development of these skills at the same time as, and because
of, balancing personal and projected manners of using energy.

Is there, within this context, a working definition of *release?*
*The Pocket Oxford Dictionary* suggests: "Set free, liberate, deliver,
unfasten (from) . . . Liberation from confinement, fixed position,
trouble, this life, etc. . . . " Other definitions might include: "To
permit that which already is to come into existence, to be;" "To
permit the full harmony and unity of body, heart, mind and
spirit;" "To permit the full acceptance of the individual 100%."
Each of these embraces the idea of release. The problem is that
release is concerned with differences in people, the individuality
of the individual, whereas much of modern education is concerned with sameness, with conformity to a norm, with judgments
based on laid down standards — and all of these contribute to the
blockages that create the need for release. On the other hand,
education that does include release will fit youngsters more for an
educative process that is genuinely developmental and not merely
a means of achieving an imposed set of products within a competitive system.

So, hypothetically, let us say that one of our aims is to realize
the genuine 100% individual, without comparisons or conformity,
and with an acceptance of that individual's personal harmony and
unity.

This aim will often be accepted in the therapeutic situation —
education and society's last battle for conformity — when it is not
acceptable in the preventive situation. Just as release is not part of
the norm of the teacher's approach, so it is not necessarily acceptable either to parents or to the youngsters themselves who, from
an early age, have already been subjected to certain fixed and
conformist attitudes. Examples of the latter proliferate according
to the age of the youngster, and to adult expectation. For a boy to
cry through pain may be acceptable at one age but, at another,
be entirely contrary to the idea that big boys do not cry; the latter
attitude has many variables according to environment, parental
ambition and so on. "Have you been good today?" is perhaps the
most harrowing example of parents' hope for a quiet and un-
complicated life, based on expectations that the child has mastered accepted standards of home and school — no matter what
areas of hypocrisy this may involve, including lying, double-

dealing, fear of punishment and the possible loss of love and its attendant security. These are all factors—there are many others—in the process of blocking "the real me" from emerging; the longer they continue the greater becomes the need for release, and the more difficult the practical approaches to it.

We must be very clear that preventive measures are as much the concern of the home and the preschool child as they are, or should be, the function of school. The major damage to the process of normal growth can take place during the preschool years. For all kinds of social reasons, parents (particularly mothers) abdicate their responsibilities in those early years, leaving as much as possible to medical advice, clinics, and then subsequently to teachers and school; and they tend to support every legislative suggestion that school should start at an earlier age. Running a home for the first seven years of a child's life is not only a full time job but, when approached with sensitivity and dedication, is probably the most dignified and constructive, with the assured outcome of the security for the children involved. Yet parents need some kind of training program provision that goes beyond medical clinics. They need to understand that their children's early struggles in the processes called play are often growth areas that they can share; that play is not just a way of passing the time, of being amused, distracted and kept out of mischief. To quote Peter Slade again:

> Play is the Child's way of thinking, proving, relaxing, working, remembering, testing, creating and absorbing. Except for the actual physical process, it is life. It may well prove in future years that if Play is the actual manner of a Child's way of life, then Play may be the correct approach to all forms of education.[3]

When the first seven years of a child's life are properly catered for, then release will take place more naturally. This will eliminate, or certainly reduce, the problem during school years.

## 2  MOVEMENT AND WORD

Without doubt, the fullest basic need and coordinator in release is movement. Through this not only will physical release arise, but also emotional, psychological, intellectual and spiritual release—together with the intuitive harmonizing of all. It is perhaps not too exaggerated to state that only through movement is full release possible.

However, we have to be quite certain what kind of movement is necessary. What exactly is meant by movement? In traditional education, with few exceptions, the answer has always safeguarded the puritanical suspicion of any venture towards a Dionysian philosophy. Thus the image of Apollo is preserved through movement which is treated as "P.T." or "Phys. Ed." — no matter how thinly disguised with various euphemisms. Then basic aims are a healthy body and the development of team spirit. They allow for the notion of a *discipline,* the mastery of *techniques,* the development of teachable *vocabularies,* time-tabling for linear growth of a *subject,* some common agreement on *standards* (which eventually can reach out towards examinations) and, within the constantly changing structures of examinations, the possibility of *optional choice* through to fully professional *specialization,* even at degree level! Once processed through these established sieves, not only are Dionysian tendencies avoided but intellectual pursuits are again given precedence over intuitive potential. The resulting by-products of Bacchanalian excesses in private lives are blamed upon many other factors, seldom on this root cause.

Much of the call for therapeutic action derives from the same root, namely: the lack of opportunity for constant experience of the harmonious unity in all facets of self, through the liberating expression of intuitively based movement, the ecstasy (in the sense of exalted feeling) of dance. The therapist who comes from the same puritan background, with the same lack of opportunity in movement, is hardly likely to introduce movement as part of the therapeutic process — particularly when confronted with a wide choice, coupled with professional disagreement regarding which is *best.*

What is meant by movement within the context of this chapter is *improvised movement:* where no vocabulary has to be mastered, particularly in the early stages; where a process of letting go must precede control, which comes eventually from within according to individual readiness, and from which control there is considerable potential for enrichment and development.

This kind of movement has as individual a style in personal activity as handwriting has in projected activity. But movement and written work have many essential differences. The principal one is that, in traditional education, writing is an act of communication between student and teacher, whereas it is essential that movement (especially until confidence is established) is freed from any intended act of communication except for the intuitive perceptions of the teacher. Written work is dominated by the mastery of spelling, punctuation, muscle control in letter formation, etc. Hence the value of the tape recorder, which permits release to some genuine moments of creative composition with words. But improvised movement, especially when free of the demands of conscious communication, has no such restrictions. Intuition can and does supersede intellect.

Rules can be applied to formal types of movement, but this means another specialization. About the only agreed official educational line with regard to movement is the rejection of improvised forms. Thus the early and inevitable scribble stages of movement are rejected as pointless, meaningless and "mucking about." The Dionysian fear embraces the fear of emotion *per se.* The sophistication and control of emotion is desirable. But the puritanical view is that the release of emotion will let loose primitive and undesirable patterns of behavior, leading to self-indulgence, and thus perpetuate a state of being that it is the business of education to change. As the head of a large girls' secondary school once said, after viewing some genuine emotional release in drama: "I have managed to get thousands of girls through this school without any signs of emotion — and we're not going to start now!"

Consequently, in most education, nearly all experiences of emotion and feelings are vicarious. Furthermore, we can believe that if we exert the right control over what young people are exposed to, we can make sure that even vicarious experiences are "ennobling" rather than ecstatic (in the sense of exalting, even). Fortunately for young people, the arts of film and TV have become domestic arts over which we have no control. No matter how much we may deplore the emotional experiences young people reach out to and receive from these media, we must, nevertheless, face the fact that there is no evidence that the vicarious does help to make emotionally happy and balanced people. We see clearly that there needs to be something more direct—less vicarious.

Drama is seen to be a more direct experience. But we have to acknowledge that for the majority of youngsters we cannot use the richest and finest of "ennobling drama" because scripts demand an ability to read—indeed to read fluently and with particular skill, if the written word is to spring alive from the printed page. Thus it has been necessary to turn to the improvised spoken word.

However, with improvised speech the same circle of dissatisfaction arises as with improvised movement. Again there is the scribble stage to be gone through before there is any real flow of words; also the presence of an audience is inhibiting for some and a stimulus to exhibitionism for others. Getting into the depth of a part with full sincerity is not just a matter of adequate rehearsal. It is the result of constant practice of many basic factors such as concentration, sensitivity, physical release, vocal confidence, intuitive awareness of structure and atmosphere and so on. All of these are as applicable to and important for improvised drama as for a scripted play. Without them, improvised drama remains shallow and superficial, and often based only on personal experiences, including TV and film. For the therapist, this basis in personal experience is often precisely what he is concerned with, even when shallow and superficial. Diagnostically much is achieved, and the emotional relief from playing out certain types of haunting situations is also of value. Drama is thus demonstrably therapeutic, especially within other aspects of treatment.

Unfortunately the achievement of the spoken word without movement is amply supported by systems of training which either keep the two activities quite separate, or else pursue one without reference to the other. Without being melodramatic, it must be said that this is not only tragic but stupid. In both educational and therapeutic terms it is a stand that is indefensible from the point of view of young people or adults, whether or not they are in need of treatment. Fortunately, many of the finest teachers of speech and voice are using improvised movement as a focus for release, thus pointing out its value in terms of releasing, energizing and enriching the improvised spoken word.

If there are regular opportunities for improvised movement and speech, we eventually see them not only as mutually supportive, but also as able to stimulate and satisfy different areas of experience (and different factors within the same experiences), having their counterpart in other creative activities. Thus improvised movement has its counterpart in poetry and painting; improvised speech has its counterpart in prose and in drawing.

Poetry has been described as saturated experience expressed in a highly economic form, often using language symbolically. Improvised movement and dance-drama can be looked on from the same viewpoint. Indeed, it can be considered as "body poetry," equally concerned with the symbolic and with economy of form. Its content of saturated experience possibly will include aspects of the conscious and unconscious, and experiences from the collective unconscious. Basically the movement is intuitive, unsubjected to intellectual scrutiny and exactness.

Vast areas of human experience — yes, vast in the literal sense — can thus be explored through improvised dance-drama, in a similar manner to the exploration through written poetry. For example, in dance-drama, groups might explore a topic or subject such as "The birth of matter to the destruction of the world." The length of the dance-drama? Perhaps, often governed by the length of the piece of music being used, no more than four and one-half to five minutes! Written poetry could approach the same subject matter within the confines of a sonnet. In either spoken improvisation or its counterpart of written prose, it would be quite impossible to work with such economy of expression, nor would there be the same intuitive call upon the symbolic.

Group dance-drama has affinities with myth and legend, with ritual, with discovery, survival and adventure, with conquest and defeat, with birth, death and resurrection. It is related to Man the Thinker, Man the Feeler, and Man the Mystic, and the involvement in all of these is intuitive. We are part of the Dionysian experience of inspiration and ecstasy, satisfactorily catering for the irrational impulses in human nature, and discovering through experience the need for the rational. Intuition fires the imagination, and the mind gives form and shape to the physical expression.

## 3 PRACTICAL SUGGESTIONS

There are many different practical approaches to the beginnings and later development of improvised dance-drama, the choice obviously depending on many circumstances regarding the size of group, available space, etc. The following suggestions are not placed in any implied developmental order:

(1) Enjoying the repetition of any single vowel or consonant one decides to make, as quietly as wished — even as a whisper in the mind; and moving one or more parts of the body with the sound, from a finger or hand to the whole body; possibly with the eyes closed.

(2) Simply point to a mark on the ceiling — then withdraw arm and finger. Repeating to a simple shaking of a tambourine. A sequence of movements can be built by pointing at different places in turn, each time withdrawing completely before going on to the next place, and with varying rhythms and pace.

(3) Start by noting the position one is sitting in; then stretching and relaxing into a different position, and again becoming fully aware of it. Then into a third position. Suggestions can be made as to the kinds of position — e.g. uncomfortable, ugly, spiky, rounded, etc. Then a sequence of moving from one position to another, to a third, and back to the original position, can be developed with sound, at various paces, including slow motion and moments of stopping movement when the sound stops.

(4) Various sporting activities, including each person's own favorite sport; try in slow motion, ultra fast and at normal pace, with different sounds or music at different speeds. Activities can be done on the spot, or, if there is space, using it. Sudden stopping of movement when the sound stops; as in (3) above, the sudden stopping and the moving at different rates are concerned with personal physical control.

(5) The development of the above working in pairs with, if possible, frequent changes of partner.

(6)    Settling into different kinds of still photographs on themes
       suggested by the teacher or leader — action arrested by a high
       speed camera. Bringing the photograph to life with action,
       and with speaking if desired, on a pre-arranged signal (such
       as a single beat on a drum or tambour) and freezing still
       again on a further signal. This can often be most useful for
       those whose concentration span is short; the signal to stop can
       be given as soon as concentration is breaking down — often
       after only a matter of seconds — thus preventing any sense of
       failure.

(7)    As in (6) above, but in pairs, or, according to readiness, in
       threes or even larger groups. Both (6) and (7) can, of course,
       be brought to life in slow or fast motion.

(8)    Being "silly people" in silent movies to silent-movie-type music,
       in groups of three or four; being an old movie, the action goes
       faster than reality. Different experiences of pace can be provid-
       ed by playing the same music at different speeds. This is also
       useful for groups who have not done much movement before
       and may feel self-conscious or "silly." The invitation to be as
       silly as possible removes the worry.

(9)    Being astronauts floating in space or on the moon. Again
       starting from a still photograph, perhaps on one's own, but
       gradually working with other people. The slow motion helps
       a strong development of personal physical control. Very slow
       music, or electronic sounds can be used. A simple story line
       can be built up after initial pre-experience.

(10)   Starting from a curled up position on the floor and, with ac-
       companying slow growth to climax sound on drum or cymbal,
       growing from this "seed" position into: large ugly monsters;
       small, fast insects; birds; apes; other animals. Next a strong
       time beat or simple rhythms for individual movement to sug-
       gestions such as walking through a forest, hunting for food,
       finding a new home, etc. Then, with slowing down of sound,
       returning to original position to rest or sleep. The growth
       from a seed helps movement to be positive within the im-
       aginative circumstances suggested. Simple story line can
       develop after pre-experience.

(11) In small groups, make a simple story about any of the creatures experienced in (10), for example: migration of the beasts; survival; the great drought, etc.

(12) As in (10) above, starting from a curled up position and growing into nightmare people, things, creatures, etc. Again adding simple story line after initial pre-experience, and then, as in (11) above, making up a simple movement story in small groups. Music should be strong in atmosphere, with a very clear time beat. If people are feeling self-conscious about early experiences of movement, it helps to work on ugly or nightmare experience as this gets rid of the worry that they cannot move "gracefully" or "beautifully."

(13) Using (10) and (11) above as pre-experience, developing a movement or dance-drama based on "The Creation" or "Evolution," perhaps developing as far as the evolution of Man. This can be built up in small groups of four or five, or as a full group experience within a story shape narrated by the teacher or leader.

(14) Developing (13) above to explore different aspects of Man: (a) Man the Hunter (including being hunter and hunted); (b) Man the Explorer and Discoverer; (c) Man and the Elements, and their external conflict; (d) Agricultural Man, including sowing and harvesting and being the seed as well as the man; (e) Industrial Man, including being and/or working machines. All of these can include beginnings with pre-experience.

(15) The journey. This is one of the most important aspects of both movement and drama, catering for the whole range of human experience from reality to symbolism, and linking naturally with (14) above and (16). The journey may involve each person working on his own, or can accommodate various sizes of group, including whole class experience. To start with a still photograph can help with swift, intuitive beginnings, leaving detail to be decided on at later stages, according to readiness. Music needs to be strongly emotional; we are concerned with the inner experience of "struggle" not the external illustration through accuracy of mime. Journeys provide a natural field of adventure, based on reality or im-

agination, and an equally natural concern with conflict, particularly with the elements and different environments.

(16) Rituals. Like the journey, the ritual is also a deep part of human experience, embracing past, present and future, and catering for the imaginative and realistic within the terms of intuitive expression. Rituals can include: supplication, prayer, thanksgiving, sacrifice, celebration. They lend themselves naturally to symbolism and the constructive use of conflicts, between Man and Man, as well as Man and the Elements, Man and the Gods, superstition, magic and so on. There are natural links with (14) and (15) above, and some of the earlier suggestions (e.g. 10 and 11) may well prove useful as pre-experience. The ritual is also a natural move towards declamatory and bold speech work, just as the sequence (10) involves the early use of vocal sounds.

(17) Conflict. In drama, fighting is often an outward sign of an inner condition, including the personal conflicts, frustrations and numerous other sources of feelings of aggression. In movement, such feelings can be catered for by the constructive build-up of various forms of fight — from the use of swords and daggers to that of fists and wrestling. The fight should be built in slow motion, blow by blow, to an intended pattern, and accompanied by a sound control such as a strong drum or cymbal beat. No props, such as sticks or rulers, should be used, as the materialism of properties takes away from the full concentration that involves inner experience; there is also the practical risk that, with properties, people may hurt one another, whereas they cannot do so with imaginary weapons. Fighting can arise naturally from many of the suggestions in (14, 15, 16 above); alternatively, the arranging of a basic fight may well stimulate stories connected with these sources or with (18) below.

(18) As a basis of dance-drama, the use of myths and legends. Much previous work (14, 15, 16, and 17) above will lend itself as a basic approach to, or pre-experience for, such use. Emphasis should be given to the emotional and symbolic experience rather than the detail of intellectual facts. Ap-

proached as dance-drama, the material is used intuitively; later, other significant detail can be added, particularly when there is confident readiness to add improvised speech. The ritual, the journey and the fight can all be significant here.

(19) Other source material for dance-dramas: proverbs; famous sayings; quotations; parables; poems; soliloquies from plays; characters and/or situations from novels; a day in the life of...; a thousand ages are but a...; contemporary problems: e.g. pollution, the third world, strikes, civil wars, refugees, old age, sickness and disease, poverty, space exploration, atomic arms race, sources of energy, color bar, medicine, TV advertisements. All of the above can be explored through spoken improvisation, extracts from poems and plays and adaptation of novels. But there are very particular intuitive experiences that arise only through the use of the material in movement.

(20) Conscious movement. In the early stages of movement, the body is stimulated by imaginative ideas. Once confidence is established through these means, then more conscious awareness of the body and its capacity to move can be introduced and, indeed, used as a stimulation to the imagination. For example: start from simple stretching and relaxing; then add the development of stretching out in every direction, to all points of the compass, high and low, in front and behind and to either side, keeping a continuous easy flow of movement throughout all of the space that surrounds oneself. Now and again, stop the movement with a signal; then invite personal and private decisions as to what one might be doing if caught by a high speed camera in that precise position while actually doing some positive activity. Repeat, including the addition of sounds or music.

(21) Where lighting is appropriately possible, repeat and develop the above with each person working to and with his own shadow.

(22) If there is a single spotlight that is maneuverable, then repeat (20) and (21) above, using all the floor space in an attempt to keep out of the light; then to try to keep in the light.

(Note: ability to change the atmosphere through the use of light can be a most important stimulus to the imagination; and the provision of areas in complete shadow, almost to the point of darkness, can help the shy and the inhibited until confidence has grown. Their use of lighted and shadowed areas will help us to see how they are feeling within the work. Our observations should not be made conscious to them.)

(23) Mirror work. In pairs, face each other with arms and hands simply extended until fingers are touching. Having thus established a physical relationship, lower arms. Now whatever movement one person makes, the other is echoing at the same moment as a reflection. Let the movement be slow and of arms only to start with. As confidence grows, then use more of the body and let the movement quicken in pace. Become still on a signal (handclap, drum beat, etc.). Decide what the shape you both make in your stillness might symbolize for a sculpture in a park, or in front of a town hall, or whatever. Find a new partner. Repeat the exercise, only this time one of you is A and the other B; A moves first, keeping his own simple flow going while B, as A's reflection, keeps absolutely with him. Again: stop on a signal, and make the imaginative decision, discussed quietly by each pair. Change partners and repeat. There are many variations, including the use of various kinds of music. The lead should constantly be changed so that A also experiences keeping with B. In this manner, each person discovers and experiences ways of moving that are new and different for him. Character, various moods and feelings, can all be added as a variation. Encourage boldness and taking risks rather than anxiety about going wrong.

(24) Develop (23) above with groups of three instead of in pairs. Then gradually increase the size of groups, according to readiness, until there are attempts with the whole group in a large circle moving together at one and the same time.

(25) Individual improvised dance. When absorption is strong and confidence established, provide opportunities for each person to improvise his own dance (though the whole group are all

working at one and the same time so that there is no audience) to a wide variety of music. Do not expect this to last for very long at the first attempts. Low or little light can be most helpful in the early stages of this quite spontaneous and intuitive personal dance.

(26) Allow, in small groups, the building up and development of their own dance-dramas to various kinds of music.

(27) Encourage through repetition and discussion the polishing of some of these. Discussion should be private to each group, and it is wise to encourage them to think first of what is going well.

(28) Develop some moments when the movement is to the group's own created simple sounds, and also the use of words.

(29) Many of the above examples lend themselves to the use of simple, creative music with soundmakers created by the group. In particular, rituals lend themselves to this use of creative and improvised music linked to movement.

(30) Many of the above examples lend themselves to program building on a theme, using improvised movement, improvised speech, extracts from poems, plays and adaptations of scenes from novels. They can also link to the use of light, creative music, the tape recorder and other media (such as the slide projector). Such program building moves into a positive area of communication based on personal creation.

# 4 LINKS WITH OTHER ARTS

Links from movement to other creative activities are essential as part of the balance between personal and projected manners of using energy. It is an easy step to move from any of the above examples to: (a) individual painting; (b) small and large group painting; (c) individual or small group use of chalks and charcoal; (d) individual use of clay, leading to group assembly; (e) model making (which, with the use of simple flashlights can be used for the development of son et lumière experiences); (f) individual and small group writing of poetry; (g) small group creation of folk songs; (h) mask making. These, in turn, can lead back to further movement work. Where music has been used for a dance-drama, the same music will invariably help creativity in other media, but needs extension in time, perhaps achieved by repetition. It is important to be able to move swiftly and easily from one activity to another by having all necessary equipment in the same working space.

## 5   SUGGESTIONS FOR BEGINNERS

The following advice may be both impertinent and presumptuous. The various points are offered with the simple hope that a few of them might be helpful to anyone new to this work. I was privileged to be one of an army of pioneers — and the privilege of pioneering is that you can fall flat on your face as often as necessary, and there is no specialist to point a finger at the error of your ways. Giving oneself permission to fail is paramount for anyone attempting this work, which is now bedeviled with specialists, esotericism and lauded authorities. Someone has wisely said: "Anything you can neatly define, you confine." Thus, it is important for newcomers to this work to trust their own intuition, to view with a mixture of objective interest and grave suspicion all proven case histories, and solemnly to give up any secret hope or desire for infallibility! Some suggestions are:

(1)   Everybody works at one and the same time; there is no audience.

(2)   The atmosphere of every session should be wholly uncritical.

(3)   An uncritical atmosphere should not be confused with a radical cry for total freedom. That kind of ill-timed and misguided freedom invariably turns to license and anarchy, which is as miserable for the participants as it is for the leader or teacher. In his or her hands, firm control should exist until there is readiness in the group for a gradual acceptance of their own personal control. Making a simple bond is important. For example: "When I touch the cymbal or drum, see if it is possible to become quite still, whatever position you are in, yes, even if one leg is off the ground; and, at the same time, see if it is possible to cut yourself off right in the middle of a sentence. Let's try it." Such an approach is quite different from: "When you hear this sound, become still and quiet and listen to me." It is also different from bruising one's hands and losing one's voice in order to

get a hearing!

(4) Avoid any kind of evaluation either during or after sessions. Particularly avoid picking on individuals for either praise or blame.

(5) With new groups, it is necessary in the early stages to give ideas about *what* to do — but never *how* to do it. Each person finds his own way, which is valid for him at that time — yes, even if out of lack of confidence he copies someone else in the group. Expect and enjoy many different approaches. There is no correct one.

(6) For people new to the work, exercises should be kept very short (sometimes literally only seconds) and gauged by the degree of concentration and capacity to sustain that concentration. Stop activities as concentration begins to fail, thus rescuing everyone from any sense of failure. Gauge time by those with least concentration. Keep atmosphere buoyant, lively, joyful and busy. Move swiftly from one exercise to the next.

(7) In early movement work, use simple instruments (e.g., a tambour, tambourine, cymbal or drum) rather than recorded music. When starting to use music, expect to use very short passages rather than whole pieces. Give opportunity for short, simple experiences of time beat, rhythm, climax and de-climax. But do not teach these experiences. If you do, you produce "Pavlov dog responses," quite different from genuine "readiness."

(8) Keep verbal instructions short, simple and clear. Check for understanding, but do not get involved in deep discussions. Do not feel the need to explain why any piece of work is being done. Certainly avoid such explanation before the work itself, otherwise some people in the group will "play the reason" rather than do the exercise. If explanation is necessary, then leave it until afterwards and keep it very simple. Seemingly deep and impressive explanations often lead to justifiable suspicions about future work.

(9) Confess, enjoy, apologize and have a sense of humor about your own mistakes, even such simple ones as putting on the wrong music or not having the phonograph switched on.

Your humanity is a greater asset than your knowledge — and everybody loves the village idiot; they only fear the lord of the manor!

(10) Try to avoid having definite end products in mind. Should this be unavoidable, then be ready for and expect something quite different.

(11) Do not impose the successes of one group upon another. Do not avoid trying something with a second group simply because it did not work with the first.

(12) If you have outside observers, make certain they know how to behave with uncritical sensitivity.

(13) Get into the habit of considering what went well (even a single moment) before lacerating yourself with what failed. When the group is ready to polish its own work by discussion and repetition, help them to feel a similar positive approach.

(14) It is necessary to have in mind, before each session, different exercises, or approaches, or intentions. But have contrasting alternatives ready at your finger tips — even the weather can completely nullify a particular plan.

(15) Whatever you have planned, be sure you know why. Yet be ready for sudden intuitive hunches that change your direction in the midst of a session.

(16) Keep reminding yourself of the incredible length of time behind all creation — the acorn to the oak tree! Expect to be tired.

(17) Constantly train your own capacity for observing without being an audience.

(18) Try to find the means, opportunity and time to do many of the exercises yourself, not in order to decide how they should be done, but so that you can feel in touch with what you are asking of others. However, generally speaking, do not join in with your group as you then lose the capacity for observing; also, if you are talented, the group may become audience to your effort.

(19) Of course you have to judge, to assess. But keep on repeating to yourself, very gently, very firmly: "Every person has his own 100%, which will be different from every other person's — but a hundred percent is a hundred percent is a . . . ."

## FOOTNOTES

1. Peter Slade, *Child Drama* (London: University of London Press, 1954), p. 29.
2. *Ibid.*, p. 35.
3. *Ibid.*, p. 42.

E. J. BURTON, a graduate of University College, London, has been a schoolmaster, college and university tutor and examiner, priest, and bishop. He is a prolific author and editor in drama, theatre, education, and theology.

*Chapter 18*

# DISADVANTAGED CHILDREN IN SCHOOLS

E. J. Burton

## 1 INTRODUCTION

Therapy concerns all human beings. It is not a term only for those so maladjusted, unhappy, or frustrated, that their needs and sickness become obvious. All of us need to find balance, fruitful relationship, with our fellows, our work in the world, and enjoy the fullness of our abilities, the satisfaction of our natural requirements.

Drama is similarly a total activity, which exercises *all* forms of evolved life. It is also concerned with our relationship to our surroundings, physical or mental, with individual life and activity, with community, with the whole human situation and potential. It may be instanced through a wide range: from kittens at play, "acting out" a hunt, stalking, attacking in mimic battle, on to human hunting rituals, to fertility dramas comprising all the actions of sowing and harvest; and on again to the struggle and quest of mankind in "religious" themes, *Man and Superman, Waiting for Godot,* the tortured spirits of *Huis Clos,* and the existential finalities of *King Lear, Peer Gynt,* and *The Flies.*

Since both drama and therapy are concerned with the "whole" of life and its active process, they will inevitably intertwine, and organically function constantly as one. Very little of each pursuit will be irrelevant to the other. Yet while it is true to say that the arts (here particularly drama with its sharing and communicating activity in theatre) are *always* therapeutic, therapy is not always

317

drama or other art. Both need to function within the wide context of human community (reflected in our imperfect societies) to
be more fully effective.

## 2   THEATRE AS THERAPY

Granted that therapy and drama both cover all human relationships, though differing in immediacy, range, or scope, let us examine some practical examples of the way in which they work
together as one process with infinite variations of emphasis.

Here we have a children's Theatre-In-Education Company which
gives its show, using the hall floor in a primary school in an urban
community. Among those watching are a class of about twenty-four
"retarded" or difficult children.

The teacher reported to me:

> "When they returned to the classroom, they talked very easily with
> one another, and then with me. Usually they are withdrawn and un-
> communicative. But now they were asking about costumes, masks,
> the lighting, not only the story and the play itself, but all the various
> elements of the experience."

Yet the class was composed of children who find difficulty in accepting or sharing normal educational patterns of school life.
Here, the actors and the play had, as it were, taken them by surprise. There was no chance to build a barrier. The immediacy,
the proximity of the actors, had taken them into experience. This
is the vitality of drama/theatre. But it has to be *basic*: plenty of
movement, music, mime, and dance, as in all "total" theatre.
The remoteness of the formal proscenium frame production may
have the effect of making such children feel uneasy and further
withdrawn. For others, that proscenium may add an extra element of wonder. But for the disadvantaged there needs to be a
warm and immediate experience in terms that do not suggest
adult approaches.

Further, the themes must not be too related to their everyday
disciplines and restraints. They may, indeed, parallel these; effort, deprivation, frustration, and struggle — fundamentals in

drama — are always important. This is a generally accepted principle in children's theatre. A play is not often aimed at the subnormal or disadvantaged. The real therapy is their special response to a play suitable for all children in its presentation and themes. So it was with the children mentioned above: they were brought into life by the talk and comment which the play initiated. Their own problems and needs were exercised in their response to the play, and not by carefully angled arguments or clinical approaches in the drama itself.

Is not this opportunity for assessment and new vision what drama affords us all (however gifted, intellectual, or successful) as human beings? There is no one, not even a Shakespeare or an Einstein, who does not experience this therapy of drama, in theatre or otherwise. From presentation there follows the ripple out into discussion, life, ideas, initiating that cross fertilization that we call creativity. Drama/theatre is there not to "smooth over" and soothe. It is there to disturb, to uncover causes of disharmony and "infertility" in life. It is the eternal probing surgeon, which is cruel only to be kind, to expose and remove the cancer so that the individual and his community may be cured. And not merely to cure, but to promote further fresh possibilities of fulfillment and wholeness which are therapy for the existing situation and participants.[1]

Drama/theatre never does this (*qua* drama/theatre) by direct preaching or instruction. It achieves its end by involving all within a healing, fulfilling, even if sometimes painful, organic activity. Life heals life; participation fosters wholeness and "health" (mental, intellectual, spiritual). Diversion from the bodily and mental tensions of the immediate moment brings adjustment, proportion, and a fresh initiative.

Louis XIV of France was tired of direct attempts to rid his courtiers of anti-social attitudes and faults. He encouraged Molière, it is said, to write *comédie* around such characters that they might see themselves (as it were) and participate in their own follies. One of the amusing results was *The Bores,* an entirely health-giving project. It may sometimes be that satire, and other attempts to integrate humanity within acceptable normality, may be used to promote attitudes which are limiting. To laugh at our own absurdities is at least a step towards being cured. It is human absurdity in itself, pride, unawareness, and pomposity, that is the disease the theatre may treat; not failure to conform to certain establishment "manners" or the amusing affectations of some authoritarian regimes. These drama reveals as stultification of life, even through their own plays when presented to following generations. Drama wins in the end.

## 3   DRAMATIC ACTIVITY AS THERAPY

### The Disadvantaged

Let us consider further our particular group of disadvantaged children. Those in the school who seem inarticulate, poor readers, socially unadjusted, individually maladjusted, often with (apparently) low I.Q., are given to one teacher, who specializes in their education. They range from seven to ten in age. They are under observation by the area psychotherapist. Their developing ability to cooperate and work with others is debatable. Many clearly are simply "backward" in learning. But backwardness (inability to read or utter) is often associated with some kind of personal disturbance. A teacher should not try to act in place of a psychotherapist. He may do great harm. He should know the analyst's diagnosis of the problem; but, knowing that problem, he has to deal with the child actively and constructively. Drama opens a way.

The children know why they are in the special class in terms *that they can accept:* they are "poor readers." That is the basis for their position. Work in the class centers nominally round "English," the ability to speak and to write. Drama motivates, activates, and brings into expression and communication, widening sensitivity and interest. The teacher was asked by the psychotherapist what other subjects were taught. She said, "None." She added that everything centered on "English" and that numeracy, history, and geography, were worked from "general knowledge." Sharing information, responding to it, were the prime concerns of the children. They had to be aligned with life. Drama was an important way of achieving this end.

So this group, varying in age, social position, needs (instead of being treated as individual "cases," marked off in their own minds as inferior or outcast), work together. As soon as competent reading and confidence are secured, they return to the mainstream of the school, normally according to their age. They can hold their own. The important factor in "holding their own" is the success of general therapy (with drama as a significant element) in the class. Failures in adjustment are few. Usually, the child plays out, comes to face, comes to terms with, problems and conflicts. Inarticulacy has been overcome because the child has expressed, argued out, the things he wanted to say, or longed to make part of his image, his dealing with people and life.

The teacher uses folk stories, narrative poetry, simple themes such as snow, exploration, shopping. After the first hesitancies, the children move quickly into the "play." *Story telling is always potential action.* Children in a congenial atmosphere respond towards "realizing" events by spontaneous move or gesture, within the group situation with leader or teacher. While not unduly discouraging such individual movement, the teacher continues with the story, holding the attention of the group. This is the art of the teacher. When the story is ended, then the group may move freely into activity. Thus the Gaelic folk story about the MacCrimmons, published in *Tocher (I)* by the School of Scottish Studies at Edinburgh, was read to the class. It concerns the young lad whose brothers went off to the "great piping," and left him alone to look after work and flocks. While he is sitting miserably, a small green man appears and asks him why he is so woebegone. The little man listens to his story and then tells him to go up to the house, get his "pipes," and be off. "But I can't play." "Never mind," says the little man. "I have no pipes." The little man shows him a chest in the house, and unlocks it. There are *golden* pipes! Off he goes, although he cannot play a note, arrives at the games, and wins the piping contest. "It's the Cinderella story," said one of the class. There is much more incident to it, opening doors as if by magic, discomfiting the big brothers, and so on. As the teacher finished reading, the children were already moving, trying to mime the playing of bagpipes (these children were southerners in

Kent, but had a general idea of the bagpipe), dancing to the imagined tune, being "green men," opening doors by magic, finding wonderful things in "kists" or "chests," and gradually filling in the action background.[2]

The relevance of the folk story or traditional fairy tale to therapy must not be underestimated. The Cinderella theme comes in many shapes and forms; it echoes a common need for recognition by the deprived, it protests (genially) about the overbearing elders, sisters or brothers. But there is at once a therapy and a hope, a *recognition* that there is for all, potentially, a quality in life of recovery and restoration—whether this power manifests as a disgustingly ornate fairy god-mother, or the much more acceptable "little green man" with his ingenious suggestions and expertise. Similarly, as I shall suggest later, therapy comes through archetypal themes, placed before the children a *general* way. Into such themes and stories the children send down roots (as it were) and find the collective unconscious of human life. Drawing upon these deeper stores of community and experience, they *transform in their own way the dramatic action* and express, objectify, and come to terms with, their own needs. This is far from fantasy in the negative sense, which is usually a pleasant (and often tragic) attempt to fulfill needs in the conscious world of events (as the pop fans in a TV interview who said frankly that they fantasized on such matters as lovemaking with their idols, and the like). The children dramatizing, on the other hand, draw on deep and hidden reserves of life energies and relationships.

Let us now examine one boy within this group of disadvantaged. I quote: "When he came to me two and a half years ago he was not only completely illiterate, but his mother (who had left him and his brother to live with another man) and his father (who opted out of responsibility and wanted to put the children in a home) had never paid any attention to his speech and he was completely unable to communicate verbally—unable to form the sounds needed for words. The other children equally were quite unable to understand him in his efforts to communicate. His grandmother saved the children from being put in a home. She was a truly wonderful woman and we worked together on his speech and he can now talk intelligibly. But he remained very much in his shell." The class was now listening to and repeating lines from *Hiawatha*, again a simple theme, almost a folk story, and, as usual, moved into the actions, miming and working as a group through various adventures. This boy began to come into a new initiative. Without aggression he gradually found tremendous happiness and a new confidence in "acting."

Now we move into that controversial area: the place of theatre for younger children. Should they be allowed to perform before an audience? The time came for the annual "folk ritual" of Christmas, with all classes expected to "get up" something for parents and friends. The disadvantaged group found enthusiasm in devising costumes and props for the Hiawatha story. They presented that. The boy was in the leading role. Foolish, you say? Hardly. It is the really shy and wounded who often enough become the most sincere actors. Without any showing off or exhibitionism; just absorption and dedication—a new unity found within themselves which they want to share. The teacher continues, "I had intended to read the poem myself." She had thought that the children could move and mime and dance, while she kept the story going. "But the children took over from me, and of their own volition recited—often in chorus—the lines of the poem." The boy "gave a remarkably sensitive performance of the leading role, though a year ago I could not have got him in the back row of the chorus. So that is another point in favor of drama in schools (even the theatre-type drama of the produced play!). Such produced drama in our school is very spontaneous and comes once a year; it would not be successful if the children were not so involved in the production. More stilted performances did come from two or three classes who perform what I call 'teacher centered' drama—and it showed! Perfect but lifeless."

There may be shaking of heads at any account given of such dramatic work. What will happen to this boy? Two thoughts emerge. *Drama is not a therapy on its own.* Such a typical case as this—I could parallel it with many from long experience, where I have been able to follow up the lasting therapy of dramatic experience, integration, confidence, and adjustment in happy lives—instances the need for "community" and "caring." Drama is part of our total relationship. Here, too, there was the remedial

treatment of other factors, such as the development of oral communication. But within such a framework, drama had its potent
healing role. It is the avoidance of any suggestion of special treatment that is important. The child must be able to feel that he is
"normal;" yes, of course, he knows when he cannot do this or
that — speak, for example. But the conviction that he is ultimately
normal, able to hold his own with others, and not an invalid — an
attitude rather encouraged by visits to special clinics and
psychiatrists — places him in a position to deal with needs and
tasks. "I can cure this, because others can — and I am as others."
The role of drama is largely to rescue children from special treatment and isolation. Such was the inordinately shy girl sent to me,
as a recruit for my drama group. Once involved with the group
and not forced to take a prominent part, her interests rapidly
developed into all associated activities, from prompter to seam-
stress. She was thirteen at the time, and we devised costumes for
our own dramas. We did not perform in public, but once a year
showed the rest of the school what we had accomplished. She
gained confidence, inhibitions died, and all her work elsewhere
improved. A story to be repeated many times.

The boy in question (given the part of Hiawatha) began to
speak now with purpose and confidence; he acquired a new
dimension and status. In a year, from being "speechless" (so far as
his fellows were concerned) he had evolved not merely into an
adequate, if at first shy, communicator, but then to "control" in a
community situation, where he was not only a person but a
positive contributor.

At the end of the enactment, parents who attended said, "What a
pity your backward children could not join in this play." The
teacher said simply, "These *are* my backward children."

We would emphasize the development of this boy in a group
situation and note the words of the teacher: "The therapy is not
the work of drama only, but within an entire situation." This we
would stress: Drama is not a single therapy; it is part of a whole
healing process. The isolated interview, intermittent treatment,
does less for children than ongoing concern, a day-to-day and
reliable pattern of living.

## The Gifted

At the other end of the I.Q. scale, we find children who are not separated and neurotic by lack of ability or hard circumstances, but isolated by awareness and intelligence. These are the so-called "gifted," I.Q. around 150 plus. Here we must distinguish those who are simply lonely because they can see so clearly, solve so readily, cut off by this almost intuitive response to life, and those who are neurotic by this isolation and unique perceptiveness. Suffering does not necessarily result, although there may be other side-effects such as contempt for their fellows or exploitation of their intelligence. They may indeed become "clever devils."

Two processes help towards therapy. One is to bring the children without any specific age grouping (from eight, say, to sixteen) into a community situation, where each may meet all and find acceptable companionship (or competition) with the group sharing its own perceptive awareness and quickness of response. This can be through a camp, with opportunities for healthy activity available in woods, lawns, and larger tents (or buildings) with raw materials for painting, pottery, constructional crafts. There may be some specialist tutors for astronomy, field craft, and what you will. Do not be too anxious to cover all fields of interest. Children respond to any possibility—they are human beings, even if already expert musicians or scientists. Among the more general provisions one includes drama and dance which will evolve normally from play, as well as opportunities for ball games and the like. Here one may observe that the whole project is to restore the children to usual concerns of human being and child growth, away from artifical urban environment and similar strains. Naturally, there must be sympathetic care for those who are at first lonely, or unused to life away from overprotective care of parents and brick walls. Such a "community" obviates incipient neuroses, the feeling of isolation from the world which the gifted child feels on his or her own. It may tend to promote elitism, but one simple fact is that these children are less elite (in their own attitude) when brought together. And another simple fact is that they *are* elite, in whatever sense the word is used—always remembering that the gifted child is like all other children, only more so. He or she is a human being, a *particularly* human being.

Secondly, there still remain the shy, the withdrawn, and the insecure. For these, drama acts as a therapy in a special way. A theme given for dramatic work, exemplified, and then left to the children's own exploration, must be general and archetypal. To attempt to play out a particular neurosis is always a way to failure; embarrassingly specific and over-precise psychotherapy is nearly always imperfect; it may *appear* to succeed, as does a surgical operation. It is not a way to real wholeness or harmony. Stanislavski's principle, that one cannot manifest or play out an emotion as such still holds. One can only give a life situation in which the emotion may be allowed scope. Give a general theme for dramatization and the child will unconsciously reveal, objectify and often resolve, his inner fears and insecurities. Again, drama is within the *whole* life pattern; let them come to "life" without your conscious intervention if possible. If that intervention is needed, provide it in terms of the dramatization which is going on. This is a most difficult task. Whether or not one succeeds, one sometimes will not know for years. One has to live with them in the work, talk *with* them, not *at* them, and again without the falsity of abandoning one's own status, or quasi-fatherhood. This again, is difficult. On the other hand, a simple week at a camp and entry upon human companionship, games, contest, and freedom from false pressures has often led them into harmony, a new initiative and understanding of themselves and others. (By understanding I indicate a practical and working relationship with their own abilities and with those they meet, a new tolerance of the human condition.)

Here is a group of "gifteds" introduced to dramatic activity, working indoors on a weekend. Their need was to use their "world" of questioning and immediate response in some way; to express, to move their knowledge and ideas, to be able to bring these into acceptance and relevance.

It would be easy to theorize on the help that drama might give towards the fulfillment and adjustment of these children. Only too easy! Let us merely note some of the things that have occurred.

With this mixed group (aged eight to twelve) who had done no dramatic work before ("I'll try anything once," said a boy), I introduced activity by the usual sitting still on the floor.[3] We explored imagined sand and mud with the hand and found "objects." Then (I skip the intermediate stages—"gifteds" like to feel something they can latch on to immediately) we moved around, journeyed to explore a sandy waste, which became a desert, struggled through under the burning sun, found an oasis, and, each for himself/herself, explored it, and found whatever we felt we should find. As each ended his exploration he sat down quietly. Then we quickly formed groups, with the idea that each group should make its own exploration—this time as a team, to rehearse and present the little play to the others. (We were working in a room where other activities were going on, constant noise and chatter, but the children never seemed to be distracted. This power of concentration on the task in hand, the exclusion of all else once attention has been focused, I have noted with these children again and again. You may say this is a mark of *all* children.)

The scenes that resulted were precisely the same in general pattern and quality as those with other children in other places. There was the same range; possibly the overall standard of the acting and the mime, gesture, and speech which emerged was rather higher, but not to any significant extent. The interesting thing was *the content*. Where other children find vague treasures or horrors in some desert temple, for example, these found (quite naturally, fitted easily into context) much more interesting things. Thus one group found a statue of the goddess Ishtar (in a small vault) which was covered with gold leaf. "Showing off," I hear some cynic say. No, they were not. The speech accompanying, and the comments as they examined the find, were easy and genuine. So, too, the question afterwards, "How did that get here—away in the desert?" They had been told to bring the scene quickly to an end, and so they simply placed the statue with their "baggage" and left the matter there.

A further example. A group at a camp demanded (though I was, to say truth, rather tired and would have dodged the work if

I could) to have a further drama session after tea. It was a wet day and all rooms were occupied. We found a small shelter, open to the air, which was used for hay, and here in a space about ten feet by six feet we built up some plays. This time I took the idea of escape as a theme, and after work in which all shared to establish the idea as a basis — traveling along narrow defiles, underground passages, rocky caves, and emerging — they made their own dramas. One boy had, on his own initiative a year before, explored certain prehistoric earthworks, and his group naturally chose to re-enact escape from such a place. But instead of the usual hectic (and "hammy") emotional striving and exaggerated gasps which sometimes result from such a situation, the group settled down quietly to consider ways of getting out. They examined the rock formation, and decided it was of a kind that would fracture if struck so as to flake. What was clear, again, was that this was all in the situation. They thought and acted their way through, discussing as they went along sensible and logical methods to get out of such a stone-capped tomb when the entrance had caved in. Watching, one felt one was seeing an actual event. The intellectual content was itself a dramatic struggle; argument developed. Rival theories were taken up.

One's own experience is the basis of any genuine acting. Imagination is the building of such experience into fresh patterns which enable one to envisage, to stretch forward into, realms as yet unknown. There may, however, be in addition a surplus of individual emotional suffering or joy; this becomes in drama an actual and more intensive "playing out," where experience is not merely used but takes over the whole scene. This occurred when I used the theme of escape.

But our whole life together in camp was largely an escape not *from* reality but *into the reality* of physical work, shared tasks, fundamental communal relationships, which enable us to adjust and to find the wholeness of human society. "Gifteds" are no more likely in *themselves* to be disturbed than others; it is only the pressures towards conformity in contemporary society which may suggest a higher rate of disturbance, especially pressures from their own highly conformist adolescent groups and fashion cliques.

However, in the play presented by one group, a house in the woods was entered through an upper window. Alas, the ladder by which they gained access was knocked away. They tried to get out by the ground floor, failed, and found a trap door. They went down this, and found, logically enough, a further door, leading up to a coal chute, a way to the outer world. But when they came to the outer world, all was worse. The ground was marshy; it became shifting sands. It was here that a girl took over. Obviously it had become her drama; the outline agreed was developing her way. She tested the ground, but she could find nowhere safe to stand; she tried again. As in a dream, she repeated, "Sinking sands, sinking sands." She told the others to keep back. The whole scene took on a fantasy quality. They were acting on the damp grass and straw (almost in the open) yet the sense of constriction and fear was enclosing the group. Everywhere they turned there seemed uncertainty. The boys took the girl back into the house. They sat there. Without breaking the mood more than necessary, I said quietly, "Try upstairs again—you may find a window *will* open." They climbed to the ground floor, and, in obedience to the "voice from beyond," did as suggested, and emerged on the other side of the house.

## 4 CONCLUSION

The psychotherapist might well analyze the experience above, the drama which was evoked, in a revealing light. He might even tell me I had acted erroneously, that I should have allowed the girl to struggle on. I would say that my simple suggestion was within my own involvement with the drama of the improvisers. This relationship is a very subtle one, as all who work thus know. However, the teacher must be aware of the analysis and judgment of the psychotherapist.

In this summary treatment I would note that I have necessarily been aware, through students and colleagues, of the use of drama in more serious cases of disturbance—in mental hospitals, for example. They seem to me always to confirm the general role of drama that, however much the individual is involved, it is a group activity, with a general theme set before those enacting which furnishes (in its own way) an opportunity for individual expression

and sublimation, easing and externalizing for assessment inner
neuroses. From the dramatization the psychotherapist may learn
much for his own use. Things will be revealed more fully than on the
psychiatrist's couch. Furthermore, the patient does not seem to
regard himself as a patient under scrutiny. He is free. One
noticeable effect during dramatization was cessation of fidgeting,
rocking movements and nervous habits. And afterwards, a greater
measure of relaxation. No one needs to be told of the stammering
boy who, put into an improvisation, immediately speaks confidently
and clearly. Something of that new and better role is brought back
into his own "daily role" as himself. There is play back. The part
they take is a step not *from* reality but *to* reality, the use of their
mental and physical equipment, the realization that they are not actually hampered by inabilities, backgrounds, or environment.

## Four principles

(1) Drama is essentially a community, group, phenomenon. Any
    effective therapy is achieved within group work, the individual
    relating to, and with, the group to environmental challenges
    and potentials.

(2) No individually angled, detailed, theme should be set; no
    specific and obvious preaching to the patient. All themes
    should be general, archetypal, possibly to be assessed in terms
    of the collective unconscious (or whatever technical phrase you
    would use). Purposely, I have avoided all such terms since I
    hold with a contemporary philosopher that whenever one at-
    tempts to impose a category or concept upon life something is
    lost. Vaguer terms contain far more, despite or because of their
    ambiguity, of what one has to communicate.

(3) For children, themes are often contained creatively within
    folklore. Indeed, is not all life potential and process contained
    within folklore? In such drama we reach back into the "soil" of
    life, even as in poetry we may envisage further reaches and in-
    herent power.

(4) Clinical treatment may be informed and guided by the drama-
    tization. At the same time, life patterns and attitudes of par-
    ticipants are harmonized (without being surgically mutilated)

by participation in life situations through the drama. Drama and theatre preserve, use, and creatively harmonize the desires, struggles, sufferings and neuroses of humanity.

## FOOTNOTES

1. The annual (or periodical) social therapy of mid-winter "saturnalia" — Lords of Misrule, Boy Bishops — is too well known to call for elaboration.
2. Such a folk tale might elicit nothing from another group or another culture. There is always a suitable theme or story, often the one the teacher least expects.
3. If you want movement, activity, start with stillness; if you want speech-flow, start with silence. With these children, anyway.

The author wishes to thank Miss Jean Allingham (Kent Education Authority), without whose collaboration this chapter could not have been written.

NELLIE McCASLIN, Ph.D., teaches educational theatre at New York University and is associate director of the University Without Walls, New York City. A past president of the Children's Theatre Association, she is the author of many books including *Creative Dramatics in the Classroom.*

*Chapter 19*

# DRAMA IN EDUCATION: OPPORTUNITY FOR SOCIAL GROWTH

Nellie McCaslin

*"Let each become all that he was created capable of being; expand if possible, to his full growth; and show himself at length in his own shape and stature, be these what they may."*

—Thomas Carlyle

## 1 INTRODUCTION

This is the goal of the teacher on all levels and in every discipline. It is also the goal of the therapist and remedial specialist. It is certainly the goal of the creative dramatics leader. I must preface all further remarks with the statement that my background is in theatre and education rather than therapy. As a teacher I have had students with problems, many of whom have been helped through participation in creative dramatics and the production of plays. I have a firm belief in the curative and restorative power of drama.

At the present time, however, there are not enough institutions offering training in drama therapy. Departments of dance, music and the visual arts are far ahead of us in establishing programs and obtaining certification of graduates. There is a growing demand for course work in drama therapy designed to help teachers working in the various areas of special education and rehabilitation.

333

This need must be met, and the drama and theatre departments must assume the responsibility. At the same time, I believe that we must exercise caution, lest harm be done through inadequate training. In other words, I see two ways in which drama therapy can be used. It can be: (1) a *specific tool*, used by psychiatrists and psychologists; and (2) a *generalized therapy*, employed by teachers, directors and recreation leaders to improve the social relationships of a group and the personal development of the members. Whereas the former requires an extensive professional background, the latter requires only enough knowledge to enable the teacher to work with a therapist and become more sensitive to the needs of the pupils. Just as a classroom teacher learns to detect a speech or reading problem and refer the child to the remedial specialist, so he or she can learn to perceive other problems and thus become equally helpful to the school psychologist or play therapist. My only concern is for those teachers and performers who are attracted to the use of drama as specific treatment, but who have had neither course work nor supervised internship as preparation.

## 2    CREATIVE DRAMATICS

A distinction must be made at this point between psychodrama and creative drama. Psychodrama may be defined as improvisation in theatrical form, used to recall and recapitulate unsolved problems. The situation is controlled by a director, assisted by several trained performers who act as auxiliary egos. No goals exist beyond the therapeutic. Creative dramatics, on the other hand, is also therapeutic, but this is not the sole aim of the leader. The goals most commonly described by teachers and leaders are educational, developmental, social and aesthetic. Play is encouraged by modern educators as a principal instrument of growth. According to Richard Courtney, "Without play, there would be no normal adult cognitive life; without play, no healthful development of affective life; without play, no full development of the power of will."[1]

The participant in creative drama builds from within as does the patient in psychodrama, but the classroom teacher is primarily interested in the child's education, creative ability and social development. Some teachers, however, who are particularly sensitive to the feelings of children, are also aware of the revelations that occur and the *catharsis* that results. Play, being spontaneous, projects the player's innermost thoughts and feelings, and his/her relationship to the world. Drama is both make-believe and reality to the player. Play represents freedom but it is not real life. According to Johan Huizinga, "It is rather a stepping out of real life into a temporary sphere of activity with a disposition all its own."[2]

The human body, including mind and speech, is the instrument used in the process. Through the body, the player communicates with others. Speech follows, but for most persons action comes first and is the more spontaneous response. "Movement, dance, mime and drama merge into one another, for any dramatic action involves movement, whether in mime, dance or acting."[3]

In creative drama, the leader tries to build an atmosphere of good feeling and trust through appreciation and constructive comment. The first few sessions, particularly with beginners, regardless of age, are usually spent working as a class. By sharing feelings and ideas, moving together and playing as a group rather than as individuals, the shy member is drawn in and the aggressive member restrained. During this period the leader replaces any attitude of competition with a spirit of cooperation. As the group moves on to the improvisation of scenes, the goals are more clearly comprehended. The encouragement of honest effort and contribution, rather than praise for individual performance, creates a climate in which all participants can feel comfortable. No one is more important than another. All play. And all enter into discussion after the playing. "What did you like about that scene? What could we add, if we play it again? Was anything important left out? Could we believe in it? What can we do to make it more interesting? What else do we need to know?" These are the kinds of questions that the teacher might ask, questions that strengthen and challenge the players.

For several years I had a class in creative dramatics for eight- to ten-year-olds on Saturday mornings. The activity was open to all interested neighborhood children but the range in maturity, self-confidence, assertiveness and ability to relate to the others varied considerably. Some of the children became involved in the first session. Others needed several weeks to develop the confidence necessary to volunteer for parts. The phenomenon that took place every fall was the sense of self that emerged in each player after his or her first successful involvement, regardless of role or length of performance. For some the effort that it took to say one word aloud or to pantomime one familiar act, was a major accomplishment. A role does not have to be large, nor a performance brilliant, to be satisfying to a player. There must, however, be sincere involvement. Both the player and the group recognize this moment of truth when it takes place. For one boy in the class, it was his convincing pantomime of pushing a heavy wheelbarrow; for another child, the caring concern she conveyed as she mimed finding a kitten. Four children gave reality to their discovery of a box and made us believe in the treasures they touched inside. Becoming involved in creative drama gave them a sense of self and the confidence to accept or share. Within the past few weeks I have encountered three young people who were once members of that Saturday class. Two are in college and the third is working. All insisted that creative dramatics had been one of their most valuable experiences. I do not take credit for this. I do, however, regard such testimony as a plea for drama in the development of personality as well as a way of learning.

Excessive emotion may be drained off through acting, and problems can be eased by involvement in drama. This is something teachers know and consider valuable. All human beings have their share of aggressive feelings and need a chance to come to grips with them. Improvisation offers that opportunity and the therapeutic effects are added benefits, and important ones. Whether it is regarded as a subject or a method, it is the process not the product that counts. It is through the process that the player is stretched and stimulated to further growth.

In his book, *Development through Drama*, Brian Way devotes much time to sensitivity and sensitivity exercises. He believes that sensitivity, a key point in child growth, cannot be achieved without practice. He summarizes in the following words: ". . . drama is perhaps the only way of helping the full development of the imaginative aspect of this process; meanwhile, the personal experience aspect is rooted in those experiences which first give rise to personal well-being and then to a sensitive awareness that each other individual can experience the same sense of well-being."[4]

## 3 PLAY PRODUCTION

The production of a play is recognized as a valuable experience for older players. Belonging to a dramatic club or a theatre group makes the member feel important and needed. Indeed, no activity in the school or community is more communal in its nature, nor more diversified in the talents it uses. According to Jack Simos, "A person's participation in a play can have curative and therapeutic effects but these are brought about by the ego building he receives from the experience and from the stimulation he gets to examine his own life objectively and to see his common bond with his fellow man."[5] For the high school or older student, the camaraderie, the sense of adventure, the opportunity to create that play production offers, add up to a satisfaction that far outlives the performance. Although the produced play for outside audiences is not generally considered desirable for children under twelve, there is no doubt that it offers a rich experience to the junior and senior high school student or adult.

In a large public high school or community center, the cast and production staff of a play are frequently strangers when they embark on the weeks of rehearsal. Through shared work and responsibility, a sense of community develops that is rarely found in any other activity. It is team work without competition. Under good leadership there is appreciation of each other's efforts as their interdependency is realized. The theatre offers the opportunity to write, act, sing, dance, build, paint, sew, design, light the stage, handle the business details and publicity—and work together as a group. Satisfaction with group success rather than pride in personal accomplishment is the hoped-for result.

I have seen growth take place in every play I have directed. In some instances it has been spectacular; in others, slight. But the experience of being in a play without pressure to compete is of incomparable value to most students.

Recent successful experiments with prison groups, patients in drug treatment centers, deaf and blind actors, and young people

from ghetto neighborhoods, prove the value of drama and theatre
as a means of expression and an effective mode of teaching. The
newest group to receive attention is the elderly. Those who are able
to read and interpret lines comprise one group; patients in nursing
homes comprise another. Creative dramatics techniques are being
used successfully with the latter.

## 4  SPECIAL EDUCATION

Special education is defined as any program of teaching techniques
designed to meet the needs of the students whose abilities deviate
markedly from those of the majority of boys and girls of their age.
Included in this group are the intellectually gifted as well as the
mentally retarded, the physically crippled, the emotionally disturbed, the culturally and economically disadvantaged, the speech
handicapped and those for whom English is a second language. For
boys and girls in all these categories, drama may prove an appropriate therapy. For some it may be highly effective. Under any
circumstances, special preparation is needed to equip the teacher
who wants to work in this area.

### The Gifted

In the case of the gifted, an opportunity to explore the
possibilities of the theatre arts may satisfy a need to create, a need
to go beyond the assignment, perhaps to produce a play, act, or
compose music. There are costumes to be made, scenery to be built
and props to find, make or invent. Some children will want to try
writing an original play. Whatever the choice, drama offers a
chance for group work, an experience that all too often eludes the
gifted who, because they are thought to be able to occupy themselves, are left to their own devices. The theatre, which is social by
nature, offers more to the loner, particularly if he or she is gifted,
than any other activity. There is a place for every interest, so the
possibilities are limitless. The theatre is highly individual yet at the
same time highly social. It is a cooperative endeavor in which the
strength of each member is necessary to the others, and to the creation of a play.

Soon after I began teaching I had a gifted eighth grade. This
was in a school in which integrated projects were encouraged and

the art, social studies, music and drama teachers enjoyed working together. We found this not only a wonderful way for children to learn but an exciting experience for all of us. Dramatic productions were developed each year with sixth, seventh and eighth grade classes. One seventh grade, fascinated by the Victorian period, worked for weeks on scenes from the play *Victoria Regina*. Their interest in the material and their grasp of history and social customs amazed me. The following year they wanted to try Shakespeare. We read *Twelfth Night* and worked on several scenes from it. In the spring, the children presented them in an assembly program for the entire school. Their enthusiasm generated an interest in Shakespeare in the next eighth grade, with the result that they selected *As You Like It* for their spring project. Through the hard work involved in the study of a classic, the education of these junior high school children took on an added dimension. It could be considered therapeutic in that it stimulated learning and helped these gifted children to work cooperatively on ambitious group projects.

The aesthetic goal, not usually given a high priority by the elementary school teacher, or by the therapist on any level, may be a primary motivation for the special child designated as gifted. Said by some to be our most neglected minority, these boys and girls can find in drama a lifelong pleasure, as well as a present means of self-expression. All too often, the teacher of large classes must spend her time with children whose learning disabilities are causing problems. The potential of the gifted, therefore, is not necessarily nourished at a time when their curiosity and energy are strongest.

## The Mentally Retarded

Creative dramatics holds just as much value for the mentally retarded as it does for the gifted; only the expectations are different. The players, whose constant dread is that of making a mistake, are freed and relaxed in an atmosphere in which there are no right or wrong answers. In an activity where all ideas are important, those of the retarded child are accepted and every effort encouraged. The retarded child also enjoys being part of a drama group but the teacher must understand what level of participation to expect. She must establish "an atmosphere of trust and mutual respect in which a child fears neither ridicule nor failure."[6] In observing creative dramatics classes, I have often been unable to distinguish the retarded child from the others. Success breeds success and the player who can make a satisfying contribution, no matter how small, will become involved again with greater ease and self-confidence.

I recall a play I once directed with a cast of college freshmen, several of whom were on academic probation. I was unaware of their status at the time of my tryouts, and it was not until I submitted the cast list to the dean's office that I discovered it. The dean, fortunately, was a woman who viewed the performing arts as a positive experience for all students, and so encouraged participation. Not only did this group do an outstanding job but not one of them was ever on probation again. All seven finished college and a number of them continued to work on theatre workshop plays as a favorite extracurricular activity. These young people were by no means retarded, but they had been marginal achievers up to this time. The success they found in drama encouraged them and strengthened them as students. Individually, and as a group, they had reached a high level of achievement, winning respect for themselves as well as from their peers. I am convinced of the creative ability possessed by every human being; and I am equally sure of the need in each of us for recognition and commendation.

## The Emotionally Disturbed

Emotional disturbance, if severe, is an area in which extreme caution must be exercised. In a hospital or therapy situation, only the trained professional should use dramatic techniques as treatment. This is the *specific* therapy referred to earlier. The classroom teacher, the recreation leader or dramatic director, on the other hand, will probably not be dealing with the seriously disturbed, though he or she will have children from time to time whose emotional stability varies from the norm. The positive results of engaging in dramatic activities are particularly important for those children whose emotional needs are so great. Being involved in a group activity, learning to share, expressing honest emotion in a socially acceptable way, making friends, creating and feeling a sense of accomplishment — all contribute to the well-being of the person who experiences difficulty in relating to others or in concentrating for any length of time. This is the *generalized* therapy that all teachers can practice, and many do.

After all, the desires and needs of the troubled child are the same as those of the so-called normal. The difference is a matter of degree. Although little research has been done in this area, one study of the effect of creative dramatics on the personality of a large group of third graders revealed "measurable changes in the personal and social adjustment aspects of personality."[7] In this study there was an indication that the free and spontaneous nature of dramatic improvisation produced an environment conducive to relaxed dynamic learning.

## The Physically Handicapped

The physically handicapped can also benefit from participation in drama, though the activities have to be adjusted to the abilities of the players. One of the best students I have ever had was a totally deaf young college woman, who attended classes with an interpreter. Through signing, she was able to follow class discussion. Her work in pantomime was superb and her satisfaction in being able to participate and communicate with her classmates on a non-verbal level was obvious. The other students got an insight into the world of the deaf through the efforts of this remarkable young woman, thus adding a dimension to their learning as well. The partially sighted and the blind, whom I have also had in class, enjoy storytelling and acting and have excelled in it. In the variety of opportunities it offers, theatre in one form or another has an advantage over crafts, writing, dance or playing a musical instrument, fine as these experiences are. There is always some element of theatre in which the handicapped can take part, if the emphasis is placed on his strength and not on his disability. For the most seriously disabled, there is puppetry. Indeed, the puppet can perform in every possible location; he is as much at home in the hospital ward as he is in a child's bedroom or wheelchair with a pillow serving as his stage.

One hears of the actor who plays a scene with his leg in a cast; or of the crippling arthritis that confines another to a wheelchair; or of the respiratory problem that besets still another but which disappears when he goes on stage. The marvel to me is not that these actors are able to perform but rather that it is in drama that they find their strength.

## The Economically Disadvantaged

The economically deprived child has been a matter of concern in America since the turn of the century, and theatre has been used as a means of reaching and educating him. The first children's theatre was established in the year 1903 at the Educational Alliance, a New York community center. The stated purpose of this organization was to teach the children of immigrants the English language and some of the literature with which people in the New World were acquainted. This first production was Shakespeare's *The Tempest,* and all performances were sold out in advance. Indeed, two thousand copies of the play were reported to have been sold in the neighborhood, indicating the effect of this event. Since that time settlement houses, community centers, civic theatres, recreation departments, government programs and organizations like the Junior League have assumed a responsibility for dramatic activities for and with ghetto children.[8] Not all of the work has been on a high artistic level, it is true, but the intent, bringing theatre to children who would otherwise have no experience of it, was a worthwhile goal.

Plays have been, and are today, presented to young audiences known as economically disadvantaged. Storytelling and story acting, creative dramatics and puppetry have been and are today still included in community programs for these boys and girls. Despite the efforts that have been made, however, it is generally conceded that we should be doing far more, both quantitatively and qualitatively, than we are in view of the benefits to be derived from dramatic activities.

Educational, social and aesthetic goals are the ones most commonly held by teachers. This means involvement both as participant and as spectator. Through seeing good plays, well produced, children are introduced to literature and the performing arts. Touring companies that perform in school assemblies, and community centers that schedule programs for school groups are the two most usual ways of accomplishing this. In the past few years "street theatre" has been bringing live entertainment to the inner city. This form of presentation, though limited in some respects, must be dynamic and relevant to the interest of the people in order to survive. By eliminating the problems of busing audiences and the expense of renting an auditorium, street theatre is one of our most effective ways of reaching these young audiences.

Through participation in creative drama, children who are disadvantaged are given a chance to work on their own. They are encouraged to think independently, release feelings, participate as a group, and make plays on topics that interest them. Again, development of the players rather than the play is the goal. The children of the inner city have the same needs and abilities as other children; too often they have no opportunity to express them. Dramatic play is a natural expression; what is done with it depends upon the opportunities and encouragement that society provides.

Later on, through the production of plays, young people may improve their skills and experience the joy of communicating with an outside audience. Some groups, established in community centers, have achieved extraordinary success. The Karamu in Cleveland, for example, has been a leading black theatre for over fifty years. Under skilled leadership, it has grown from a small neighborhood drama group into a renowned company of actors with a theatre building of their own. Not every group reaches this level of professionalism but all stand to gain from the experience of producing a play.

The White House Conference of 1960 recommended that "Every child should be given the opportunity to participate in creative dramatics under the guidance of qualified leadership for basic understanding and critical appreciation of the theatre arts and as an adjunct to constructive learning."[9] We have not yet reached that goal, but with the help of arts councils, university theatre departments, community centers and regional conferences of the American Theatre Association, new programs are being established and public consciousness raised.

## 5  SUMMARY

As I look back over a long career in the teaching profession, I find that my greater satisfactions have come from the development of my students than from the plays we have produced, although the success of the process is measured in part at least by the the success of the product. In its power to make us feel, think, move, and interact with others; in its power to reach an audience and, thereby, effect change; in its power to relieve and restore, drama/theatre is therapy. I am not speaking of drama only as a specific method of treatment but theatre as an art form that has survived more than two thousand years, perhaps for these very reasons. It involves the emotions, the mind and the body of the player. Properly guided, it is a cooperative rather than a competitive experience, replacing pressure to win with desire to create. And for those who love and take it seriously, there is the added promise of achieving an even higher standard of performance with time and practice.

Through drama the player assumes a variety of roles and in the process learns more about himself. For the older, more experienced actor, there is the additional satisfaction of communicating with an audience.

Invariably, when I meet former students whom I have not seen for several years, the conversation begins with the lively recollection of a play in which they once took part. They talk of the fun they had; the ideas, shared with sandwiches at rehearsal breaks; the arguments about plays and playwrights; the personal confidences; audience reactions. These were the fringe benefits of the weeks of work. And because they became a part of the players themselves, they were lasting benefits.

During this period, we, the directors, see change taking place. We watch groups as they form and grow. We find intellectual curiosity stimulated and, we hope, satisfied. We are aware of deepening involvement on the part of each player and we know that he/she will not be the same again. Maslow said that "education through art may be especially important not so much for turning out artists or art products, as for turning out better people."[10] If this is so, and I believe that it is, then the classroom teacher and dramatic director have important roles. Through creative drama and the production of plays, they can prevent problems from developing, ease those that exist, and help further the growth of full human beings.

# FOOTNOTES

1. Richard Courtney, *Play, Drama & Thought: The Intellectual Background to Dramatic Education*, 3d ed. (London: Cassell; New York: Drama Book Specialists, 1974), p. 204.
2. Johan Huizinga, *Homo Ludens* (Boston: Beacon, 1955), p. 8.
3. Audrey G. Wethered, *Drama and Movement in Therapy* (London: Macdonald & Evans, 1973), p. 61.
4. Brian Way, *Development through Drama* (London: Longman; New York: Humanities Press, 1968), p. 160.
5. Jack Simos, *Social Growth through Play Production* (New York: Association Press, 1957), p. 19.
6. Emily Pribble Gillies, *Creative Dramatics for All Children* (Washington, D.C.: Association for Childhood Education International, 1974), p. 21.
7. Mabel Wright Henry, *Creative Experiences in Oral Language* (Champagne, Ill.: National Council of Teachers of English, 1967), p. 73.
8. Nellie McCaslin, *Theatre for Children in the United States: A History* (Norman, Okla.: University of Oklahoma Press, 1971), p. 15.
9. Henry, *Creative Experiences in Oral Language*, p. 71.
10. A. Maslow, *The Farther Reaches of Human Nature* (New York: Viking, 1971), p. 57.

# INDEX OF NAMES AND TITLES

# GENERAL INDEX

Abreaction, 123
Addiction, *see* Alcoholism, Narcotics
Adolescents, 74, 207, 298, 328; *see also*
　Preadolescents
Adults, 18, 63, 78, 85, 86
Affective, *see* Feelings
Aggression, 2, 10, 32, 33, 44, 45, 46, 48,
　50, 66, 68, 69, 80, 81, 86, 90, 96, 118,
　120, 122, 132, 134, 141, 143, 145,
　146, 151, 165, 168, 169, 170, 172,
　199, 200, 203, 204, 205, 215, 216,
　251, 253, 260, 262, 272, 273, 308,
　323, 335, 336
Alcoholism, 121, 127, 129, 143
Alienation, 13, 61
American Sign Language, *see* Sign
　Language
Analysis, 9–10
Anger, *see* Aggression
Anlage, 253
Anxiety, 85, 112, 114, 117, 118, 119,
　121, 122, 130, 199, 207, 213, 251,
　253, 254, 255, 258, 259, 260, 266, 310
Apperception test, 256
Approval, 34, 37
Art, *see* Visual art expression
Art therapy, 56, 64, 197
Articulation, *see* Pronunciation
Assessment, 1–50, 313;　descriptive,
　11–12;
　developmental, 14–20;
　dramatic, 12–14;
　extrinsic, 10–11;
　phenomenological, 11;
　*see also* Index of Names and Titles
Audio tape, *see* Tape recorder
Auditory-oral, *see* Oral training
Autism, 43, 52, 53, **95–109,** 155, 194
Auxiliary ego, 334
Awareness, *see* Perception

Back Projection, *see* Rear projection
Backward children, 85, 86–87, 90, 324;
　*see also* Educationally subnormal,
　mentally handicapped, retarded, slow
　learner, Special Education

Backward readers, 84, 320; *see also*
　Special Education
Bedwetting, *see* Enuresis
Behavior modification, 8–9
Bioenergetics, 56
Black theatre, 343
Blind, 52, 89, **162–72,** 280, 286, 337,
　341
Blindfold, 156
Body, *see* Movement expression
Box test, 81
Brain damage, 52, 70, 74, 79, 86,
　**151–60,** 219, 223

Camera, *see* Videotape; high speed, 306,
　309
Carpeting, 152
Catatonia, 69
Categories, 9–10, 31
Catharsis, 7, 13, 91, 114, 117, 135, 266,
　290, 335; *see also* Release
Check list, 12, 20, **21–26,** 195
Child drama, see Creative drama
Child guidance, 238
Children's theatre, 278–86, 291, 319,
　342
Clay, *see* Visual art expression
Cleft palate, *see* Speech defects
Color, 74
*Comédie,* 319
*Commedia dell'arte,* 19
Communication, 19, 31, 33, 34, 35, 37,
　**38,** 39, 43, 47, 58, 59, 63, 66, 67, 69,
　74, 89, 98, 109, 112, 130, 177, 178,
　180, 181, 182, 183, 185, 187, 207,
　212, 216, 217, 218, 237, 240, 241,
　247, 248, 251, 252, 253, 255, 256,
　258, 259, 261, 262, 263, 266, 267,
　276, 291, 302, 311, 317, 320, 322,
　324, 330, 335, 341, 344; *see also* Total
　communication
Completion, 12
Concentration, 19, 32, 41, 47, 48, 50, 52,
　77, 80, 153
Confidence, 37, 45, 52, 66, 67, 77, 85,
　103, 104, 262, 321, 323, 340

355